Zeitoun

Dave Eggers

Zeitoun

Annotations by
Mechthild Hesse

Ernst Klett Sprachen
Stuttgart

Bildquellennachweis:
340 Corbis (Maps.com), Düsseldorf; **341** Geoatlas, Hendaye; **342** Fotolia.com (pavalena), New York

1. Auflage 1 [6 5 4 3 2] | 2016 15 14 13

Internetadresse: www.klett.de / www.lektueren.com

Herausgegeben von Mechthild Hesse
Redaktion: Paul Newcomb
Layoutkonzeption: Elmar Feuerbach
Gestaltung und Satz: bostext, 71229 Leonberg
Umschlaggestaltung: Elmar Feuerbach
Titelbild: Martin Scheuermann, Frankfurt/Main
Fotos: The Whylie Agency, London WC1B 3JA
Druck und Bindung: Print Consult GmbH, München
Printed in Slovakia

ISBN 978-3-12-579884-7

9 783125 798847

Contents

Dave Eggers © Michelle Quint

About the author

Dave Eggers is the author of six previous books, including *What Is the What*, a finalist for the 2006 National Book Critics Circle Award and winner of France's Prix Medici. That book, about Valentino Achak Deng, a survivor of the civil war in southern Sudan, gave birth to the Valentino Achak Deng Foundation, run by Mr. Deng and dedicated to building secondary schools in southern Sudan.

Eggers is the founder and editor of McSweeney's, an independent publishing house based in San Francisco. In 2002, Eggers co-founded 826 Valencia, a nonprofit writing and tutoring center for youth in the Mission District of San Francisco. Local communities have since opened sister 826 centers in seven cities across the United States.

In 2004, Eggers taught at the University of California–Berkeley Graduate School of Journalism, and there, with Dr. Lola Vollen, he co-founded Voice of Witness, a series of books using oral history to illuminate human rights crises around the world.

A native of Chicago, Eggers graduated from the University of Illinois with a degree in journalism. He now lives in the San Francisco Bay Area with his wife and two children.

About the book

This is a work of nonfiction, based primarily on the accounts of Abdulrahman and Kathy Zeitoun (pronounced "Zay-toon"). Dates, times, locations, and other facts have been confirmed by independent sources and the historical record. Conversations have been recounted as best as can be remembered by the participants. Some names have been changed.

This book does not attempt to be an all-encompassing book about New Orleans or Hurricane Katrina. It is only an account of one family's experiences before and after the storm. It was written with the full participation of the Zeitoun family, and reflects their view of the events.

1 **account** narrative version, story – 6 **to recount** to re-tell – 9 **all-encompassing** including every detail

For Abdulrahman, Kathy, Zachary, Nademah,
Aisha, Safiya, and Ahmad in New Orleans

For Ahmad, Antonia, Lutfi, and Laila in Malaga

For Kousay, Nada, Mahmoud, Zakiya, Luay, Eman,
Fahzia, Fatimah, Aisha, Munah, Nasibah, and all the
Zeitouns of Jableh, Lattakia, and Arwad Island

For the people of New Orleans

Abbreviations used in the annotations

abb	abbreviation
adj	adjective
AE	American English
a.m.	ante meridian (before midday)
b	born
etc.	et cetera
fml	formal
Fr	French
i.e.	id est (that is)
inf	informal
old	old-fashioned
opp of	opposite of
sb	somebody
sth	something
usu	usually

...in the history of the world it might even be
that that there was more punishment than crime...
Cormac McCarthy, *The Road*

To a man with a hammer,
everything looks like a nail.
Mark Twain

PART I

FRIDAY AUGUST 26, 2005

On moonless nights the men and boys of Jableh, a dusty fishing town on the coast of Syria, would gather their lanterns and set out in their quietest boats. Five or six small craft, two or three fishermen in each. A mile out, they would arrange the boats in a circle on the black sea, drop their nets, and, holding their lanterns over the water, they would approximate the moon.

The fish, sardines, would begin gathering soon after, a slow mass of silver rising from below. The fish were attracted to plankton, and the plankton were attracted to the light. They would begin to circle, a chain linked loosely, and over the next hour their numbers would grow. The black gaps between silver links would close until the fishermen could see, below, a solid mass of silver spinning.

Abdulrahman Zeitoun was only thirteen when he began fishing for sardines this way, a method called *lampara,* borrowed from the Italians. He had waited years to join the men and teenagers on the night boats, and he'd spent those years asking questions. Why only on moonless nights? Because, his brother Ahmad said, on moon-filled nights the plankton would be visible everywhere, spread out all over the sea, and the sardines could see and eat the glowing organisms with ease. But without a moon the men could make their own, and could bring the sardines to the surface in stunning concentrations. You have to see it, Ahmad told his little brother. You've never seen anything like this.

And when Abdulrahman first witnessed the sardines circling in the black he could not believe the sight, the beauty of the undulating silver orb below the white and gold lantern light. He said nothing, and the other fishermen were careful to be quiet, too, paddling without motors, lest they scare away

2 **Jableh** Syrian city on the Mediterranean, 80,000 inhabitants (2008) – 7 **to approximate** to simulate, look like, come near – 11 **plankton** organisms, such as algae, that float on the surface of the sea and serve as food for fish – 15 **solid** firm, not liquid *(fest)* – 24 **with ease** easily – 25 **stunning** very surprising – 30 **undulating silver orb** moving silver circle – 32 **lest** *(old)* so that they don't

the catch. They would whisper over the sea, telling jokes and talking about women and girls as they watched the fish rise and spin beneath them. A few hours later, once the sardines were ready, tens of thousands of them glistening in the refracted light, the fishermen would cinch the net and haul them in.

They would motor back to the shore and bring the sardines to the fish broker in the market before dawn. He would pay the men and boys, and would then sell the fish all over western Syria — Lattakia, Baniyas, Damascus. The fishermen would split the money, with Abdulrahman and Ahmad bringing their share home. Their father had passed away the year before and their mother was of fragile health and mind, so all funds they earned fishing went toward the welfare of the house they shared with ten siblings.

Abdulrahman and Ahmad didn't care much about the money, though. They would have done it for free.

Thirty-four years later and thousands of miles west, Abdulrahman Zeitoun was in bed on a Friday morning, slowly leaving the moonless Jableh night, a tattered memory of it caught in a morning dream. He was in his home in New Orleans and beside him he could hear his wife Kathy breathing, her exhalations not unlike the shushing of water against the hull of a wooden boat. Otherwise the house was silent. He knew it was near six o'clock, and the peace would not last. The morning light usually woke the kids once it reached their second-story windows. One of the four would open his or her eyes, and from there the movements were brisk, the house quickly growing loud. With one child awake, it was impossible to keep the other three in bed.

3 **to spin beneath** to twist *(sich drehen)* under – 4 **to glisten** ['glisən] **in the refracted light** *im gebrochenen Licht glänzen* – 5 **to cinch** to get a tight grip on – 8 **broker** salesperson – 10 **Lattakia** city in northern Syria, 50 km from the Turkish border – 12 **to pass away** to die – 14 **funds** income, money – 14 **welfare** well-being – 15 **siblings** brothers and sisters – 20 **tattered** *here:* disordered – 23 **exhalation** breathing out – 24 **hull** body of a boat – 29 **brisk** quick

Kathy woke to a thump upstairs, coming from one of the kids' rooms. She listened closely, praying silently for rest. Each morning there was a delicate period, between six and six-thirty, when there was a chance, however remote, that they could steal another ten or fifteen minutes of sleep. But now there was another thump, and the dog barked, and another thump followed. What was happening in this house? Kathy looked to her husband. He was staring at the ceiling. The day had roared to life.

The phone began ringing, today as always, before their feet hit the floor. Kathy and Zeitoun — most people called him by his last name because they couldn't pronounce his first — ran a company, Zeitoun A. Painting Contractor LLC, and every day their crews, their clients, everyone with a phone and their number, seemed to think that once the clock struck six-thirty, it was appropriate to call. And they called. Usually there were so many calls at the stroke of six-thirty that the overlap would send half of them straight to voicemail.

Kathy took the first one, from a client across town, while Zeitoun shuffled into the shower. Fridays were always busy, but this one promised madness, given the rough weather on the way. There had been rumblings all week about a tropical storm crossing the Florida Keys, a chance it might head north. Though this kind of possibility presented itself every August and didn't raise eyebrows for most, Kathy and Zeitoun's more cautious clients and friends often made preparations. Throughout the morning the callers would want to know if Zeitoun could board up their windows and doors, if he would be clearing his equipment off their property before the winds

3 **delicate** ['delɪkət] fragile *(zerbrechlich)* – 4 **however remote** *here: auch wenn unwahrscheinlich* – 9 **to roar** to make a loud noise – 13 **Painting Contractor LLC** the name of the painting company – 16 **appropriate** suitable *(angebracht)* – 20 **to shuffle** *here:* to go slowly – 21 **given the rough weather** *here: bei dem stürmischen Wetter* – 22 **rumblings** *here:* rumor, talk – 23 **Florida Keys** chain of islands at the southernmost tip of Florida – 26 **cautious** very careful – 28 **to board up** to cover with wooden boards – 29 **to clear ... off the property** to take ... away from the land

came. Workers would want to know if they'd be expected to come in that day or the next.

"Zeitoun Painting Contractors," Kathy said, trying to sound alert. It was an elderly client, a woman living alone in a Garden District mansion, asking if Zeitoun's crew could come over and board up her windows.

"Sure, of course," Kathy said, letting her feet drop heavily to the floor. She was up. Kathy was the business's secretary, bookkeeper, credit department, public-relations manager — she did everything in the office, while her husband handled the building and painting. The two of them balanced each other well: Zeitoun's English had its limits, so when bills had to be negotiated, hearing Kathy's Louisiana drawl put clients at ease.

This was part of the job, helping clients prepare their homes for coming winds. Kathy hadn't given much thought to the storm this client was talking about. It took a lot more than a few downed trees in south Florida to get her attention.

"We'll have a crew over this afternoon," Kathy told the woman.

Kathy and Zeitoun had been married for eleven years. Zeitoun had come to New Orleans in 1994, by way of Houston and Baton Rouge and a half-dozen other American cities he'd explored as a young man. Kathy had grown up in Baton Rouge and was used to the hurricane routine: the litany of preparations, the waiting and watching, the power outages, the candles and flashlights and buckets catching rain. There seemed to be a half-dozen named storms every August, and they were rarely worth the trouble. This one, named Katrina, would be no different.

5 **Garden District** an area of New Orleans - 5 **mansion** a large, expensive house - 13 **to negotiate bills** *über Rechnungen verhandeln* - 13 **Louisiana drawl** language accent typical of the state of Louisiana - 13 **to put sb at ease** to calm sb down - 24 **Baton Rouge** [ˌbæt'nru:ʒ] capital of Louisiana, big city on the Mississippi - 26 **power outage** electricity failure

Downstairs, Nademah, at ten their second-oldest, was helping get breakfast together for the two younger girls, Aisha and Safiya, five and seven. Zachary, Kathy's fifteen-year-old son from her first marriage, was already gone, off to meet friends before school. Kathy made lunches while the three girls sat at the kitchen table, eating and reciting, in English accents, scenes from *Pride and Prejudice.* They had gotten lost in, were hopelessly in love with, that movie. Dark-eyed Nademah had heard about it from friends, convinced Kathy to buy the DVD, and since then the three girls had seen it a dozen times — every night for two weeks. They knew every character and every line and had learned how to swoon like aristocratic maidens. It was the worst they'd had it since *Phantom of the Opera,* when they'd been stricken with the need to sing every song, at home or at school or on the escalator at the mall, at full volume.

Zeitoun wasn't sure which was worse. As he entered the kitchen, seeing his daughters bow and curtsy and wave imaginary fans, he thought, *At least they're not singing.* Pouring himself a glass of orange juice, he watched these girls of his, perplexed. Growing up in Syria, he'd had seven sisters, but none had been this prone to drama. His girls were playful, wistful, always dancing across the house, jumping from bed to bed, singing with feigned vibrato, swooning. It was Kathy's influence, no doubt. She was one of them, really, blithe and girlish in her manner and her tastes — video games, Harry Potter, the baffling pop music they listened to. He knew she was determined to give them the kind of carefree childhood she hadn't had.

7 **Pride and Prejudice** *here:* film version of the classic English novel by Jane Austen – 12 **to swoon** *(old)* to become unconscious *(ohnmächtig werden)* – 14 **to strike, struck, (be) stricken with the need to do sth** to suddenly feel the need to do sth – 18 **to bow and curtsy** *sich verbeugen und einen Knicks machen* – 22 **to be prone to sth** to have a tendency to do sth – 23 **wistful** full of longing – 24 **feigned** [feɪnd] false – 25 **blithe** [blaɪð] lighthearted

"That's all you're eating?" Kathy said, looking over at her husband, who was putting on his shoes, ready to leave. He was of average height, a sturdily built man of forty-seven, but how he maintained his weight was a puzzle. He could go without breakfast, graze at lunch, and barely touch dinner, all while working twelve-hour days of constant activity, and still his weight never fluctuated. Kathy had known for a decade that her husband was one of those inexplicably solid, self-sufficient, and never-needy men who got by on air and water, impervious to injury or disease — but still she wondered how he sustained himself. He was passing through the kitchen now, kissing the girls' heads.

"Don't forget your phone," Kathy said, eyeing it on the microwave.

"Why would I?" he asked, pocketing it.

"So you don't forget things?"

"I don't."

"You're really saying you don't forget things."

"Yes. This is what I'm saying."

But as soon as he'd said the words he recognized his error.

"You forgot our firstborn child!" Kathy said. He'd walked right into it. The kids smiled at their father. They knew the story well.

It was unfair, Zeitoun thought, how one lapse in eleven years could give his wife enough ammunition to needle him for the rest of his life. Zeitoun was not a forgetful man, but whenever he did forget something, or when Kathy was trying to prove he had forgotten something, all she had to do was remind him of the time he'd forgotten Nademah. Because he had. Not for such a long time, but he had.

She was born on August 4, on the one-year anniversary of their wedding. It had been a trying labor. The next day, at

3 **sturdy** heavy and strong – 5 **barely** almost not *(kaum)* – 9 **impervious to** not affected by – 10 **to sustain oneself** to keep oneself in existence, to support oneself – 24 **lapse** mistake – 32 **trying labor** *heftige Wehen und Geburt*

home, Zeitoun helped Kathy from the car, closed the passenger door, and then retrieved Nademah, still in her carseat. He carried the baby in one hand, holding Kathy's arm with the other. The stairs to their second-floor apartment were just inside the building, and Kathy needed help getting up. So Zeitoun helped her up the steep steps, Kathy groaning and sighing as they went. They reached the bedroom, where Kathy collapsed on the bed and got under the covers. She was relieved beyond words or reason to be home where she could relax with her infant.

"Give her to me," Kathy said, raising her arms.

Zeitoun looked down to his wife, astonished at how ethereally beautiful she looked, her skin radiant, her eyes so tired. Then he heard what she'd said. The baby. Of course she wanted the baby. He turned to give her the baby, but there was no baby. The baby was not at his feet. The baby was not in the room.

"Where is she?" Kathy asked.

Zeitoun took in a quick breath. "I don't know."

"Abdul, where's the baby?" Kathy said, now louder.

Zeitoun made a sound, something between a gasp and a squeak, and flew out of the room. He ran down the steps and out the front door. He saw the carseat sitting on the lawn. He'd left the baby in the yard. *He'd left the baby in the yard.* The carseat was turned toward the street. He couldn't see Nademah's face. He grabbed the handle, fearing the worst, that someone had taken her and left the seat, but when he turned it toward him, there was the tiny pink face of Nademah, scrunched and sleeping. He put his fingers to her, to feel her heat, to know she was okay. She was.

He brought the carseat upstairs, handed Nademah to Kathy, and before she could scold him, kid him, or divorce him, he ran down the stairs and went for a walk. He needed a walk that day, and needed walks for many days following, to work

13 **ethereal** [ɪˈθɪriəl] heavenly – 32 **to scold** to criticize harshly – 32 **to kid** *(inf)* to tease

out what he'd done and why, how he had forgotten his child while aiding his wife. How hard it was to do both, to be partner to one and protector to the other. What was the balance? He would spend years pondering this conundrum.

This day, in the kitchen, Zeitoun wasn't about to give Kathy the opportunity to tell the whole story, again, to their children. He waved goodbye.

Aisha hung on his leg. "Don't leave, Baba," she said. She was given to theatrics — Kathy called her Dramarama — and all that Austen had made the tendency worse.

He was already thinking about the day's work ahead, and even at seven-thirty he felt behind.

Zeitoun looked down at Aisha, held her face in his hands, smiled at the tiny perfection of her dark wet eyes, and then extracted her from his shin as if he were stepping out of soggy pants. Seconds later he was in the driveway, loading the van.

Aisha went out to help him, and Kathy watched the two of them, thinking about his way with the girls. It was difficult to describe. He was not an overly doting father, and yet he never objected to them jumping on him, grabbing him. He was firm, sure, but also just distracted enough to give them the room they needed, and just pliant enough to let himself be taken advantage of when the need arose. And even when he was upset about something, it was disguised behind those eyes, grey-green and long-lashed. When they met, he was thirteen years older than Kathy, so she wasn't immediately sold on the prospect of marriage, but those eyes, holding the light the way they did, had seized her. They were dream-filled, but discerning, too, assessing — the eyes of an entrepreneur. He

2 **to aid** to help – 4 **to ponder a conundrum** to think about a complicated problem – 15 **soggy** wet through and through – 19 **overly doting** too loving – 22 **pliant** ['plaɪənt] flexible – 29 **to discern** to comprehend, able to differentiate *(abwägen)* – 29 **to assess** to determine the value of – 29 **entrepreneur** businessman

could see a run-down building and have not only the vision to see what it might become, but also the practical knowledge of what it would cost and how long it would take.

Kathy adjusted her hijab in the front window, tucking in stray hairs — it was a nervous habit — while watching Zeitoun leave the driveway in a swirling grey cloud. It was time for a new van. The one they had was a crumbling white beast, long-suffering but dependable, filled with ladders and wood and rattling with loose screws and brushes. On the side was their ubiquitous logo, the words ZEITOUN A. PAINTING CONTRACTOR next to a paint roller resting at the end of a rainbow. The logo was corny, Kathy admitted, but it wasn't easy to forget. Everyone in the city knew it, from bus stops and benches and lawn signs; it was as common in New Orleans as live oak or royal fern. But at first it was not so benign to all.

When Zeitoun first designed it, he'd had no idea that a sign with a rainbow on it would signify anything to anyone — anything other than the array of colors and tints from which clients might choose. But soon enough he and Kathy were made aware of the signals they were sending.

Immediately they began getting calls from gay couples, and this was good news, good business. But at the same time, some potential clients, once they saw the van arrive, were no longer interested in Zeitoun A. Painting Contractor LLC. Some workers left, thinking that by working under the Zeitoun Painting rainbow they would be presumed to be gay, that somehow the company managed to employ only gay painters.

When Zeitoun and Kathy finally caught on to the rainbow's signifying power, they had a serious talk about it. Kathy wondered if her husband, who did not at that point have any

4 **hijab** [hɪʒa:b] headscarf worn by Muslim women – 12 **corny** old-fashioned, dated – 14 **live oak, royal fern** plants typical of the region – 15 **benign** [bɪ'naɪn] kind – 18 **array** arrangement, range, number – 18 **tints** *Farbabstufungen* – 21 **gay** *(inf)* homosexual

gay friends or family members, might want to change the logo, to keep their message from being misconstrued.

But Zeitoun barely gave it a thought. It would cost a lot of money, he said — about twenty signs had been made, not to mention all the business cards and stationery — and besides, all the new clients were paying their bills. It wasn't much more complicated than that.

"Think about it," Zeitoun laughed. "We're a Muslim couple running a painting company in Louisiana. Not such a good idea to turn away clients." Anyone who had a problem with rainbows, he said, would surely have trouble with Islam.

So the rainbow remained.

Zeitoun pulled onto Earhart Boulevard, though a part of him was still in Jableh. Whenever he had these morning thoughts of his childhood, he wondered how they all were, his family in Syria, all his brothers and sisters and nieces and nephews scattered up and down the coast, and those who had long ago left this world. His mother died a few years after his father passed on, and he'd lost a treasured brother, Mohammed, when he was very young. But the rest of his siblings, those still in Syria and Spain and Saudi Arabia, were all doing well, extraordinarily so. The Zeitouns were a high-achieving clan, full of doctors and school principals and generals and business owners, all of them with a passion for the sea. They had grown up in a big stone house on the Mediterranean, and none had strayed far from the shore. Zeitoun made a note to call Jableh sometime that day. There were always new babies, always news. He only had to reach one of his brothers or sisters — there were seven still in Syria — and he could get the full report.

Zeitoun turned on the radio. The storm that people were talking about was still far down in Florida, moving slowly west. It wasn't expected to make it up the Gulf for another few

2 **to misconstrue** to misinterpret – 5 **stationery** writing paper and envelopes – 22 **high-achieving clan** capable, successful family – 33 **Gulf** Gulf of Mexico

days, if at all. As he drove to his first job of the day, the restoration of a wonderful old mansion in the Garden District, he turned the dial on the radio, looking for something, anything, else.

Standing in her kitchen, Kathy looked at the clock and gasped. It was all too rare that she got the kids to school on time. But she was working on it. Or planned to work on it as soon as the season calmed down. Summer was the busiest time for the business, with so many people leaving, fleeing the swamp heat, wanting these rooms or that porch painted while they were away.

With a flurry of warnings and arm movements, Kathy herded the girls and their gear into the minivan and headed across the Mississippi to the West Bank.

There were advantages to Zeitoun and Kathy running a business together — so many blessings, too many to name — but then again, the drawbacks were distinct and growing. They greatly valued being able to set their own hours, choose their clients and jobs, and be at home whenever they needed to be — their ability to be there, always and for anything relating to their children, was a profound comfort. But when friends would ask Kathy whether they, too, should start their own business, she talked them out of it. You don't run the business, she would say. The business runs you.

Kathy and Zeitoun worked harder than anyone they knew, and the work and worry never ended. Nights, weekends, holidays — respite never came. They usually had eight to ten jobs going at any one time, which they oversaw out of a home office and a warehouse space on Dublin Street, off Carrollton. And that was to say nothing of the property-management aspect of the business. Somewhere along the line they started

10 **to flee the swamp heat** New Orleans is built on a swamp; it is very hot and humid in the summer. – 10 **porch** verandah – 12 **flurry** large number and very quickly – 16 **blessing** advantage – 17 **drawback** disadvantage – 27 **respite** relaxation, recovery

buying buildings, apartments, and houses, and now they had six properties with eighteen tenants. Each renter was, in some ways, another dependent, another soul to worry about, to provide with shelter, a solid roof, air-conditioning, clean water. There was a dizzying array of people to pay and collect from, houses to improve and maintain, bills to deal with, invoices to issue, supplies to buy and store.

But she cherished what her life had become, and the family she and Zeitoun had created. She was driving her three girls to school now, and the fact that they could go to a private school, that their college would be taken care of, that they had all they needed and more — she was thankful every hour of every day.

Kathy was one of nine children, and had grown up with very little, and Zeitoun, the eighth of thirteen children, had been raised with almost nothing. To see the two of them now, to stand back and assess what they'd built — a sprawling family, a business of distinct success, and to be woven so thoroughly into the fabric of their adopted city that they had friends in every neighborhood, clients on almost any block they passed — these were all blessings from God.

How could she take Nademah, for instance, for granted? How had they produced such a child — so smart and self-possessed, so dutiful, helpful, and precocious? She was practically an adult now, it seemed — she certainly spoke like one, often more measured and circumspect than her parents. Kathy glanced at her now, sitting in the passenger seat playing with the radio. She'd always been quick. When she was five, no more than five, Zeitoun came home from work for lunch one day and found Nademah playing on the floor. She looked up at him and declared, "Daddy, I want to be a dancer." Zeitoun took off his shoes and sat on the couch. "We have too

2 **tenant** sb who rents an apartment or house from sb else *(Mieter)* – 7 **to issue an invoice** to write a bill – 8 **to cherish** to like a lot, dearly *(sehr schätzen)* – 17 **sprawling** large and growing – 18 **to be woven into the fabric of** to be part of – 23 **smart** *(inf)* intelligent – 24 **dutiful** responsible – 24 **precocious** [prɪˈkoʊʃəs] mature for her age – 26 **circumspect** wise

many dancers in the city," he said, rubbing his feet. "We need doctors, we need lawyers, we need teachers. I want you to be a doctor so you can take care of me." Nademah thought about this for a moment and said, "Okay, then I'll be a doctor." She went back to her coloring. A minute later, Kathy came downstairs, having just seen the wreck of Nademah's bedroom. "Clean up your room, Demah," she said. Nademah didn't miss a beat, nor did she look up from her coloring book. "Not me, Mama. I'm going to be a doctor, and doctors don't clean."

In the car, approaching their school, Nademah turned up the volume on the radio. She'd caught something on the news about the coming storm. Kathy wasn't paying close attention, because three or four times a season, it seemed, there was some early alarmist talk about hurricanes heading straight for the city, and always their direction changed, or the winds fizzled in Florida or over the Gulf. If a storm hit New Orleans at all, it would be greatly diminished, no more than a day of grey gusts and rain.

This reporter was talking about the storm heading into the Gulf of Mexico as a Category 1. It was about 45 miles north-northwest of Key West and heading west. Kathy turned the radio off; she didn't want the kids to worry.

"You think it'll hit us?" Nademah asked.

Kathy didn't think much of it. Who ever worried about a Category 1 or 2? She told Nademah it was nothing, nothing at all, and she kissed the girls goodbye.

With the thrump of three car doors, Kathy was suddenly and definitively alone. Driving away from the school, she turned the radio on again. City officials were giving the usual recommendations about having three days' worth of supplies on hand — Zeitoun had always been vigilant about this — and then there was some talk about 110-mile-per-hour winds and storm surges in the Gulf.

18 **gust** *here:* strong wind – 31 **vigilant** ['vɪdʒələnt] watchful *(wachsam)* – 33 **surge** sudden increase (*here*: of wind and high waves)

She turned it off again and called Zeitoun on his cell phone.

"You hear about this storm?" she asked.

"I hear different things," he said.

"You think it's serious?" she asked.

"Really? I don't know," he said.

Zeitoun had reinvented the word "really," prefacing a good deal of his sentences with "Really?" as a kind of throat-clearer. Kathy would ask him any question, and he would say, "Really? It's a funny story." He was known for anecdotes, and parables from Syria, quotations from the Qur'an, stories from his travels around the world. All of it she'd gotten used to, but the use of "Really?" — she'd given up fighting it. For him it was equivalent to starting a sentence with "You know," or "Let me tell you." It was Zeitoun, and she had no choice but to find it endearing.

"Don't worry," he said. "Are the kids at school?"

"No, they're in the lake. My God."

The man was school-obsessed, and Kathy liked to tease him about it and any number of other things. She and Zeitoun spoke on the phone throughout every day, about everything — painting, the rental properties, things to fix and do and pick up, often just to say hello. The banter they'd developed, full of his exasperation and her one-liners, was entertaining to anyone who overheard it. It was unavoidable, too, given how often they talked. Neither of them could operate their home, their company, their lives or days without the other.

That they had come to such symbiosis continually surprised Kathy. She had been brought up a Southern Baptist in suburban Baton Rouge with dreams of leaving home — she did so just after high school — and running a daycare center.

11 **Qu'ran** Koran (the holy book of Moslems) – 14 **equivalent to** [ɪ'kwɪvələnt] the same as – 16 **endearing** charming – 23 **banter** good-humored, playful conversation – 24 **exasperation** annoyance, desparation – 29 **Southern Baptist** Christian denomination known for their strict beliefs – 31 **daycare center** nursery *(Kinderkrippe)*

Now she was a Muslim married to a Syrian American, managing a sprawling painting and contracting business. When Kathy met her husband, she was twenty-one and he was thirty-four and a native of a country she knew almost nothing about. She was recovering from an unsuccessful marriage and had recently converted to Islam. She wasn't even vaguely interested in getting married again, but Zeitoun had turned out to be everything she had not believed possible: an honest man, honest to the core, hardworking, reliable, faithful, devoted to family. And best of all, he very much wanted Kathy to be who and how she wanted to be, nothing more or less.

But it didn't mean there wasn't some fussing. Kathy called it that, their spirited back-and-forth about everything from what the kids ate for dinner to whether they should enlist a collection agency to help with a particular client.

"We're just fussin'," she would tell her kids when they heard the two of them. Kathy couldn't help it. She was a talker. She couldn't hold anything in. I'm going to speak my mind, she told Abdul early in their relationship. He shrugged; that was fine with him. He knew that sometimes she just needed to blow off steam, and he let her. He would nod patiently, sometimes thankful that his English wasn't as quick as hers. While he searched for the right words to respond with, she would go on, and often enough, by the time she was finished, she had tired herself out, and there was nothing left to say.

In any case, once Kathy knew that she would be heard, and heard to the end, it softened the tone of her arguments. Their discussions became less heated, and often more comical. But the kids, when they were young, sometimes couldn't tell the difference.

Years before, while Kathy was driving and fussing about something with Zeitoun, Nademah spoke up. Strapped into a

9 **honest to the core** very deeply honest – 9 **reliable** [rɪ'laɪəbl] dependable *(zuverlässig)* – 12 **to fuss** to argue (*usu* unnecessarily) – 13 **spirited back-and-forth** lively discussion – 14 **to enlist a collection agency** to get/ask a group of people to help (the client)

car seat in the back, she had had enough. "Dad, be nice to Mom," she said. And then she turned to Kathy. "Mom, be nice to Dad." Kathy and Zeitoun stopped cold. They looked at each other, and then, in unison, back to little Nademah. They already knew she was smart, but this was something different. She was only two years old.

After she hung up with Zeitoun, Kathy did what she knew she shouldn't do, because clients no doubt needed and expected to reach her in the morning. She switched off her phone. She did this every so often, after the kids had left the car and she'd turned toward home. Just to have that thirty minutes of solitude during the drive — it was decadent but essential. She stared at the road, in total silence, thinking of nothing at all. The day would be long, it would be nonstop until the kids went to bed, so she allowed herself this one extravagance, an uninterrupted, thirty-minute expanse of clarity and quiet.

Across town, Zeitoun was at his first job of the day. He loved this place, a magisterial old house in the Garden District. He had two men on the job and was stopping by to make sure they were there, that they were busy, that they had what they needed. He jumped up the steps and strode into the house. It was easily 120 years old.

He saw Emil, a painter and carpenter from Nicaragua, kneeling in a doorway, taping off a baseboard. Zeitoun snuck up behind him and grabbed his shoulders suddenly.

Emil jumped.

Zeitoun laughed.

He wasn't even sure why he did things like this. It was hard to explain — sometimes he just found himself in a playful mood. The workers who knew him well were unsurprised,

10 **every so often** occasionally, sometimes – 16 **expanse** space, amount – 19 **magisterial** big, majestic – 25 **to tape off** to cover with tape – 25 **to snick, snuck, snuck** to appear suddenly and quietly – 27 **to jump** *here: sich erschrecken*

while the newer ones would often be startled, thinking his behavior a bizarre sort of motivational method.

Emil managed a smile.

In the dining room, applying a second coat to the wall, was Marco, originally from El Salvador. The two of them, Marco and Emil, had met at church and had gone looking for work as a team of housepainters. They'd shown up at one of Zeitoun's job sites, and because Zeitoun nearly always had more work than he could handle, he'd taken them on. That had been three years ago, and Marco and Emil had worked for Zeitoun consistently since then.

Outside of employing a number of New Orleans natives, Zeitoun had hired men from everywhere: Peru, Mexico, Bulgaria, Poland, Brazil, Honduras, Algeria. He'd had good experiences with almost all of them, though in his business there was an above-average rate of attrition and turnover. Many workers were transient, intending only to spend a few months in the country before returning to their families. These men he was happy to hire, and he'd learned a fair bit of Spanish along the way, but he had to be prepared for their short-notice disappearances. Other workers were just young men: irresponsible and living for today. He couldn't blame them — he'd been young and untethered once, too — but he tried, whenever he could, to instill in them the knowledge that if they kept their heads down and saved a few dollars a week, they could live well, could raise a family doing this kind of work. But he rarely saw a young man in this business who had an eye to the future. Just keeping them in food and clothing, chasing them down when they were late or absent — all of it was exhausting and occasionally disheartening. He felt, sometimes, as if he had not four children but dozens, most of them with paint-covered hands and mustaches.

4 **coat** *here:* layer *(Lage)* – 11 **consistently** often, regularly – 16 **attrition** reduction, natural wastage (because Zeitoun trains men then they leave) – 21 **short-notice** *kurzfristig* – 23 **untethered** unrestricted – 24 **to instill in them** to give them – 30 **disheartening** frustrating

His phone rang. He looked at the caller ID and picked up.

"Ahmad, how are you?" Zeitoun said in Arabic.

Ahmad was Zeitoun's older brother and closest friend. He was calling from Spain, where he lived with his wife and two children, both in high school. It was late where Ahmad was, so Zeitoun worried that the call might bring grave news.

"What is it?" Zeitoun asked.

"I'm watching this storm," he said.

"You scared me."

"You should be scared," Ahmad said. "This one could be for real."

Zeitoun was skeptical but paid attention. Ahmad was a ship captain, had been for thirty years, piloting tankers and ocean liners in every conceivable body of water, and he knew as much as anyone about storms, their trajectories and power. As a young man, Zeitoun had been with him for a number of those journeys. Ahmad, nine years older, had brought Zeitoun on as a crewman, taking him to Greece, Lebanon, South Africa. Zeitoun had gone on to work on ships without Ahmad, too, seeing most of the world in a ten-year period of wanderlust that eventually brought him to New Orleans and to his life with Kathy.

Ahmad clicked his tongue. "It really does seem unusual. Big and slow-moving. I'm watching it on the satellite," he said.

Ahmad was a technophile. At work and in his spare time he paid close attention to the weather, to developing storms. At the moment he was at his home in Malaga, a beach town on the Spanish Mediterranean, in his cluttered office, tracking this storm making its way across Florida.

"Have they begun evacuating?" Ahmad asked.

"Not officially," Zeitoun said. "Some people are leaving."

"And Kathy, the kids?"

Zeitoun told him they hadn't thought about it yet.

Ahmad sighed. "Why not go, just to be safe?"

6 **grave** bad – 14 **conceivable** possible – 15 **trajectory** course – 28 **cluttered** untidy, full of stuff

Zeitoun made a noncommittal sound into the phone.
"I'll call you later," Ahmad said.

Zeitoun left the house and walked to the next job, one block over. It was often like this, multiple jobs in close proximity. Clients seemed so surprised to work with a painter or contractor they could trust and recommend that through referrals and in rapid succession Zeitoun would get a half-dozen jobs in any given neighborhood.

This next house, which he'd worked on for years, was across the street from the home of Anne Rice, the writer — he had not read her work, but Kathy had; Kathy read everything — and was as stately and gorgeous a home as existed in New Orleans. High ceilings, a grand winding staircase descending into the foyer, hand-carved everything, each room themed and with a distinct character. Zeitoun had painted and repainted probably every room in the house, and the owners showed no signs of stopping. He loved to be in that house, admiring the craftsmanship, the great care put into the most eccentric details and flourishes — a mural over the mantel, one-of-a-kind ironwork on every balcony. It was this kind of willful, wildly romantic attention to beauty — crumbling and fading beauty needing constant attention — that made this city so unlike any other and such an unparalleled sort of environment for a builder.

He walked in, straightened the drop cloth in the front hall, and made his way to the back of the house. He peeked in on Georgi, his Bulgarian carpenter, who was installing new

1 **noncommittal** neutral – 4 **multiple** several – 4 **in close proximity** nearby (to each other) – 7 **referral** reference, recommendation – 7 **succession** sequence – 10 **Anne Rice** (b 1941) best-selling Southern American author of gothic fiction, Christian literature and erotica. Her books have sold nearly 100 million copies; she is one of the most widely read authors in modern history. She moved to New Orleans in 1978, leaving in Spring 2005, shortly before Katrina struck. – 13 **winding staircase** *Wendeltreppe* – 18 **craftmanship** *Handwerkskunst* – 19 **flourish** ['flʌrɪʃ] *here:* eccentric style – 19 **mural over the mantel** wall painting above the shelf over the fireplace – 20 **willful** playful – 21 **crumbling and fading beauty** a beauty that is in danger of going away

molding near the kitchen. Georgi was a good worker, about sixty, barrel-chested and tireless, but Zeitoun knew not to get him talking. Once Georgi started you were in for a twenty-minute discourse on the former Soviet Union, waterfront property in Bulgaria, and his various cross-country motorhome trips with his wife Albena, who had passed away years ago and was greatly missed.

Zeitoun got in his van and the radio assaulted him with more warnings about this storm called Katrina. It had formed near the Bahamas two days earlier and had scattered boats like toys. Zeitoun took note, but thought little of it. The winds were still many days from being relevant to his life.

He made his way to the Presbytere Museum on Jackson Square, where he had another crew working on a delicate restoration of the two-hundred-year-old building. The museum had been a courthouse long ago and was now home to a vast and extraordinary collection of Mardi Gras artifacts and memorabilia. It was a high-profile job and Zeitoun wanted to get it right.

Kathy called from home. She had just heard from a client in the Broadmoor neighborhood. Zeitoun's men had painted a window shut and someone needed to come unstick it.

"I'll go," he said. Easier that way, he figured. He would go, he would do it, it would be done. Fewer phone calls, no waiting.

"You hear about the winds?" Kathy said. "Killed three in Florida so far."

Zeitoun dismissed it. "This is not the storm for us," he said.

Kathy often poked fun at Zeitoun's stubbornness, at his unwillingness to bow before any force, natural or otherwise.

1 **molding** *here:* framework – 2 **barrel-chested** his chest looks like a barrel *(Fass)* – 8 **to assault** to attack – 10 **to scatter** to throw about – 13 **Presbytere** museum – part of the Louisiana State Museum – 29 **to poke fun at sb** to make fun of sb; to laugh at sb (but in a kind way)

But Zeitoun couldn't help it. He had been raised in the shadow of his father, a legendary sailor who had faced a series of epic trials, and had always, miraculously, survived.

Zeitoun's father, Mahmoud, had been born not far from Jableh, on Arwad Island, the only island off Syria, a landmass so small it didn't appear on some maps. There, most boys grew up to be shipbuilders or fishermen. As a teenager Mahmoud began crewing on shipping routes between Lebanon and Syria, on large sail-powered cargo boats, bringing timber to Damascus and other cities along the coast. He had been on such a ship during World War II, sailing from Cyprus to Egypt. He and his shipmates were vaguely aware of the danger of Axis forces targeting them as potential suppliers to the Allies, but they were astounded when a squadron of German planes appeared on the horizon and bore down on them. Mahmoud and the rest of the crew dove into the sea just before the planes began strafing. They managed to detach an inflatable lifeboat before their ship sank, and were crawling into it when the Germans returned. They were intent, it seemed, on killing all the crew members who had survived. Mahmoud and his fellow sailors were forced to dive from the dinghy and wait underwater until the Germans were satisfied that the crew had all been shot or drowned. When the surface seemed safe again, the sailors returned to their lifeboat and found it full of holes. They stuffed their shirts into the gaps and paddled by hand, for miles, until they reached the Egyptian shore.

But the story Mahmoud told most often when Zeitoun was growing up, the story he told when forbidding his children to live on the sea, was this one:

Mahmoud was returning from Greece on a thirty-six-foot schooner when they ran into a black and tortuous storm. They sailed through it for hours until the main mast cracked and dropped the sail into the water, threatening to drag the whole

13 **Axis forces** Germany, Italy, Japan were Axis forces in WWII

ship into the sea. Without thinking, Mahmoud climbed up the mast, intending to free the sail and right the hull. But when he reached the crack in the mast, it gave way completely, and he fell into the ocean. The ship was traveling at eight knots and there was no chance of turning it around, so the crew threw what they could to Mahmoud — a few planks and a barrel — and in minutes the boat was gone into the darkness. He was alone at sea for two days, with sharks below and storms above, clinging to the remnants of the barrel, when he finally washed ashore near Lattakia, fifty miles north of Arwad Island.

No one, including Mahmoud, could believe he had survived, and thereafter he vowed never to take the chance again. He quit sailing, moved his family from Arwad onto the mainland, and forbade his children to work on the sea. He wanted good schooling for them all, opportunities apart from fishing and shipbuilding.

Mahmoud and his wife went looking all over Syria for a new home, a place far from the water. They spent months traveling with their small children, inspecting this town and that house. But nothing seemed right. Nothing, that is, until they found themselves inside a two-story home, with enough room for all their current and future children. When Mahmoud declared that this was the place for them, his wife laughed. They were facing the sea, not fifty feet from shore.

There, in Jableh, Mahmoud opened a hardware store, sent his sons and daughters to the best schools, and taught his boys every trade he could. Everyone knew the Zeitouns, all of them hardworking and quick, and they all knew Abdulrahman, the eighth-born, a young man who wanted to know everything and who feared no kind of labor. As a teenager, he watched the tradesman in town whenever he could, studying their craft. And once they realized he was serious and a quick learner, they'd teach him whatever they knew. Over the years he'd learned every trade he could get close to — fishing, ship rigging, painting, framing, masonry, plumbing, roofing, tile work, even auto repair.

Zeitoun's father would likely be both proud and bemused by the trajectory of his son's life. He hadn't wanted his kids to work on the sea, but many of them, including Zeitoun, had. Mahmoud wanted his children to be doctors, teachers. Zeitoun, though, was too much like his father: first a sailor, then, to provide for a family and to ensure that he lived to watch them grow up, a builder.

Zeitoun called Kathy at eleven. He'd freed the window in Broadmoor and now was at Home Depot.

"You hear anything new?" he asked.

"Looks bad," she said.

She was online. The National Hurricane Center had upgraded Katrina to a Category 2. They had shifted the possible track of the storm from the Florida panhandle to the Mississippi—Louisiana coast. The storm was crossing southern Florida with winds around ninety miles an hour. At least three people had been killed. Power was out for 1.3 million households.

"People here are worried," Zeitoun said, looking around the store. "A lot of people buying plywood." The lines were long. The store was running low on plastic sheeting, duct tape, rope—anything that would protect windows from the winds.

"I'll keep watching," Kathy said.

In the parking lot, Zeitoun looked to the sky for signs of the coming weather. He saw nothing unusual. As he pushed his cart to his van, a young man, pushing his own cart full of supplies, approached Zeitoun.

1 **ship rigging** providing ships with sails etc. – 1 **masonry** stonework (e.g. in housebuilding) – 1 **plumbing** ['plʌmɪŋ] *Klempnerarbeiten* – 2 **tile work** *Fliesenarbeiten* – 11 **Home Depot** big American warehouse – 22 **plywood** *Sperrholz* – 23 **duct tape** strong silver tape used for sealing – 28 **cart** *(AE)* shopping cart *(Einkaufswagen)*

"How's business?" the man asked.

Probably an electrician, Zeitoun figured.

"Not bad," Zeitoun said. "You?"

"Could be better," he said, and introduced himself and his trade: he was indeed an electrician. He was parked next to Zeitoun, and began helping Zeitoun unload his cart. "You ever need one," he said, "I show up when I say I'll show up, and I finish what I start." He handed Zeitoun his card. They shook hands, and the electrician got into his own van, which Zeitoun noticed was in better shape than his own.

"Why do you need me?" Zeitoun asked. "Your van's newer than mine."

They both laughed, and Zeitoun put the card on his dashboard and pulled out. He would call the young man, he figured, sooner or later. He always needed electricians, and he liked the man's hustle.

When he began working in New Orleans, eleven years earlier, Zeitoun labored for just about every contractor in the city, painting, hanging Sheetrock, tiling — anything they needed — until he was hired by a man named Charlie Saucier. Charlie owned his own company, had built it from scratch. He'd become wealthy, and was hoping to retire before his knees gave out on him.

Charlie had a son in his late teens, and he wanted nothing more than to leave the company to this son. He loved his son, but his son was not a worker; he was shifty and ungrateful. He failed to show up for work, and when he did, he worked listlessly, and condescended to his father's employees.

2 **to figure** *(AE)* ['fɪgʊr] to think – 14 **dashboard** board inside a car, under the windshield, where the instruments are *(Armaturenbrett)* – 16 **hustle** ['hʌsl] *(inf)* eagerness, energy – 19 **Sheetrock** material used for plastering *(Verputzen)* – 21 **from scratch** from nothing – 22 **to retire** *here:* to stop working *usu* because of old age (or ill health) – 22 **his knees gave out on him** his knees stopped functioning properly – 26 **shifty** unsteady; cannot be trusted – 26 **ungrateful** not thankful – 28 **listless** not paying attention; without any enthusiasm – 28 **to condescend** to look down upon

At the time, Zeitoun didn't have a car, so he rode to Charlie's work sites on a bike — a ten-speed he bought for forty dollars. One day, when Zeitoun was already in danger of being late, the bike blew a tire. After riding on the rim for half a mile, he gave up. He needed to get four miles across the city in twenty minutes, and it was looking like he would be late for work for the first time in his life. He couldn't leave the bike and run — he needed that bike — and he couldn't ride on the flat tire, so he threw the bike over his shoulders started jogging. He was panicking. If he was late for this job, what would happen to his reputation? Charlie would be disappointed, and he might not hire him again. And what if Charlie talked to other contractors, and found he couldn't recommend Zeitoun? The consequences could be far-reaching. Work was a pyramid, he knew, built on day after solid day.

He ran faster. He would be tardy, but if he sprinted, he had a shot at being no more than fifteen minutes late. It was August and the humidity was profound. A mile or so into his run, already soaked in sweat, a truck pulled up next to him.

"What are you doing?" a voice asked. Without breaking stride, Zeitoun turned to see who it was. He figured it was some smart aleck poking fun at the man running along the road with a bike over his shoulders. But instead it was his boss, Charlie Saucier.

"I'm going to the job," Zeitoun said. He was still running; in hindsight he should have stopped at this point, but he was in a rhythm and he continued, with the truck puttering beside him.

Charlie laughed. "Throw your bike in the back."

As they drove, Charlie looked over to Zeitoun. "You know, I've been at this for thirty years, and I think you're the best worker I've ever had."

4 **the bike blew a tire** the tire had a puncture (a hole) in it – 16 **tardy** *(usu AE)* arriving late – 17 **to have a shot at doing sth** to have a chance of achieving sth – 20 **to break stride** to stop – 22 **smart aleck** ['ælɪk] *(inf)* impolite person because they are showing off how much they know *(Klugscheißer)* – 25 **in hindsight** looking back

They were driving to the job site and Zeitoun had finally managed to relax, knowing he wouldn't be fired that day.

"I have one guy," Charlie continued, "he says he can't come to work because his car won't start. I have another guy, he doesn't come because he slept late. He slept late! Another guy, his wife kicked him out of the house or something. So he doesn't show. I have twenty or thirty employees, and ten of them show up to work any given day."

They were at a stop sign, and Charlie took a long look at Zeitoun. "Then there's you. You have the perfect excuse. All you have is a bike, and the bike has a flat. But you're carrying your bike on your back. You're the only guy I've ever known who would have done something like that."

After that day, things moved quickly forward and upward for Zeitoun. Within a year, he had saved enough to buy his own truck. Two years later, he was working for himself and employing a dozen men.

At noon Zeitoun made his way to the Islamic Center on St. Claude — a humble-looking mosque and community gathering place downtown. Though his siblings worshiped in a variety of ways, Zeitoun was perhaps the most devout, missing none of his daily prayers. The Qur'an asked Muslims to worship five times daily: once between first light and dawn; again after midday; at mid-afternoon; at sunset; and lastly an hour and a half after sunset. If he found himself near home during the afternoon prayers, he would stop, but otherwise he prayed wherever he was, on any job. He had worshiped all over the city by now, at job sites, in parks, and in the homes of friends, but on Fridays he always stopped here, to meet friends for the *jumu'ah,* a ritual gathering of all the Muslim men in the community.

19 **humble** *here:* small, modest – 19 **mosque and community gathering place** *Moschee und Gemeindezentrum* – 20 **to worship** to pray to God / Allah – 21 **devout** very religious

Inside, he first washed in a ritual cleansing called *wuduu*, required of worshipers. Then he began his prayers:

In the name of God, the Most Beneficent,
the Most Merciful:
Praise be to God, the Lord of the Heavens and the Earth.
The Most Beneficent, the Most Merciful.
Master of the Day of Judgment.
You alone we worship, and You alone we ask for help
Guide us to the straight way;
the way of those whom you have blessed,
not of those who have deserved anger,
nor of those who are astray...

Afterward he called Kathy.

"It'll be a Category 3 soon," she said.

Kathy was at home, checking the weather online.

"Coming at us?" he asked.

"They say it is."

"When?"

"Not sure. Maybe Monday."

Zeitoun dismissed it. Monday, to him, meant never. This had happened before, Zeitoun noted, so many times. The storms always raged across Florida, wreaking havoc, and then died somewhere overland or in the Gulf.

Kathy's call waiting went off; she said goodbye to Zeitoun and switched over. It was Rob Stanislaw, a longtime client and friend.

"You leaving or are you crazy?" he asked.

Kathy cackled. "I want to leave. Of course. But I can't speak for my husband."

Rob had a similar predicament. His husband, Walt Thompson, was like Zeitoun — bullheaded, always feeling

1 **to cleanse** [klenz] to clean – 2 **required of worshippers** what believers have to do – 3 **beneficent** [bɪˈnefɪsənt] *(AE)* kind – 4 **merciful** full of mercy *(Gnade)* – 12 **astray** away from the correct path – 20 **to dismiss** to not take seriously – 22 **to wreak havoc** to cause chaos – 28 **to cackle** to make a shrill cry (like a hen) – 30 **predicament** [prɪˈdɪkəmənt] situation

like his information was better than what anyone else had access to. Rob and Walt had been together for fifteen years, and had been close with the Zeitouns since 1997. They had hired the Zeitouns to help with the renovation of a house they'd bought, and immediately the two couples had clicked. Over the years they'd grown to depend on each other.

Walt's family was in Baton Rouge, and it was likely that Rob and Walt would go there for the weekend, he said. Rob and Kathy agreed to update each other throughout the day.

She was about to take a break from the internet when something caught her attention. A news item, just posted: a family of five was missing at sea. The details were few — two parents, three kids aged four, fourteen, and seventeen. They had been sailing in the Gulf, and had been expected Thursday in Cape Coral. But when the storm came, they'd lost contact. Family and friends had notified the Coast Guard, and boats and planes were searching as best they could. That was all anyone knew for now, and it looked bad.

Kathy was a mess. Stories like this just wrecked her.

Kathy called her husband. "Rob and Walt are leaving."

"Really? Walt wants to leave?"

Zeitoun trusted Walt's judgment on just about everything.

Kathy thought she might have her husband tilting her way. "Fifteen inches of rain, I hear."

Silence from Zeitoun.

"Twenty-five-foot waves," Kathy added.

Zeitoun changed the subject. "Did you get the DeClercs to approve that paint sample?"

"I did," Kathy said. "Did you hear about this family of five?"

1 **had access to** *here:* could get – 5 **to click** *(inf)* to understand each other – 11 **a news item** *eine Nachricht* – 15 **Cape Coral** city in Florida on the Gulf coast – 19 **to be a mess** *(inf)* to be worried and confused – 23 **to tilt one's way** *here:* to listen to her and be convinced by her opinion – 26 **twenty-five foot waves** waves more than 7 meters high

He had not, so in a breathless rush Kathy told him what she knew about the family lost at sea in their tiny boat, swept away in the hurricane, just as the Zeitouns might be swept away if they didn't flee its path.

"We're not at sea, Kathy," Zeitoun said.

Zeitoun had spent the better part of ten years on ships, carrying everything from fruit to oil. He worked as a crewman, an engineer, a fisherman — he'd been everywhere from Japan to Cape Town. All along, his brother Ahmad had told him that "If a sailor finds the right port or the right woman, he'll drop anchor." In 1988 Zeitoun came to the United States on a tanker carrying oil from Saudi Arabia to Houston. He began working for a contractor in Baton Rouge, and it was there that he met Ahmaad, a Lebanese American who became one of his closest friends and the conduit through which he met his bride.

Ahmaad was working at a gas station at the time, and Zeitoun was hanging drywall. They bonded over common ancestry, and one day Zeitoun asked Ahmaad if he knew any single women who might be appropriate for him. Ahmaad was married to a woman named Yuko, an American of Japanese ancestry who had converted to Islam. And Yuko, it turned out, had a friend. Ahmaad was conflicted, though, because while he liked and trusted Zeitoun and wanted to help, he was hoping this friend of Yuko's might be a match for another friend of his. If it didn't work out between his friend and Yuko's, he said, he would surely introduce her to Zeitoun. Zeitoun was willing to respect that boundary, but at the same time his interest was piqued. Who was this woman who was so prized that Ahmaad would not even mention her name?

14 **Lebanese American** American originally from Lebanon – 15 **conduit** ['kɑ:nduɪt] channel; means – 18 **drywall** ceiling constructed from prefabricated material – 18 **to bond** to connect – 19 **ancestry** *Vorfahren* – 28 **boundary** limit – 29 **to pique** [pi:k] *here:* to arouse

That year Zeitoun became increasingly determined to find the right woman. He told friends and cousins he was looking for a down-to-earth Muslim woman who wanted a family. Knowing he was a serious and hardworking man, they provided many introductions. He was sent to New York to meet the daughter of an acquaintance. He went to Oklahoma to meet the cousin of a friend. He went to Alabama to meet the sister of a coworker's roommate.

Meanwhile, Yuko's friend had been set up with Ahmaad's friend, and though they courted for a few months, that relationship came to an end. Ahmaad, as promised, let Zeitoun know that Yuko's friend was now single. It was only then that Zeitoun was told her name: Kathy.

"Kathy?" Zeitoun asked. He hadn't known too many Muslims named Kathy. "Kathy what?"

"Kathy Delphine," Ahmaad said.

"She's American?"

"She's from Baton Rouge. She converted."

Zeitoun was more intrigued than ever. It took a courageous and self-possessed woman to take such a step.

"But listen," Ahmaad said. "She's been married. She has a two-year-old son."

This did nothing to dissuade Zeitoun.

"When can I see her?" he asked.

Ahmaad told him she worked at a furniture store, and gave Zeitoun the address. Zeitoun formulated a plan. He would park out front and observe her unnoticed. This was, he told Ahmaad, Jableh style. He didn't want to make a move, or allow anyone representing him to mention his intentions, before he could see her. This was the way of doing things where he'd come from: observe from afar, make inquiries, gather information, then meet. He wanted no confusion, no hurt feelings.

6 **acquaintance** distant friend *(Bekannte/r)* – 19 **intrigued** [ɪn'tri:gd] interested – 23 **to dissuade** to discourage, turn away

He pulled into the furniture store's parking lot at about five o'clock one day, planning to wait and watch as she left at the end of her shift.

He was just settling in for his stakeout when a young woman burst through the door, wearing jeans and a hijab. She was striking, and very young. She tucked a few strands of hair into her scarf and looked around the parking lot. And then she was walking again, striding with a powerful confidence, her hands flying about as if she were drying just-painted fingernails. Then she broke into a private smile, as if recounting something that had made her laugh. *What was it?* Zeitoun wondered. She was beautiful, fresh-faced, and the smile was everything — wide, shy, electric. *I want to make her smile like that,* he thought. *I want to be the one. I want to be the reason.* He liked her more with every step she took toward him. He was sold.

But she was getting too close. She was heading straight for him. Did she know he had come to see her? How was this possible? Someone had told her. Ahmaad? Yuko? She was almost at his car. He would look foolish. Why was she coming right at him? He wasn't ready to meet her.

Not knowing what else to do, he ducked. Crouching below his dashboard, he held his breath and waited. *Please God,* he thought. *Please.* Would she pass by, or would she appear at his window, wondering about the man trying to disappear below her? He felt ridiculous.

Kathy, though, had no idea she was passing a man hiding under his steering wheel. Her car just happened to be parked next to his. She unlocked her door, got in, and drove off.

When she was gone, Zeitoun righted himself, breathed a sigh of relief, and tried to settle his stampeding heart.

"I need to meet her," he told Ahmaad.

4 **stakeout** surveillance *(Überwachung)* – 8 **to stride** to walk quickly and confidently – 10 **to recount** to remember

It was agreed that they would meet at Ahmaad and Yuko's house. There would be a casual dinner, with Ahmaad and Yuko's kids and Kathy's son Zachary. It would be low-pressure, just an opportunity for the two of them to talk a bit and for Kathy, who had yet to even see Zeitoun, to meet this man who had inquired about her.

When she saw him, she liked his eyes, his handsome, gold-skinned face. But he seemed too conservative, and he was thirty-four to her twenty-one — well beyond the age she had imagined for a husband. Besides, it had been just two years since she'd left her first marriage, and she felt unready to begin again. She could think of nothing she needed from a man. She could certainly raise Zachary herself; the two of them had become a very good and streamlined team, and there seemed no reason to upset the balance of her life. She couldn't risk the chaos that her first marriage had wrought.

After he left that night, Kathy told Yuko that he was a nice enough man, but she didn't think it was a good match.

But over the next two years, she and Zeitoun saw each other occasionally. He would be at a barbecue at Ahmaad and Yuko's, but out of deference to her — he didn't want her to feel uncomfortable — when Kathy arrived, he would leave. He continued to ask about her, and once a year he sent an offhand inquiry through Yuko, just to be sure she hadn't changed her mind.

Meanwhile, Kathy's outlook was evolving. As Zachary grew, she began to feel guilty. She would take him to the park and watch the other boys playing with their fathers, and she began to wonder if she was being selfish. *A boy needs a dad,* she thought. Was it unfair to dismiss the possibility of a father figure in Zachary's life? Not that she was ready to act on these notions, but there was a slow thaw occurring within her. As

2 **casual** ['kæʒju:l] easy-going, not formal – 16 **wrought** *here:* brought, caused – 21 **deference** ['defərənts] respect – 26 **her outlook was evolving** her view on things was changing – 32 **thaw** [θɑ:] melting

the years went by, as Zachary turned three and then four, she grew more open to the idea of someone new.

Kathy called Zeitoun in the early afternoon.

“Let’s wait and see,” he said.

“That isn’t why I’m calling,” she said.

A client on the West Bank wanted a bathroom repainted.

“Really? We just finished that one,” he said.

“She doesn’t like how it looks.”

“I told her that color was wrong. Tangerine.”

“Well, now she agrees with you.”

“I’ll go now,” he said.

“Don’t rush,” she said.

“Well, make up your mind.”

“I just don’t want you driving fast,” she said. Kathy worried about his driving, especially when there were people worried about a coming storm. She knew Zeitoun considered himself a good driver, but when they rode together she was a jumble of nerves.

“Kathy, please—” he started.

“I just get scared when you drive!”

“I ask you,” he said, beginning what Kathy knew was one of his frequent thought experiments. “Let’s say the average person drives maybe two hours a day, every day, and that person gets, on average, two tickets a year. I drive maybe six hours each day. How many tickets should I have? This is what I ask.”

“I’m just saying, I personally get scared.”

“I get only two, three tickets a *year,* Kathy! I knew this man, a cab driver in New York for thirty years. No license, and this man—“

Kathy didn’t want to hear about the man in New York. “I’m just saying...”

“Kathy. Kathy. In Syria we have a saying, ’The crazy person talks, the wise person listens.’”

9 **tangerine** [ˌtændʒəˈriːn] orange – 17 **a jumble of nerves** very nervous

"But you're the one talking."

Zeitoun had to laugh. She always got the best of him.

"I'll call you later," she said.

Zeitoun headed to the West Bank to get a look at the tangerine bathroom. He tried to be amused by the fickle nature of clients' tastes; it was part of the job, and if he got exasperated every time someone changed their mind, he'd never survive. The upshot was that it ensured no day was dull. The intensely personal nature of his business, the subjectivity of taste, the variables of light and curtains and carpets, guaranteed that minds would reevaluate and work would have to be redone.

Still, the most unusual requests often came from the most normal-seeming people. One customer, a Southern belle in her sixties, had called Zeitoun Painting and had been happy to talk with Kathy, with her chatty demeanor and familiar accent. But when the painters showed up to begin work on the exterior of her home, the woman immediately called Kathy.

"I don't like these men," she said.

"What's wrong with 'em?" Kathy asked.

"They're swarthy," she said. "I only want white people working on my house." She said it like she was choosing a kind of dressing for her salad.

"White people?" Kathy laughed. "Sorry, we're fresh out of those."

She convinced the woman that the men who had been sent — all of them Latino, in this case — were skilled professionals who would do an excellent job. The woman assented, but continued to call. "He's too short to be a painter," she said about one worker, Hector, who was over six feet tall. Realizing

2 **to get the best of sb** to beat sb in an argument or discussion – 5 **fickle** unstable, changing quickly – 7 **exasperated** [ɪg'zæspəreɪt̬ɪd] angry – 8 **upshot** *(inf)* result – 11 **to reevaluate** [ri:ɪ'væljuːeɪt] *here:* to change – 14 **Southern belle** *(old)* a rich, beautiful woman from the South with a Southern accent – 16 **chatty demeanor** [dɪ'mi:nɚ] love of chatting – 21 **swarthy** ['swɔ:rθi] with dark skin color – 28 **to assent** to agree

that no matter how much she complained, she would not be able to replace these painters with taller, Caucasian ones, the Southern belle resigned herself to watching the men, checking on them frequently.

Of course, every so often, would-be clients could not get past Zeitoun's last name. They would call for an estimate and ask Kathy, "Zeitoun, where's that name come from? Where is he from?" And Kathy would say, "Oh, he's Syrian." Then, after a long pause or a shorter one, they would say, "Oh, okay, never mind." It was rare, but not rare enough.

Kathy sometimes told Zeitoun about such incidents, sometimes not, and never at dinner. Usually he just laughed it off, but occasionally it got under his skin. His frustration with some Americans was like that of a disappointed parent. He was so content in this country, so impressed with and loving of its opportunities, but then why, sometimes, did Americans fall short of their best selves? If you got him started on the subject, it was the end of any pleasant meal. He would begin with a defense of Muslims in America and expand his thesis from there. Since the attacks in New York, he would say, every time a crime was committed by a Muslim, that person's faith was mentioned, regardless of its relevance. When a crime is committed by a Christian, do they mention his religion? If a Christian is stopped at the airport for trying to bring a gun on a plane, is the Western world notified that a Christian was arrested today and is being questioned? And what about African Americans? When a crime is committed by a black man, it's mentioned in the first breath: "An African American man was arrested today..." But what about German Americans? Anglo Americans? A white man robs a convenience store and do we hear he's of Scottish descent? In no other instance is the ancestry mentioned.

Then Zeitoun would quote the Qur'an.

2 **Caucasian** white person – 6 **estimate** idea about how much a job will cost *(Kostenvoranschlag)* – 17 **to fall short of one's best self** to not be as good as they could be – 30 **convenience store** small food shop

Be one who is staunch in equity,
witnesses for God
even against yourselves
or ones who are your parents or nearest of kin;
whether rich or poor,
for God is closer to both than you are;
so follow not your desires
that you become unbalanced;
and if you distort or turn aside,
then truly God is aware of what you do.

Kathy was astonished at how well he knew the book, and how quickly he could quote a passage appropriate for any occasion. Still, though, these monologues at dinner? It was good for the kids to have some awareness of such prejudices, but to see Zeitoun disappointed, to get him so worked up after a long day — it wasn't worth it. In the end, though, Zeitoun could laugh this kind of thing off, but the one thing he could not abide was a client raising their voice to Kathy.

There had been one client, a young woman married to a doctor. She was thin, pretty, immaculately put together. She had not set off any alarm bells when Zeitoun had provided an estimate and begun work on painting her stairway and guest bedroom. She told him that she and her husband were expecting houseguests, and she wanted the stairway and guest room painted in five days' time. Zeitoun said the timetable would be tight, but would present no problems on his end. She was thrilled. No other painter had been able to commit to such a deadline.

Zeitoun sent a crew of three over the next day. The client, seeing the quick and efficient work Zeitoun's team was doing, asked him if they could paint her husband's office and her daughter's bedroom, too. He said they could. He sent more

1 **staunch** firm – 1 **equity** fairness, justice – 4 **nearest of kin** closest family member – 9 **to distort** to lie – 18 **to abide** to stand, to bear – 20 **immaculately** perfectly

painters to the house, and she continued to add rooms and jobs — including re-tiling and painting a bathroom — and Zeitoun's men continued to execute the work quickly.

But not quickly enough. On the third day, Kathy phoned Zeitoun, near tears. The woman had called Kathy four times in rapid succession, cursing and carrying on. The house wasn't ready, the client had screamed, and her guests were coming in less than two days. Kathy had told her that Zeitoun's crew had finished the original work on the guest room in plenty of time. But this wasn't what the client wanted. She wanted everything — all seven rooms and their myriad tasks — done in five days. She wanted three times the work done in the same amount of time.

Kathy had tried to reason with her. She and Zeitoun had never promised that he could finish all of the additional work in five days. That schedule was irrational; no one, not even Zeitoun A. Painting Contractor LLC, could complete the work on that timetable. But the client was beyond reason. She barked at Kathy, hanging up, calling again, hanging up. She was loud, condescending, and cruel.

Kathy, in tears, reached Zeitoun on his cell phone while he was driving to a job on the other side of the city. Even before they hung up, he had turned his truck around and was barreling to the client's house as fast as was legal. When he got there, he walked calmly into the house and told his crew they were leaving. In the space of ten minutes, they packed their paint, ladders, brushes, and tarps, and loaded them into the bed of Zeitoun's truck.

As Zeitoun was backing out, the client's husband ran out to the truck. What's wrong? he asked. What happened? Zeitoun was so angry he could barely think of the words in English. It was better, in fact, that he did not speak. He waited a few

3 **to execute** to carry out – 11 **myriad** [ˈmɪriəd] very large number of – 20 **condescending** [ˌkɑːdɪˈsendɪŋ] arrogant – 27 **tarp** (*abb* for "tarpaulin") waterproof material *(Plane)*

seconds to say only that no one talked that way to his wife, that he was leaving the job, that this was over and good luck.

When he arrived at the tangerine-bathroom house, he called Kathy to run through the prices for the materials they'd need. Looking around the orange room — it really was difficult to look at — he noted the clients' new tub, a huge claw-footed antique.

"It's big, but isn't it beautiful?" Kathy asked.

"Yes, like you!" he joked.

"Watch it," she said. "I can lose this weight, but you're never growing that hair back."

When they'd met, Kathy had been weight-obsessed, and was far too thin. She had been chubby as a child, at least to some eyes, and in her teens her weight fluctuated wildly. She binged and dieted and then cycled through it all again. When she and Zeitoun were married, he insisted that she get beyond the weight issues and eat like a normal person. She did, and now joked that she'd gone too far. "Thank God for the abaya," she told friends. When she didn't want to bother worrying about clothes or how they looked on her, the shoulder-to-floor Islamic dress solved the problem, and tidily.

There was a knock on the door. Kathy went to answer it and found Melvin, a Guatemalan painter. He was looking to get paid before the weekend.

Zeitoun was relentless in his efforts to pay the workers well and promptly. He always quoted the Prophet Muhammad: "Pay the laborer his wages before his sweat dries." Zeitoun used that as a bedrock and constant guide in the way he and Kathy did business, and the workers took note.

7 **claw-footed tub** bathtub with feet looking like animal claws – 13 **chubby** rounded (nice/polite word for "overweight") – 15 **to binge** [bɪndʒ] to eat too much (in an uncontrolled way) – 16 **to get beyond weight issues** to not worry about body weight any more – 25 **relentless** non-stop; he always tried his hardest to do it – 28 **bedrock** basis

Still, Zeitoun preferred to pay on Sundays or Mondays — because when he paid on Fridays, too many of the workers would disappear all weekend. But Kathy's heart was soft, her resolve to withhold payment even an hour weakened in the presence of these workers soaked with sweat, knuckles bleeding, forearms yellow with sawdust.

"Don't tell Zeitoun," she said, and wrote him a check.

Kathy turned on the TV and flipped through the channels. Every station was covering the storm.

Nothing had changed: Katrina was still headed their way, and it was losing no power. And because the hurricane as a whole was traveling so slowly, about eight miles per hour, the sustained winds were causing, and would continue to cause, catastrophic damage.

The coverage was just background noise, though, until Kathy caught the words "family of five." They were talking about the family lost at sea. *Oh no,* she thought. *Please.* She turned up the sound. They were still missing. The father's name was Ed Larsen. He was a construction supervisor. *You're kidding me,* she thought. He had taken the week off to take his family sailing on his yacht, the *Sea Note.* They had been at Marathon and were sailing back to Cape Coral when they'd lost radio contact. His wife and three kids were with him. They were on their way back to shore for a family reunion. The extended family had gathered only to realize that the Larsens were missing; the celebration turned into a vigil of worry and prayer.

Kathy couldn't stand it.

She called her husband. "We have to go."

"Wait, wait," he said. "Let's wait and see."

"Please," she said.

"Really?" he said. "You can go."

4 **resolve** decision – 4 **to withhold payment** not to pay immediately – 13 **sustained** *here:* constant – 15 **coverage** *here:* TV report – 22 **Marathon** town on an island of the Florida Keys

Kathy had taken the kids north a handful of times when storms had gotten close. But she was hoping she wouldn't have to make the trip this time. She had work to do over the weekend, and the kids had plans, and she always came back from those trips more exhausted than when she'd left.

Almost without exception, whether it was fleeing a storm or for a weekend vacation, Kathy and the kids had to go without Zeitoun. Her husband had trouble leaving the business, had trouble relaxing for days on end, and after years of this vacationless life Kathy had threatened to pack the kids and just leave for Florida some Friday after school. At first Zeitoun hadn't believed her. Would she really pack up and leave with or without him?

She would, and she did. One Friday afternoon, Zeitoun was checking on a nearby job and decided to stop at home. He wanted to see the kids, change his shirt, pick up some paperwork. But when he pulled into the driveway, there was Kathy, loading up the minivan, the two youngest already buckled inside.

"Where you going?" he asked.

"I told you I'd go with or without you. And we're going."

They were going to Destin, Florida, a beach town on the Gulf about four hours away, with long white beaches and clear water.

"Come with us, Daddy!" Nademah pleaded. She had just come out of the house with their snorkeling gear.

Zeitoun was too stunned to react. He had a hundred things on his mind, and a pipe at one of the rental properties had just burst. How could he go?

Nademah got in the front seat and put on her seatbelt.

"Bye bye," Kathy said, backing out. "See you Sunday."

And they were gone, the girls waving as they left.

19 **to buckle** to fasten a seat belt – 27 **stunned** extremely surprised

He didn't go that Friday, but after that, he no longer doubted Kathy's resolve. He knew she was serious — that in the future he'd be consulted on vacation plans, but that trips to Florida or beyond could and would happen with or without him. So over the years there were other trips to Destin, and he even made it on a few of them.

But always his decision was made at the last minute. One time Kathy was late in getting started, and he was so late in deciding that he couldn't even pack. She was in the driveway, backing out, when he pulled in.

"Now or never," she said, barely stopping the car.

And so he jumped in the car. The girls giggled to see their dad in the back seat, still in his work clothes, dirty and sweating — as much from the stress of the decision as from the day's work. Zeitoun had to buy beach clothes when they got to Florida.

Kathy was proud that she'd gotten him to Destin once a year. Zeitoun didn't mind going too much because, given how close it was, he knew he could come back at any time — and more than once, he had cut a vacation short because of some problem at one of the work sites.

By 2002, though, Kathy wanted something that really felt like a vacation. And she knew she had to do something drastic. In all their time together — eight years at that point — he had never taken more than two days off in a row. She knew that she had no choice but to kidnap him.

She started by planning a weekend in Destin. She chose a weekend when she knew things would be calm at work; it was just after Christmas, and there was rarely much work till well after New Year's. As usual, Zeitoun wouldn't commit till the last minute, so she took the precaution of actually packing a bag for him and hiding it in the back of the mini-van. Because she had made sure the weekend was quiet, he came along —

2 **resolve** determination – 31 **to take the precaution** to prepare *(Vorsorge treffen)*

as always, at the last minute. Kathy told him she'd drive, and because he was exhausted, he agreed. She made sure the kids were quiet — they were in on the plan — and he soon fell asleep, drooling on his seatbelt. While he slept, Kathy drove right on through Destin and onward down the paunch of Florida. Each time he woke up she would say, "Almost there, go back to sleep," and thankfully he would — he was so tired — and it wasn't until an hour north of Miami that he realized they weren't going to Destin. Kathy had driven straight down to Miami. Seventeen hours. She'd checked on the computer for the warmest place in the country that week, and Miami was it. Being that far away was the only way to ensure he would take a real vacation, a full week's worth of rest. Every time she thought back on the gambit, and how well it had worked, Kathy smiled to herself. A marriage was a system like any other, and she knew how to work it.

At about two-thirty, Ahmad called Zeitoun again. He was still tracking the storm from his computer in Spain.

"Doesn't look good for you," he said.

Zeitoun promised he would keep watch on it.

"Imagine the storm surges," Ahmad said.

Zeitoun told him he was paying close attention.

"Why not leave, just to be safe?" Ahmad said.

Kathy decided to go to the grocery store before picking up the girls from school. You could never tell when people would make a run on the basics before a storm arrived, and she wanted to avoid the crush. She went to the mirror to adjust her hijab, brushed her teeth, and left the house. Not that she thought about it much, but any trip to the grocery store or the mall presented the possibility that she would encounter some kind of ugliness. The frequency of incidents seemed tied, to

4 **to drool** to have spit run from one's mouth – 5 **paunch** belly – 14 **gambit** trick; maneuver – 21 **to surge** to rise, increase in force – 31 **incidents** *here:* anti-Muslim activities

some extent, to current events, to the general media profile of Muslims that week or month. Certainly after 9/11 it was more fraught than before, and then it had calmed for a few years. But in 2004 a local incident had stoked the fire again. At West Jefferson High School, a tenth grader of Iraqi descent had been repeatedly harassed by her history teacher. He had called Iraq a "third-world country," had worried that the student would "bomb us" if she ever returned to Iraq. In February of that year, while passing out tests, the teacher had pulled back the girl's hijab and said, "I hope God punishes you. No, I'm sorry, I hope Allah punishes you." The incident was widely reported. The student filed a lawsuit against him, and his termination was recommended by the Jefferson Parish School District superintendent. The school board overruled; he was given a few weeks' suspension and returned to the classroom.

After the decision, there had been an uptick in minor harassment of Muslims in the area, and Kathy was aware of the invitation she was providing in going out in her hijab. There was a new practice in vogue at the time, favored by adolescent boys or those who thought like them: sneak up behind a woman wearing a headscarf, grab it, and run.

One day it happened to Kathy. She was shopping with Asma, a friend who happened to be Muslim but who wore no hijab. Asma was originally from Algeria, and had been living in the U.S. for twenty years; she was usually taken for Spanish. Kathy and Asma were leaving the mall, and outside, Kathy was trying to remember where she'd parked her car. She and

3 **fraught** [frɑːt] intense, out of control – 12 **to file a lawsuit** to go to court *(anklagen)* – 13 **termination** *here:* the end of his work contract – 14 **superintendent** head, boss – 14 **the school board overruled** the people on the school board changed the decision – 15 **to give a few weeks' suspension** to be not allowed to work for a few weeks – 17 **uptick** increase – 18 **harassment** [həˈræsmənt] bullying

Asma were on the sidewalk, Kathy squinting at the rows of gleaming cars, when Asma gave her a funny look.

"Kathy, there's a girl behind you —"

A girl of about fifteen was crouched behind Kathy, her arm raised, about to yank the hijab off Kathy's head.

Kathy cocked her head. "You got a problem?" she barked.

The girl cowered and slunk away, joining a group of boys and girls her age, all of whom had been watching. Once back with her friends, the girl directed some choice words Kathy's way. Her friends laughed and echoed her, cursing at Kathy in half a dozen different ways.

They could not have expected Kathy to return the favor. They assumed, no doubt, that a Muslim woman, presumably submissive and shy with her English, would allow her hijab to be ripped from her head without retaliation. But Kathy let loose a fusillade of pungent suggestions, leaving them dumbfounded and momentarily speechless.

On the drive home, even Kathy was shocked by what she'd said. She had been brought up around plenty of cursing, and knew every word and provocative construction, but since she'd become a mother, since she'd converted, she hadn't sworn more than once or twice. But those kids needed to learn something, and so she'd obliged.

In the weeks after the attacks on the Twin Towers, Kathy saw very few Muslim women in public. She was certain they were hiding, leaving home only when necessary. In late September, she was in Walgreens when she finally saw a woman in a hijab. She ran to her. *"Salaam alaikum!"* she said, taking the woman's hands. The woman, a doctor studying at Tulane, had been feeling the same way, like an exile in her

1 **to squint** to look with the eyes partly closed as if looking into a bright light *(die Augen zukneifen)* – 5 **to yank** *(inf)* to tear violently – 6 **to cock one's head** to turn around – 9 **choice words** *here:* swear words – 15 **retaliation** revenge – 16 **pungent suggestions** [ˈpʌndʒənt] sharp words – 17 **dumbfounded** [ˈdʌmfaʊndɪd] silent with surprise; perplexed – 24 **Twin Towers** New York World Trade Center – 27 **Walgreens** drugstore chain – 30 **Tulane** Tulane University in New Orleans

own country, and they laughed at how delirious they were to see each other.

On this day in August, the grocery-store trip went off without confrontation, and she picked up her girls.

"You hear about the storm?" Nademah asked.

"It's coming toward us," Safiya added from the back seat.

"Are we going to leave?" Nademah asked.

Kathy knew that her kids wanted to. They could go to one of their cousins' homes, in Mississippi or Baton Rouge, and it would be a vacation, a two-day sleepover. Maybe school would be canceled on Monday as the city cleaned up? This was surely what they were thinking and hoping. Kathy knew the workings of her children's minds.

When they got home, it was five o'clock and Katrina was all over the news. The family watched footage of enormous waves, uprooted trees, whole towns washed grey with torrential rain. The National Hurricane Center was suggesting that Katrina would soon become a Category 3. Governor Blanco held a press conference to declare a state of emergency for Louisiana. Governor Barbour did the same for Mississippi.

Kathy was rattled. Sitting on the arm of the couch, she was so distracted that soon it was six o'clock and she hadn't started dinner. She called Zeitoun.

"Can you get Popeyes on your way home?" she asked.

At home, Nademah arranged the tablecloth and placemats. Safiya and Aisha set out the silverware and glasses. Kathy threw together a salad and poured milk for the kids and juice for herself and Zeitoun.

1 **delirious** extremely excited – 15 **footage** films – 16 **uprooted** blown over, fallen – 17 **torrential** extemely heavy – 19 **state of emergency** very dangerous situation *(Notstand)* – 22 **rattled** *(inf)* scared, nervous – 25 **Popeyes** name of restaurant chain that makes Louisiana Cajun fried chicken

Zeitoun arrived with the chicken, showered, and joined the family for dinner.

“Finish, finish,” he said to his daughters, who were picking at their food, leaving huge swaths of it uneaten.

He had gotten used to it after all these years, but still, there were times when the waste got to him. The disposability of just about everything. Growing up in Syria he had often heard the expression “If your hand doesn’t work for it, your heart doesn’t feel sorry for it.” But in the U.S., it wasn’t just the prosperity — because New Orleans was not uniformly prosperous, to be sure — there was a sense that everything could be replaced, and on a whim. In his children he was trying to instill a sense of the value of work, the value of whatever came into their house, but he knew that much would be lost in the context, the waste and excess of the culture at large. He had been brought up to know that what God hates as much as anything is waste. It was, he had been told, one of the three things God *most* hated: murder, divorce, and waste. It destroyed a society.

After dinner the girls asked if they could watch *Pride and Prejudice* again. It was Friday night, so Zeitoun had no school-related reasons to block the movie. Still, it didn’t mean he had to sit and watch it again. He’d liked the movie fine the first time, but the need to watch it a dozen times in as many days was beyond him. In the past week, he and Zachary had retired to other rooms to do something, anything, else. Kathy, though, was right there with the girls each time, and this time all of them draped over each other on the couch, misting up at the same parts they always did. Zeitoun shook his head and went into the kitchen to fix a cabinet door that had gotten loose.

4 **swath** [swɑːθ] large piece, strip – 6 **to get to sb** to anger sb – 6 **disposability** the fact that sth can be thrown away – 10 **prosperity** wealth – 12 **to replace on a whim** to substitute immediately – 24 **the need to watch … was beyond him** he did not understand why people needed to watch… – 28 **to mist up** *here:* to cry – 30 **cabinet** cupboard

All evening they paused the movie to watch the news reports about the storm's intensity and direction. Still moving slowly, the hurricane was heading up the coast with winds over one hundred miles per hour. The longer it lingered over any region, the more destruction it would bring. All the news was terrible, and when Kathy saw the picture of the family of five she was ready to turn it off. She was sure they were gone, and she would obsess over this family for weeks, thinking about all their relatives gathered for the reunion, now forced to mourn the loss of so many at once — but then Kathy realized that the family was not lost. She turned up the volume. They had been rescued. They had docked their boat on a mangrove island near Ten Thousand Islands, and had ridden out the storm in the cabin of the yacht, praying and taking turns climbing up to look for help in the skies. Just hours earlier, the Coast Guard had spotted their boat and lifted them all to safety. The family of five had been saved.

Later, after kissing Zachary goodnight, Kathy lay down in Nademah's bed and the girls arranged themselves around her, a mess of overlapping limbs and pillows.

"Who wants to start?" Kathy asked.

Safiya began a story about Pokemon. The stories, which the girls told collaboratively, were often about Pokemon. After Aisha introduced the protagonist, Safiya provided the setting and central conflict, and Nademah took it from there. They continued, taking turns advancing the plot, until Aisha was asleep and Nademah and Safiya were drifting off. Kathy looked up to find Zeitoun in the doorway, leaning against the frame, watching them all. He did this often, just watching, taking it all in. The scene was almost too much, too beautiful. It was enough to burst a man's heart wide open.

4 **to linger** to stay in one place (often for a long time) – 13 **mangrove** tree which grows in salt water in the (sub-) tropics – 13 **Ten Thousand Islands** group of islands on the southwest coast of Florida near Naples – 16 **Coast Guard** branch of the US armed service responsible for safety at sea – 16 **to spot** to see – 22 **Pokemon** ['poʊkeɪmɑːn] pocket monster – 23 **collaborative** [kə'læbɚət̬ɪv] together

SATURDAY AUGUST 27

Zeitoun and Kathy woke late, after eight. When they turned on the TV they saw Michael Brown, director of the Federal Emergency Management Agency, telling all residents of New Orleans to leave as soon as they could, to head inland with all possible haste. The National Hurricane Center had issued a watch for central Louisiana and warned that the hurricane could become a Category 5 by the time it made landfall. Category 5 hurricanes had only struck the United States mainland three times before, and never New Orleans.

"Honey," Kathy said, "I think we should go."

"You go," Zeitoun said. "I'll stay."

"How can you stay?" she asked.

But she knew the answer. Their business wasn't a simple one, where you could lock an office door and leave. Leaving the city meant leaving all their properties, leaving their tenants' homes, and this they couldn't do unless absolutely necessary. They had job sites all over the city, and any number of things could happen in their absence. They would be liable for damage if their equipment caused harm to clients' property. It was yet another hazard of the company they'd built.

Kathy was leaning strongly toward fleeing, and watching the news throughout the day it seemed that there were so many new indicators that this storm was unique that she didn't feel she could even contemplate staying in the city. They'd already closed down most operations at Louis Armstrong International Airport. The Louisiana National Guard had called four thousand troops into service.

6 **to issue** to publish officially – 7 **watch** period of close observation – 8 **to make landfall** to reach land – 10 **mainland** the land not including islands and peninsulas – 19 **liable** ['laɪəbl] legally responsible – 21 **hazard** danger – 28 **National Guard** military reserve unit of every state

Mid-morning, it was at least ninety-five degrees, the air leaden with humidity. Zeitoun was in the backyard, running around with the kids and Mekay, the dog. Kathy opened the back door.

"You're really staying?" Kathy asked him. Somehow she thought that he might be wavering. She was wrong.

"What're you worried about?" he said.

She wasn't worried, in fact. She didn't fear for her husband's safety, really, but she did have the feeling that life in the city would be very trying during and after the storm. The electricity would go. The roads would be covered with debris, impassable for days. Why would he want to struggle through all that?

"I have to watch the house," he said. "The other houses. One small hole in the roof — if I fix it, no damage. If not, the whole house is wrecked."

By the early afternoon Mayor Nagin and Governor Blanco had called for a voluntary evacuation of the city. Nagin told residents that the Superdome would be open as a "shelter of last resort." Kathy shuddered at the thought; the year before, with Hurricane Ivan, that plan had been a miserable failure. The Superdome had been ill-supplied and overcrowded then and in '98, with Hurricane Georges. She couldn't believe the place was being used again. Maybe they'd learned from the last time and better provisioned the stadium? Anything was possible, but she was doubtful.

Kathy planned to leave as soon as the contraflow took effect, supposedly around four o'clock. The contraflow would allow all lanes of every highway to flow outward from the city.

1 **ninety-five degrees Fahrenheit** 35 degrees Celsius – 2 **leaden** ['ledən] very heavy – 6 **to waver** to hesitate – 11 **debris** [də'bri:] rubble, litter – 19 **Superdome** large convention center also used for NBA games etc. – 19 **shelter of last resort** place to go if you have nowhere else *(letzter Zufluchtsort)* – 22 **ill-supplied** with too few supplies

By then Kathy would have the Odyssey packed and ready in the driveway.

But where would she be going? She knew well that every hotel within two hundred miles would be booked already. So it was a matter of deciding which family member she'd impose on. She had thought first of her sister Ann, who lived in Poplarville, Mississippi. But when she called, Ann was considering leaving, too. Her home was technically within the area that would be affected by the high winds, and it was surrounded by old trees. Given the likelihood that one of them might fall through her roof, Ann wasn't sure she should stay there herself, let alone with Kathy and her kids.

The next option was the family headquarters in Baton Rouge. Owned by her brother Andy, it was a three-bedroom ranch in a subdivision outside the city. Andy traveled frequently and was currently in Hong Kong, working on a construction project. While he'd been gone, two of Kathy's sisters, Patty and Mary Ann, had moved in.

Kathy knew they would allow her family to stay, but it would be cramped. The house wasn't so big to begin with, and Patty had four kids of her own. With Kathy's family there, all told there would be eight kids and three sisters living together in a house that would likely lose electricity in the high winds.

Still, it had been some time since the families had gotten together. This might bring them closer. They could all eat out, maybe go shopping in Baton Rouge. Kathy knew her kids would endorse the plan. Patty's kids were older, but they got along well with the Zeitouns, and anyway, eight kids always found something to do together. It would be cramped and loud, but Kathy found herself looking forward to it.

5 **to impose on sb** *here:* to disturb, to burden sb – 10 **likelihood** probability – 20 **cramped** crowded

Throughout the afternoon, Kathy tried to convince her husband to come with them. When had officials suggested an all-city evacuation before? she asked. Wasn't that reason enough to go?

Zeitoun agreed that it was unusual, but he had never evacuated before and he saw no need to do so now. Their home was elevated three feet above the ground, and rose two stories on top of that, so there would be no danger of getting stuck in an attic or on a roof, even if the worst happened. Zeitoun could always retreat to the second floor. And they lived nowhere near any levees, so they wouldn't get any of the flash flooding that might hit some of the other neighborhoods. It was East New Orleans, or the Lower Ninth, with its one-story houses so close to the levees, that were in the gravest danger.

And he certainly couldn't leave before he secured all his job sites. No one else would do it, and he wouldn't ask anyone else to do it. He'd already told his workers and his foremen to leave, to be with their families, to get a head start on the traffic. He planned to go to every one of the nine job sites to gather or tie down his equipment. He had seen what happened when a contractor failed to do this: ladders careening through windows and walls, tools damaging furniture, paint all over the lawn and driveway.

"I better go," he said.

He set out, visiting the work sites, tying down ladders, packing up tools, brushes, loose tiles, Sheetrock. He was through about half the sites when he headed home to say goodbye to Kathy and the kids.

7 **elevated three feet above** one meter up (from the ground) – 9 **attic** place directly below the roof of a building – 11 **levee** ['levi] *(AE)* wall that blocks water from flooding an area *(Damm)* – 16 **to secure** [sɪ'kjʊr] to (try to) fix things so that nothing gets damaged in the storm – 19 **to get a head start** to leave early (so that he's in front of the traffic) – 22 **to careen** *(AE)* to move forward suddenly and in an uncontrolled way

Kathy was loading up a few small bags in the back of the Odyssey. She had packed enough clothes, toiletries, and food for two days. They would return on Monday night, she figured, after the storm had come and gone.

Kathy had the minivan's radio on and heard Mayor Nagin repeat his instructions for residents to leave the city, but she noted that he had stopped short of a mandatory evacuation. This would embolden her husband, she was certain. She switched to another station, where they were issuing a warning that anyone who planned to ride out the storm in New Orleans should be prepared for a flood. Levee breaches could happen, they said. Storm surges might cause flooding. Ten or fifteen feet of water would be a possibility. Any diehards staying home should have an axe, in case they needed to chop through their attic to reach the roof.

Zeitoun pulled up and parked the van on the street in front of the house. Kathy watched him approach. She never doubted his ability to care for himself in any situation, but now her heart was jumping. She was leaving him to fend for himself, leaving him to chop holes in the attic with an axe? It was insane.

He and Kathy stood in the driveway, as they had many other times when she and the family were leaving and he was staying.

"Better hurry," Zeitoun said. "Lot of people leaving at once."

Kathy looked at him. Her eyes, much to her own frustration, teared up. Zeitoun held her hands.

"C'mon, c'mon," he said. "Nothing's going to happen. People are making a big deal for no reason."

7 **to stop short of mandatory evacuation** evacuation is strongly recommended, but still voluntary – 8 **to embolden** to encourage – 10 **to ride out the storm** to stay in the storm – 11 **breach** the act of breaking – 13 **diehard** sb who stubbornly resists change – 14 **to chop** to cut with an axe – 19 **to fend for oneself** to look after oneself – 21 **insane** mad, stupid

"Bye, Daddy!" Aisha sang from the back seat.

The kids waved. They always waved, all of his children, as he stood on the driveway. None of this was new. A dozen times they had lived this moment, as Kathy and his children drove off in search of sanctuary or rest, leaving Zeitoun to watch over his house and the houses of his neighbors and clients all over the city. He had keys to dozens of other houses; everyone trusted him with their homes and everything in them.

"See you Monday," he said.

Kathy drove away, knowing they were all mad. Living in a city like this was madness, fleeing it was madness, leaving her husband alone in a home in the path of a hurricane was madness.

She waved, her children waved, and Zeitoun stood in the driveway waving until his family was gone.

Zeitoun set out to finish securing the rest of his job sites. The air was breezy, the low sky smudged brown and grey. The city was chaotic, thousands of cars on the road. Traffic was worse than he expected. Brake lights and honking, cars running red lights. He took streets that no one fleeing would use.

Downtown, hundreds of people were walking to the Superdome carrying coolers, blankets, suitcases. Zeitoun was surprised. Previous experiments using the stadium as shelter had failed. As a builder, he worried about the integrity of the stadium's roof. Could it really withstand high winds, torrential rain? You couldn't pay him enough to hide there from the storm.

And anyway, in the past it had been little more than a few hours of squealing winds, some downed trees, a foot or two of water, some minor damage to fix once the winds had passed.

He already felt good. New Orleans would soon be largely vacated, and being in the empty city always felt good, at least

5 **sanctuary** place of refuge, safe place – 17 **smudged** dirty – 20 **to run red lights** to ignore red lights (by driving right past them)

for a day or two. He continued to make his rounds, secured the last few sites, and arrived home just before six.

Kathy called at six-thirty.

She was stuck in traffic a few miles outside the city. Worse, between her own confusion and the unprecedented volume of cars, she had gone the wrong way. Instead of taking the I-10 west directly to Baton Rouge, she was on I-10 heading east, with no way to correct her error. She would have to cross Lake Pontchartrain and swing all the way back through Slidell and across the state. It was going to add hours. She was harried and exhausted and the trip had barely begun.

Zeitoun was sitting at home, his feet up on the table, watching TV. He made a point of telling her so.

"Told you so," he said.

Kathy and the kids were expected at her brother's house for dinner, but at seven o'clock she'd traveled less than twenty miles. Just short of Slidell, she pulled into a Burger King drive-through. She and the kids ordered cheeseburgers and fries and got back onto the road. A little while later, a foul odor overtook the Odyssey.

"What is that?" Kathy asked her kids. They giggled. The smell was fecal, putrid. "What *is* that?" she asked again. This time the girls couldn't breathe they were laughing so hard. Zachary shook his head.

"It's Mekay," one of the girls managed, before collapsing again into hysterics.

The girls had been sneaking the dog pieces of their cheeseburgers, and the cheese was clogging her pipes. She'd been farting for miles.

"That is awful!" Kathy wailed. The kids giggled more. Mekay continued to suffer. She was hiding under the seat.

5 **unprecedented** never seen before – 10 **harried** distressed, stressed – 19 **odor** [ˈoʊdɚ] bad smell – 22 **fecal** [fiːkəl] smelling of feces, excrement – 22 **putrid** rotten – 28 **to clog** to block *(verstopfen)* – 29 **to fart** *furzen*

They passed Slidell and soon met up with I-190, a smaller road Kathy figured would have less traffic. But it was just as bad, an endless stream of brake lights. Ten thousand cars, twenty thousand lights, she guessed, extending all the way to Baton Rouge or beyond. She had become part of the exodus without entirely registering the enormity and strangeness of it. A hundred thousand people on the road, all going north and east, fleeing winds and water. Kathy could only think of beds. Where would all these people sleep? A hundred thousand beds. Every time she passed a driveway she looked at the home longingly. She was so tired, and not even halfway there.

She thought again of her husband. The images she'd seen on the news were absurd, really — the storm looked like a white circular saw heading directly for New Orleans. On those satellite images the city looked so small compared to the hurricane, such a tiny thing about to be cut to pieces by that gigantic spinning blade. And her husband was just a man alone in a wooden house.

Zeitoun called again at eight o'clock. Kathy and the kids had been on the road for three hours and had only gotten as far as Covington — about fifty miles. Meanwhile, he was watching television, puttering around the house, enjoying the cool night.

"You should have stayed," he said. "It's so nice here."

"We'll see, smart guy," she said.

Though she was exhausted, and was being driven near-crazy by her flatulent dog, Kathy was looking forward to a few days in Baton Rouge. At certain moments, at least, she was looking forward to it. Her family was not easy to deal with, this was certain, and any visit could take a wrong turn quickly

18 **blade** sharp part of a knife or saw *(Klinge)* – 23 **to putter** ['pʌţɚ] *(AE)* to do odd jobs – 28 **flatulent** bloated *(an Blähungen leidend)*

and irreparably. *It's complicated,* she would tell people. With eight siblings, it had been turbulent growing up, and when she converted to Islam, the battles and misunderstandings multiplied.

It often started with her hijab. She'd come in, drop her bags, and the suggestion would come: "Now you can take that thing off." She'd been a Muslim for fifteen years and they still said this to her. As if the scarf was something worn under duress, only in the company of Zeitoun, a disguise she could shed when he was not around. As if only in the Delphine household could she finally be herself, let loose. This was actually the command her mother had given the last time Kathy had visited: "Take that thing off your head," she'd said. "Go out and have a good time."

There were times, however, when her mother's loyalty to Kathy trumped her issues with Islam. Years earlier, Kathy and her mother had gone to the DMV together to have Kathy's license renewed. Kathy was wearing her hijab, and had already received a healthy number of suspicious looks from DMV customers and staff by the time she sat down to have her picture taken. The employee behind the camera did not disguise her contempt.

"Take that thing off," the woman said.

Kathy knew that it was her right to wear the scarf for the photo, but she didn't want to make an issue of it.

"Do you have a brush?" Kathy asked. She tried to make a joke of it: "I don't want to have my hair all matted for the photo." Kathy was smiling, but the woman only stared, unblinking. "Really," Kathy continued, "I'm okay with taking it off, but only if you have a brush..."

That's when her mother jumped to the rescue — in her way.

"She can wear it!" her mother yelled. "She can if she wants to!"

8 **under duress** by force – 9 **to shed** to get rid of – 16 **to trump** to win over *(übertrumpfen)* – 17 **DMV** Department of Motor Vehicles

Now it was a scene. Everyone in the DMV was watching. Kathy tried to diffuse the situation. "Mama, it's okay," she said. "Really, it's okay. Mama, do you have a brush?"

Her mother barely registered Kathy's question. She was focused on the woman behind the camera. "You can't make her take it off! It's her constitutional right!"

Finally the DMV woman disappeared into the back of the office. She returned with permission from a superior to take the photo with Kathy wearing her scarf. As the flash went off, Kathy tried to smile.

Growing up in Baton Rouge, it was a crowded house, full of clamor and extremes. Nine kids shared a one-story, 1,400-square-foot home, sleeping three to a room and squabbling over one bathroom. They were content, though, or as content as could be expected, and the neighborhood was tidy, working-class, full of families. Kathy's house backed up against Sherwood Middle School, a big multiethnic campus where Kathy felt overwhelmed. She was one of a handful of white students, and she was picked on, pushed around, gawked at. She grew to be quick to fight, quick to argue.

She must have run away from home a dozen times, maybe more. And almost every time she did, from age six or so on, she ran to her friend Yuko's house. It was just a few blocks away, on the other side of the high school, and given that she and Yuko were among the few non-African American kids in the neighborhood, they had bonded as outsiders. Yuko and her mother Kameko were alone in their house; Kameko's husband had been killed by a drunk driver when Yuko was small. Even though Yuko was three years older, she and Kathy grew inseparable, and Kameko was so welcoming and dedicated to Kathy's well-being that Kathy came to call her Mom.

27 **matted** tangled, in a mess – 6 **constitutional** based on the law (the constitution) *(verfassungsgemäß)* – 12 **clamor** noise – 13 **1,400 square feet** app. 130 square meters – 19 **to pick on** to bully – 20 **to gawk** *(inf)* to stare in an unfriendly way

Kathy was never sure why Kameko took her in, but she was careful not to question it. Yuko joked that her mom just wanted to get close enough to Kathy to bathe her. As a kid Kathy didn't like baths much, and they weren't a great priority in her house, so every time she was at Yuko's, Kameko filled the tub. "She looks greasy," Kameko would joke to Yuko, but she loved to make Kathy clean, and Kathy looked forward to it — Kameko's hands washing her hair, her long fingernails tickling her neck, the warmth of a fresh, heavy towel around her shoulders.

After high school Kathy and Yuko grew closer. Kathy moved into an apartment off Airline Highway in Baton Rouge, and they began working together at Dunkin' Donuts. The independence meant everything to Kathy. Even in her small apartment off a six-lane interstate, there was a sense of order and quiet to her life that she had never known.

A pair of Malaysian sisters used to come into the shop, and Yuko began talking to them, questioning them. "What does that scarf mean?" "What do you see in Islam?" "Are you allowed to drive?" The sisters were open, low-key, never proselytizing. Kathy had no real inkling that they had made a great impression on Yuko, but Yuko was captivated. She began reading about Islam, investigating the Qur'an. Soon the Malaysian sisters brought Yuko pamphlets and books, and Yuko delved deeper.

When she caught on to how serious Yuko was about it, it drove Kathy to distraction. They'd both been brought up Christian, had gone to a rigorous Christian elementary school. It was baffling to see her friend dabbling in this exotic

3 **to bathe** [beɪð] to give a bath to sb – 13 **Dunkin Donuts** American donut chain – 20 **low-key** relaxed – 21 **to proselytize** ['prɑːselɪtaɪz] to make sb convert to another faith – 21 **inkling** idea – 22 **captivated** very impressed – 25 **to delve deeper** to get more interested – 26 **to catch on** to learn – 27 **to drive sb to distraction** to confuse sb, make sb worried and nervous (they can think of nothing else) – 29 **baffling** very surprising – 29 **to dabble** to explore sth in a light-hearted way (i.e. not seriously, and it may be dangerous to do this)

faith. Yuko had been as devout a Christian as walked the Earth — and Kameko was even more so.

"What would your mom think?" she asked.

"Just keep an open mind," Yuko said. "Please."

A few years passed, and Kathy, through a series of missteps and heartbreaks, was divorced and living alone with Zachary, who was less than a year old. She was renting the same apartment off Airline Highway and working two jobs. In the mornings she was a checkout clerk at K&B, a chain drugstore on the highway. One day the manager of Webster Clothes, a menswear store across the road, had come into the drugstore and, admiring Kathy's ebullient personality, asked her if she'd be willing to quit K&B or, if not, take a second job at Webster. Kathy needed the money, so she said yes to the second job. After finishing in the early afternoon at K&B, she would walk across the highway to Webster and work there until closing. Soon she was working fifty hours a week and making enough to cover health insurance for herself and Zachary.

But her life was a struggle, and she was looking for some order and answers. Yuko, by contrast, seemed peaceful and confident; she'd always been centered, so much so that Kathy had been envious, but now Yuko really seemed to have things figured out.

Kathy began borrowing books about Islam. She was just curious, having no particular intention to leave the Christian faith. At first she was simply intrigued by the basic things she didn't know, and the many things she'd wrongly presumed. She had no idea, for instance, that the Qur'an was filled with the same people as the Bible — Moses, Mary, Abraham, Pharaoh, even Jesus. She hadn't known that Muslims consider the Qur'an the fourth book of God to His messengers, after the Old Testament (referred to as the *Tawrat,* or the Law), the

12 **ebullient** bubbling, enthusiastic – 26 **intrigued** [ɪnˈtriːgd] interested – 27 **to presume** to think *(annehmen, glauben)* – 31 **messenger** prophet (human being that receives and passes on messages from a divine *(göttlich)* being

Psalms (the *Zabur)*, and the New Testament *(Injeil)*. The fact that Islam acknowledged these books was revelatory for her. The fact that the Qur'an repeatedly reaches out to the other, related faiths, knocked her flat:

We have believed in God
and what has been sent forth to us,
and what was sent forth to Abraham,
Ishmael, Isaac, Jacob,
and the Tribes
and what was given the Prophets
from their Lord;
we separate and divide not
between any one of them;
and we are the ones who submit to Him.

She was frustrated that she hadn't known any of this, that she'd been blind to the faith of a billion or so people. How could she not know these things?

And Muhammad. She'd been so misinformed about Him. She'd thought He was the actual god of Islam, the one whom Muslims worshiped. But he was simply the messenger who related the word of God. An illiterate man, Muhammad was visited by the angel Gabriel *(Jibril* in Arabic), who related to him the words of God. Muhammad became the conduit for these messages, and The Qur'an, then, was simply the word of God in written form. *Qur'an* meant "Recitation."

There were so many basic things that defied her presumptions. She'd assumed that Muslims were a monolithic group, and that all Muslims were made of the same devout and unbending stock. But she learned that there were Shiite and Sunni interpretations of the Qur'an, and within

2 **to acknowledge** to accept (*here:* as holy) – 2 **revelatory** ['rəvələtɔ:ri] *(adj)* a revelation; insightful – 21 **illiterate** [ɪ'lɪt̬ərət] unable to read or write – 26 **to defy** to challenge; to go against, contradict *(widersprechen)* – 27 **monolithic** same, uniform – 28 **devout** religious – 29 **stock** origin, family ancestors

any mosque there were the same variations in faith and commitment as there were in any church. There were Muslims who treated their faith lightly, and those who knew every word of the Qur'an and its companion guide to behavior, the Hadith. There were Muslims who knew almost nothing about their religion, who worshiped a few times a year, and those who obeyed the strictest interpretation of their faith. There were Muslim women who wore T-shirts and jeans and Muslim women who covered themselves head to toe. There were Muslim men who modeled their lives on the life of the Prophet, and those who strayed and fell short. There were passive Muslims, uncertain Muslims, borderline agnostic Muslims, devout Muslims, and Muslims who twisted the words of the Qur'an to suit their temporary desires and agendas. It was all very familiar, intrinsic to any faith.

At the time, Kathy was attending a large evangelical church not far from her jobs. Though not always full, it could seat about a thousand parishioners. She felt a need to connect with her faith; she needed all the strength she could find.

But there were things about this church that bothered her. She was accustomed to the kind of fiery preaching that the church offered, the extremes of showmanship and drama, but one day, she thought, they crossed a line. They had just passed the collection plates, and after they had gathered and counted the funds donated, the preacher — a short man with a rosy face and a mustache — seemed disappointed. His expression was pained. He couldn't hold it in. He chastised the congregation calmly at first, and then with increasing annoyance. Did they not love this church? Did they not appreciate the connection this church created with their lord

11 **to stray** to move away from; (*here:* to sin, no longer follow the religion of Islam) – 12 **agnostic** skeptical about the existence of God – 15 **intrinsic** *here:* part of – 16 **evangelical** fundamentalist – 18 **parishioner** member of a church – 21 **to be accustomed to sth** to be used to sth – 27 **pained** showing pain – 27 **to chastise** [tʃæsˈtaɪz] to scold *(beschimpfen)* – 29 **annoyance** anger

Jesus Christ? He went on and on, shaming the congregants for their miserly ways. The lecture lasted twenty minutes.

Kathy was aghast. She'd never seen the collection counted during a Sunday service. And to ask for more! The congregants were not wealthy people, she knew. This was a working-class church, a middle-class church. They gave what they could.

She left that day shaken and confused by what she'd seen. At home, after putting Zachary to bed, she turned again to the materials Yuko had given her. She flipped through the Qur'an. Kathy wasn't sure that Islam was the way, but she knew that Yuko had never misled her before, that Yuko was the most grounded and sensible person she knew, and if Islam was working for her, why wouldn't it work for Kathy? Yuko was her sister, her mentor.

Kathy struggled with the question of faith all week. She lived with the questions in the morning, at night, all day through work. She had just started her shift at Webster one day when a familiar man walked in.

Kathy recognized him immediately as one of the preachers at the church. She came over to help him with a new sport coat.

"You know," he said, "you should come to our church! It's not far from here."

She laughed. "I know your church! I'm there all the time. Every Sunday."

The man was surprised. He hadn't seen her before.

"Oh, I sit in the back," she said.

He smiled and told her that next time he'd look for her. He made it his business to make sure everyone felt welcome.

"You know," Kathy said to him, "this must be a sign from God, seeing you here."

"How so?" he asked.

She told him about her crisis, how she had been disappointed with aspects of the Christianity she knew, in some of the

1 **congregants** people in the church – 2 **miserly** ['maɪzɚli] mean with money *(geizig)* – 3 **aghast** [ə'gæst] shocked

things she'd seen, in fact, at his own church. She told him that she had actually been considering converting to Islam.

He was listening closely, but he didn't seem worried about losing a member of the congregation.

"Oh, that's just the devil toying with you," he said. "He'll do that, try to tempt you away from Christ. But this'll only make your faith stronger. You'll see come Sunday."

When he left, Kathy already felt more certain about her faith. How could his visit not be a sign from God? Just at the moment she was having doubts about her church, a messenger from Jesus walked straight into her life.

She went to church that Sunday with a renewed sense of purpose. Yuko may have found comfort and direction in Islam, but Kathy was sure that she herself had been personally called by Christ. She walked in and sat near the front, determined that her new friend should see her and know that he had made a difference.

It didn't take long. When he looked down at the congregation and upon her, his eyes opened wide. He gave her an expression that made clear that she was the one he'd been looking for all day. She'd seen the same expression on kids spotting a birthday cake with their name on it.

And then suddenly, in the middle of the service, her name was being called. The preacher, in front of a full room of almost a thousand people, was saying her name, Kathy Delphine.

"Come up here, Kathy," the preacher commanded.

She rose from her seat and stepped toward the blinding lights of the pulpit. Onstage, she didn't know where to look, how to avoid the glare. She shielded her eyes. She squinted and looked down — at her shoes, at the people in the front row. She had never stood in front of so many people. The closest thing had been her wedding, and that had been only

12 **sense of purpose** a meaning in life – 29 **pulpit** the place in a church from where the leader of that church preaches *(Kanzel)* – 30 **glare** angry stare

fifty or so friends and family. What was this? Why had she been called forth?

"Kathy," the preacher said, "tell them what you told me. Tell us all."

Kathy froze. She didn't know if she could do this. She was a talkative person, rarely nervous, but to recount something she'd said privately to the reverend in front of a thousand strangers — it didn't seem right.

Still, Kathy had faith that he knew what he was doing. She believed she'd been chosen to remain in this church. And she wanted to serve. To help. Perhaps, like Reverend Timothy entering the store that day, this was another event that was meant to be, meant to bring her closer to Christ.

She was given a microphone and she spoke into it, telling the congregation what she'd told the reverend, that she had been investigating Islam, and that —

The preacher cut her off. "She was looking to Islam!" he said with a sneer. "She was considering" — and here he paused — "the worship of Allah!" And with that, he made a snorting, derisive sound, the sort of sound an eight-year-old boy would make on a playground. This preacher, this leader of this church and congregation, was using this tone to refer to Allah. Did he not know that his God and Islam's were one and the same? That was one of the first and simplest things she'd learned from the pamphlets Yuko had given her: Allah is just the Arabic word for God. Even Christians speaking Arabic refer to God as Allah.

He went on to praise Kathy and Jesus and reaffirm the primacy of his and their faith, but by then she was hardly listening. Something had ruptured within her. When he was done, she sat down in a daze, bewildered but becoming sure about something right there and then. She smiled politely

30 **to shield** to protect – 18 **sneer** the sound a voice makes when it expresses scorn *(Verachtung)* – 20 **snorting** rough, noisy sound – 20 **derisive** [dɪˈraɪsɪv] mocking – 25 **pamphlet** brochure – 29 **primacy** [ˈpraɪməsi] state of being first; great importance – 30 **to rupture** to break – 31 **daze** shock – 31 **bewildered** [bɪˈwɪldɚd] confused

through the rest of the service, already knowing she would never come back.

She thought about the episode while driving home, and that night, and all the next day. She talked to Yuko about it and they realized that this man, preaching to a thousand impressionable and trusting parishioners, didn't know, or didn't care, that Islam, Judaism, and Christianity were not-so-distantly related branches of the same monotheistic, Abrahamic faith. And to dismiss all of Islam with a playground sound? Kathy could not be part of what that man was preaching.

So by fits and starts, she followed Yuko into Islam. She read the Qur'an and was struck by its power and lyricism. The Christian preachers she'd heard had spent a good amount of time talking about who would and wouldn't go to hell, how hot it burned and for how long, but the imams she began to meet made no such pronouncements. Will I go to heaven? she asked. "Only God knows this," the imam would tell her. The various doubts of the imams were comforting, and drew her closer. She would ask them a question, just as she had asked questions of her pastors, and the imams would try to answer, but often they wouldn't know. "Let's look at the Qur'an," they would say. She liked Islam's sense of personal responsibility, its bent toward social justice. Most of all, though, she liked the sense of dignity and purity embodied by the Muslim women she knew. To Kathy they seemed so wholesome, so honorable. They were chaste, they were disciplined. She wanted that sense of control. She wanted the peace that came with that sense of control.

The actual conversion was beautifully simple. With Yuko and a handful of other women from the mosque present, she pronounced the *shahadah*, the Islamic pledge of conviction of faith. "AshHadu An La Ilaha Il-lallah, Wa Ash Hadu Anna

12 **by fits and starts** irregularly – 13 **lyricism** poetry – 16 **imam** Muslim preacher – 26 **wholesome** healthy – 27 **chaste** [tʃeɪst] morally pure *(keusch)* – 32 **pledge** a solemn promise to do sth

Muhammadar Rasul-allah." That was all she needed to say. *I bear Witness that there is no deity but Allah and I bear witness that Muhammad is His Messenger.* With that, Kathy Delphine had become a Muslim.

When she tried to explain it to friends and family, Kathy fumbled. But she knew that in Islam she had found calm. The doubt sewn into the faith gave her room to think, to question. The answers the Qur'an provided gave her a way forward. Even her view of her family softened through the lens of Islam. She was less aggressive. She had always fought with her mother, but Islam taught her that "heaven is at the feet of your mother," and this reined her in. She stopped talking back and learned to be more patient and forgiving. *It brought back a purity in me,* she would say.

Her conversion might have been a step forward in her eyes, but in the eyes of her mother and siblings it was as if she'd renounced her family and all they stood for. Kathy tried to get along with them nevertheless, and her family tried too. There were times when all was good, visits were enjoyable, uneventful. But for every one of those, there was one that spiraled into sniping and accusations, slammed doors and quick departures. There were a few of her eight siblings she wasn't in touch with at all.

But she wanted extended family. She wanted her own kids to know their aunts and uncles and cousins, and so the relief was profound when the Odyssey arrived at her brother's house in Baton Rouge at eleven-thirty. She unpacked the kids and they fell asleep, on couches and floors, in minutes.

Settled, she called Zeitoun.

"Winds come?"

"Nothing yet," he said.

2 **to bear witness** *bezeugen* – 2 **deity** ['di:əti] divine being, God – 6 **to fumble** to have difficulty; be clumsy – 9 **lens** eyes – 12 **to rein sth in** to bring sth under control – 17 **to renounce** to give up – 21 **sniping** *here:* making bad remarks – 26 **profound** deep

"I'm gonna pass out," Kathy said. "Never been so tired."

"Get some rest," he said. "Sleep in."

"You too."

They said good night and turned out the lights.

SUNDAY AUGUST 28

Kathy woke before dawn and turned on the TV. Katrina was now a Category 5 storm with winds over 150 miles an hour. It was heading almost directly toward New Orleans, with the brunt of it expected to strike about sixteen miles west of the city. Meteorologists were predicting furious winds, ten-foot storm surges, possibilities of levee breaches, flooding everywhere along the coast. It was estimated that the storm would reach the New Orleans area that night.

Throughout the day, as news of the hurricane grew more dire, clients called Kathy or Zeitoun, asking them to secure their windows and doors. Kathy collected requests and relayed them to Zeitoun. Zeitoun discovered that one of his carpenters, James Crosso, was still in the city, so the two of them spent the day driving around, rigging the houses on the list. James's wife worked for one of the hotels downtown, and the couple was planning to ride the storm out there. Zeitoun and James drove from job to job, a quarter ton of plywood in the back of the truck, doing what they could before the winds came. The roads were still crowded, a new surge of cars leaving, but Zeitoun didn't consider it. He would be safe in their house on Dart Street, he figured, far from any levees, with two stories, plenty of tools, and food.

Mid-morning, Mayor Nagin ordered the city's first-ever mandatory evacuation. Anyone who could leave must leave.

9 **brunt** the main force – 15 **dire** bad – 17 **to relay** to send – 19 **to rig** to fix

All day Zeitoun and James saw people lined up at bus stops — those who planned to stay in the Superdome. Families, couples, elderly men and women carrying their belongings in backpacks, suitcases, garbage bags. Seeing them exposed like that, as the winds picked up and the sky darkened, worried Zeitoun. He and James passed the same groups, waiting patiently, on the way to their job sites and on their way back.

In Baton Rouge, the weather was dark and unruly. High winds, black skies at noon. The kids played outside for a while, but then came inside to watch DVDs while Kathy caught up with Patty and Mary Ann. The trees in the neighborhood swung wildly.

The power went out at five o'clock. The kids played board games by candlelight.

Kathy periodically went out to the car to listen to the news on the radio. The winds were smashing windows in New Orleans, knocking down trees and power lines.

Kathy tried to call Zeitoun, but the call went straight to his voice-mail. She tried the home phone. Nothing. The lines were down, she assumed. The hurricane had not hit the city yet, and already she had no way to reach her husband.

By six o'clock, Zeitoun had dropped James off and was home and ready. He watched the news on TV; the reports had not changed much. The outermost edge of the hurricane was expected about midnight. He assumed that would be the end of the electrical grid for a few days.

Walking through the darkening rooms, Zeitoun assessed all the possible dangers he would face during the storm. The house had four bedrooms — the master bedroom on the first floor and the kids' rooms upstairs. He expected leaks up there.

8 **unruly** impossible to control – 26 **grid** network – 30 **leak** small hole that lets sth in or out (*usu* water)

Portions of the roof might be compromised. A few windows might break — the front sitting room, with its bay window, was at risk. There was an outside chance the tree in the backyard would fall on the house. If that happened, there could be significant damage, because nothing, then, could keep the water out.

But he was optimistic. And in any case he wanted to be in the house, on which he had spent untold thousands for improvements, to protect it in whatever way possible. His grandmother had stayed put during countless storms in her home on Arwad Island, and he planned to do the same. A home was worth fighting for.

The only thing that concerned him was the levees. Again and again the news reports warned of the storm surge. The levees were meant to hold back fourteen feet of water, and the storm surges in the Gulf were already nineteen, twenty feet high. If the levees were breached, he knew the battle would be lost.

He called Kathy at eight o'clock.

"There you are," she said. "You disappeared."

He looked at his phone and saw that he'd missed three calls from her.

"Coverage must be spotty already," he said. His phone had not rung. He told her that nothing significant had happened yet. Just strong winds. Nothing new.

"Stay away from the windows," she said.

He said he would try.

Kathy wondered aloud if there was something foolish in what they were doing. Her husband was in the path of a Category 5 hurricane and they were talking about staying away from the windows.

"Say goodnight to the kids," he said.

1 **compromised** *here:* exposed to danger – 2 **bay window** rounded window *(Erkerfenster)* – 11 **Arwad Island** island off the Syrian coast – 23 **spotty** *here:* uneven, unreliable

She said she would.

"Better go. To save the battery," he said.

They said goodnight.

The kids asleep, Kathy sat on the couch in her brother Andy's house and stared at the candle in front of her. It was the only light left on in the house.

Just after eleven o'clock, the front end of the storm arrived at Zeitoun's house. The sky was a brutal grey, the winds swirling and cool. Rain came in sheets. Every half hour brought an escalation in the mayhem outside. At midnight the power went out. The leaks began at about two or three. The first was in the corner of Nademah's bedroom. Zeitoun went down to the garage and retrieved a forty-gallon garbage can to catch the water. Another leak opened a few minutes later, this one in the upstairs hallway. Zeitoun found another garbage can. A window in the master bedroom broke just after three o'clock, as if a brick had been thrown through the glass. Zeitoun gathered the shards and stuffed the opening with a pillow. Another leak opened in Safiya and Aisha's room. He found another, bigger garbage can.

He dragged the first two garbage cans outside and dumped them on the lawn. The sky was a child's fingerpainting, blue and black hastily mixed. The wind was cooler. The neighborhood was utterly dark. As he stood on the lawn, he heard a tree fall somewhere on the block — a crack and then a shush as the branches pushed down through other trees and rested against the side of a house.

He went inside.

Another window had broken. He stuffed another pillow into it. Branches clawed at the walls, the roof. There were unknown thumps everywhere. The bones of the house seemed to be

10 **mayhem** ['meɪhem] violent disorder, confusion – 13 **to retrieve** to get, fetch – 15 **hallway** open place in a house that isn't a room *(Flur)* – 18 **shard** piece of broken glass – 24 **utterly** extremely

moaning under the strain of it all. The house was under assault.

When he next checked, it was four o'clock in the morning. He hadn't stopped moving in five hours. If the damage continued at this pace, it would be worse than he had predicted. And the real storm hadn't come yet.

In the small hours, Zeitoun had a thought. He didn't expect the city to flood, but he knew a flood was not impossible. So he walked outside, tasting the cool wind, and dragged his secondhand canoe from the garage and righted it. He wanted to have it ready.

If Kathy could only see him now. She had rolled her eyes when she saw him come home with that canoe. He'd bought it a few years before, from a client in Bayou St. John. When the client was moving, Zeitoun had seen it on his lawn, a standard aluminum model, and asked him if he was selling it. The client laughed. "You want *that?*" he asked. Zeitoun bought it on the spot for seventy-five dollars.

Something about the canoe had intrigued him. It was well-made, undamaged, with a pair of wooden benches inside. It was about sixteen feet long, built for two people. It seemed to speak of exploration, of escape. He tied it to the top of his van and brought it home.

Through the living room window, Kathy saw him pull up. She met him at the door.

"No way," she said.

"What?" Zeitoun said, smiling.

"You're crazy," she said.

Kathy liked to act exasperated, but Zeitoun's romantic side was central to why she loved him. She knew that any kind of boat reminded him of his childhood. How could she deny him a used canoe? She was fairly certain he would never use it, but having it in the garage, she knew, would mean something to

1 **to moan** to cry – 1 **strain** stress – 2 **assault** attack

him — a connection to the past, the possibility of adventure. Whatever it was, she wouldn't stand in the way.

He did try, two or three times, to get his daughters interested in the canoe. He brought them to Bayou St. John, put the canoe in the water, and sat down inside. When he reached for Nademah, standing on the grass, she refused. The younger girls weren't having it, either. So for half an hour, as the girls watched from the grass, he paddled around by himself, trying to make it all look fun, irresistible. When he returned, they still wanted no part of it, so he put the canoe back on the roof of the van and they all went home.

The wind picked up after five o'clock. He couldn't tell when the hurricane actually made landfall, but the day barely brightened that morning. It went from black to a charcoal grey, the rain like pebbles thrown against glass. He could hear tree limbs succumbing to the wind, great exhalations as their trunks fell on streets and roofs.

Eventually he could not stay awake. Though his house was under attack, he lay down, knowing something would awaken him soon enough, and so, surrendering for now, he fell into a shallow sleep.

MONDAY AUGUST 29

Zeitoun woke late. He couldn't believe his watch. It was after ten a.m. He hadn't slept that late in years. All the clocks had stopped. He got up, tried the light switches in three rooms. The power was still out.

The wind was strong outside, the sky still dark. The rain was coming down — not heavily, but enough to keep Zeitoun inside much of the day. He ate breakfast and checked for any

15 **pebble** small stone – 16 **to succumb** [se'kʌm] to give in – 16 **exhalation** sighing, emitting air as if in pain – 20 **to surrender** to give up – 21 **shallow** *opp of* deep

other damage to the house. He put buckets under two new leaks. Overall the damage had remained at about the level it had been at before he fell asleep. He had slumbered through the worst of the hurricane. Through the windows he could see the streets were covered with downed power lines and fallen trees and about a foot of water. It was bad, but not much worse than a handful of storms he could remember.

In Baton Rouge, Kathy brought her kids to Wal-Mart to stock up on supplies and buy flashlights. Inside, there seemed to be more people than products. She'd never seen anything like it. The place had been bought out, the shelves nearly bare. It looked like the end of the world. The kids were scared, holding on to her. Kathy looked for ice and was told that the ice was long gone. Improbably, she found a package of two flashlights, the last one, and reached for it a split second before another woman did. She gave the woman an apologetic smile and went to the check-out counter.

In the afternoon the wind and rain calmed. Zeitoun went outside to explore. It was warm, over eighty degrees. He estimated there were eighteen inches of water on the ground. It was rainwater, murky and grey-brown, but soon, he knew, it would drain away. He looked in the backyard. There was the canoe. It called to him, floating and ready. It was a rare opportunity, he thought, to be able to glide over the roads. He had only this day. He bailed the water resting in the hull, and in his T-shirt and shorts and sneakers, he stepped in.

Leaving the yard was difficult. A tree across the street had been ripped from its roots and lay across the road, branches spread over his driveway. He paddled around them and looked back to the house. No great damage to the exterior. Some shingles missing from the roof. The windows broken. A

3 **to slumber** to sleep – 16 **apologetic smile** in the smile you could see that he was saying sorry – 25 **to bail** to scoop out *(löffeln)* – 31 **shingle** *(AE)* tile *(Dachziegel)*

gutter that would need remounting. Nothing too bad, three days' work.

In the neighborhood, other homes had been hit by all manner of debris. Windows had been blown out. Wet, black branches covered cars, the street. Everywhere trees had been pulled out of the earth and lay flat.

The quiet was profound. The wind rippled the water but otherwise all was silent. No cars moved, no planes flew. A few neighbors stood on their porches or waded through their yards, assessing damage. No one knew where to start or when. He knew he would be giving many estimates in the coming weeks.

He paddled only a few blocks before he began to have second thoughts. There were power lines down everywhere. What would exposed lines do if they made contact with his aluminum canoe? Besides, there wasn't enough water to paddle much. In some parts of the neighborhood, there was scarcely any water at all — only a few inches. He ran aground, got out, turned the canoe around, and paddled back home.

Throughout the afternoon, the water fled from the streets, a few inches an hour. The drainage system was working. By that evening, the water had receded completely. The streets were dry. The damage was extensive, but really no worse than a handful of other storms he could remember. And it was over.

He called Kathy.

"Come back," he said.

Kathy was tempted, but it was already seven o'clock, they were about to eat dinner, and she knew she wasn't about to drive through the night again with four kids and a flatulent dog. Besides, there was no power in New Orleans, so they

1 **gutter** the channel at the bottom of a roof which leads to a pipe to allow rainwater to flow away *(Abfluss)* – 1 **to remount** to fix again – 28 **to be tempted** to feel that you want to do sth even though you know you shouldn't

would be returning to the same situation they were suffering through in Baton Rouge. The kids were still enjoying the time spent with their cousins — the laughter rattling the house was testament to it.

She and Zeitoun agreed to talk about it again in the morning, though they both expected Kathy to be packing up the kids sometime the next day.

She went inside and the combined families, three adults and eight kids, ate hot dogs by candlelight. That her sisters had put pork on the table did not go unnoticed, but Kathy vowed not to make an issue of it. *Better to let it go,* she said to herself. *Let it go, let it go.* She had so many battles to fight. There would be so many more in the coming days, she was sure, that she couldn't expend her energy on her sisters, on hot dogs. If they wanted to serve her children pork, they could try.

Later, when Kathy went to the car to steal a few moments with the radio, she heard Mayor Nagin echoing her reluctance to return. Don't come back yet, he said. Wait to see what the damage is, until everything is settled and cleaned up. Give it a day or two.

In the afternoon, Zeitoun got a call from Adnan, a second cousin on Zeitoun's mother's side. Adnan had done well since emigrating over a decade earlier; he owned and managed four Subway franchises in New Orleans. His wife Abeer was six months pregnant with their first child.

"You still in the city?" he asked, assuming Zeitoun was.

"Of course I am. You in Baton Rouge?" Zeitoun asked.

"I am." Adnan had driven up the night before with Abeer and his elderly parents. "How is it there?"

"Windy," Zeitoun said. "Really? It's a little scary." He would never have admitted this to Kathy, but he could confide in Adnan.

10 **pork** meat from a pig – 11 **to vow** to promise earnestly – 18 **reluctance** unwillingness – 32 **to confide in sb** to tell sth to sb that you trust

"You think you'll stay?" Adnan asked.

Zeitoun said he planned to, and offered to look after Adnan's shops. Before Adnan had left the city, he'd emptied the cash register at the City Park Avenue location and made sure bread was baked; he'd assumed he'd be back on Tuesday.

"You know any mosques in Baton Rouge?" Adnan asked. All the motels were booked, and he and Abeer knew no one in Baton Rouge. They'd been able to place Adnan's parents in a mosque the previous night, but there were already hundreds of people there, sleeping on the floors, and they couldn't accommodate more. Adnan and Abeer had spent the night in their car.

"I don't," Zeitoun said. "But call Kathy. She's with family. They'll take you in, I'm sure." He gave Adnan her cell phone number.

Zeitoun emptied all of the buckets in the house, put them under the holes in the roof again, and got ready for bed. It was warm outside, stifling inside. He lay in the dark. He thought about the strength of the storm, its duration, how oddly minimal the damage had been to this house. He went to the front window. Already, at eight o'clock, the streets were dry as bone. All that effort to flee, and for what? Hundreds of thousands of people rushing north for this. A few inches of water, all of it now gone.

It was quiet that night. He heard no wind, no voices, no sirens. There was only the sound of a city breathing as he breathed, weary from the fight, grateful it was over.

TUESDAY AUGUST 30

Zeitoun woke up late again. He squinted at the window above, saw the same grey sky, heard the same strange quiet. He had never known a time like this. He couldn't drive anywhere,

19 **stifling** *here:* unbearably hot – 28 **weary** tired

couldn't work. For the first time in decades, there was nothing to do. It would be a day of calm, of rest. He felt strangely lethargic, ethereally content. He fell back into a shallow sleep.

Arwad Island, his family's ancestral home, was soaked in light. The sun was constant there, a warm white light that bleached the stone buildings and cobblestone alleys, that brought incredible clarity to the surrounding cobalt sea.

When Zeitoun dreamt of Arwad, it was the Arwad he visited during the summers of his boyhood, and in these dreams he was doing boyish things: sprinting around the island's tiny perimeter, scaring seagulls to flight, searching in the tide pools for crabs and shells or whatever oddities had been thrown onto the island's rocky shore.

By the outer wall, facing the western expanse of the sea, he and Ahmad chased a lone chicken through the ruins around the outermost homes. The scrawny bird raced up a pile of garbage and rubble and into a cave of coral and masonry. They turned at the sound of a frigate dropping anchor, waiting to land at Tartus, the port city a mile east. There were always a half-dozen ships, tankers, and freighters waiting for a berth at the busy port, and often they would anchor close enough to cast a shadow over the tiny island. Abdulrahman and Ahmad would stare up at them, the hulls rising twenty, thirty feet over the sea. The boys would wave to the crew and dream of being aboard. It seemed a life of impossible romance and freedom.

Even then, when Ahmad was a skinny, tanned boy of fifteen, he knew he would be a sailor. He was careful not to tell his father, but he was certain he wanted to steer one of those ships. He wanted to guide great vessels around the world,

5 **soaked** bathed – 7 **to bleach** to whiten – 7 **cobblestone** *(adj)* rounded paving stone – 12 **perimeter** closed curve, boundary – 12 **tide pool** small puddles of water left by the sea – 13 **oddity** strange thing – 15 **expanse** wide, open landscape – 17 **scrawny** thin (*usu* unhealthily so) – 21 **berth** space for a ship to anchor – 30 **vessel** ship

to speak a dozen languages, to know the people of every nation.

Abdulrahman never doubted that Ahmad would do this. Ahmad was, in Abdulrahman's eyes, capable of anything. He was his best friend, his hero and teacher. Ahmad taught him how to spear a fish, how to row a boat alone, how to dive from the great Phoenician stones on the island's southern wall. He would have followed Ahmad anywhere, and often did.

The boys stripped to their underwear and set out for a narrow archipelago of rocks. Abdulrahman and Ahmad found the spear they kept hidden in the stones and took turns diving for fish. Swimming came naturally to the boys of the Zeitoun family, and to all the children of Arwad. They could swim as soon as they could walk and would stay in the water, swimming and treading, for hours. When Ahmad and Abdulrahman emerged they would lay on a low stone wall, the sea on one side and the town's outer promenade on the other.

The promenade wasn't much to look at, a wide, crumbling paved area, dotted with litter, evidence of the island's half-hearted attempts to attract tourists. Most of the residents of Arwad didn't much care if visitors came or not. It was home, and a place where real industry happened: fish were caught, cleaned, and brought to the mainland, and ships, strong wooden sailboats of one or two or three masts, were built using methods perfected on the island centuries before.

Arwad had been a strategic military possession for an endless succession of sea powers: the Phoenicians, the Assyrians, the Achaemenid Persians, the Greeks under

7 **Phoenician** [fə'niːʃən] relating to ancient Phoenicia, a civilisation which existed between the mountains of Lebanon and the Mediterranean. Some of the most important contributions to western culture came from Phoenicia, e.g. the phonetic alphabet, generally held to be the first of all modern alphabets, including ours (the Roman alphabet). – 10 **archipelago** [ˌɑːrkə'peləgoʊ] group of islands – 15 **to tread water** [tred] to swim, but not to move through the water *(Wasser treten)* – 16 **to emerge** to come out or up – 16 **lay** *here:* lie – 20 **dotted with** full of – 28 **succession** series *(Abfolge)* – 29 **Achaemenid** relating to the dynasty of the Persian Empire

Alexander, the Romans, the Crusaders, the Mongols, the Turks, the French, and the British. Various walls and battlements, in pieces and all but gone, spoke of past fortresses. Two small castles, scarcely altered since the Middle Ages, stood in the center of the island and could be explored by curious children. Abdulrahman and Ahmad often ran up the smooth stone stairs of the lookout tower by their home, pretending they were spotting invaders, sounding bells of warning, planning their defenses.

But usually their games took place in the water. They were never more than a few steps from the cool Mediterranean, and Abdulrahman would follow Ahmad to the shore and up the great Phoenician stones of the wall. From the top they could see into the windows of the higher-sitting dwellings of the town. Then they would turn to the sea and dive. After swimming, they would lay on the stone wall, the surface polished by the crashing waves and the feet of uncountable children. They warmed themselves with the heat of the rocks and the sun above. They would talk of heroes who had defended the island, of armies and saints who had stopped there. And they would talk of their plans, their own great deeds and explorations.

Soon the two of them would grow quiet, near sleep, hearing the waves push against the island's outer walls, the ceaseless shushing of the sea. But in Zeitoun's half-dream, the sound of the ocean seemed wrong. It was both quieter and less rhythmic — not an ebb and flow, but instead the constant whisper of a river.

The dissonance woke him.

3 **battlement** low wall around the top of a castle which helps to defend it in a battle – 3 **all but** almost completely – 22 **deed** action – 27 **ebb and flow** rhythmic movement of the sea – 29 **dissonance** harsh sound

PART II

TUESDAY AUGUST 30

Zeitoun opened his eyes again. He was home, in his daughter Nademah's room, under her covers, looking through the window at a dirty white sky. The sound continued, something like running water. But there was no rain, no leaks. He thought a pipe might have broken, but that couldn't be it; the sound wasn't right. This was more like a river, the movement of great volumes of water.

He sat up and looked down through the window that faced the backyard. He saw water, a wide sea of it. It was coming from the north. It flowed into the yard, under the house, rising quickly.

He couldn't make sense of it. The day before, the water had receded, as he had expected it to, but now it had returned, far stronger. And this water was different from the murky rainwater of the day before. This water was green and clear. This was lake water.

At that moment, Zeitoun knew that the levees had been overtopped or compromised. There could be no doubt. The city would soon be underwater. If the water was here, he knew, it was already covering most of New Orleans. He knew it would keep coming, would likely rise eight feet or more in his neighborhood, and more elsewhere. He knew the recovery would take months or years. He knew the flood had come.

He called Kathy.

"The water's coming," he said.

"What? No, no," she said. "Levees broke?"

"I think so."

"I can't believe it."

He heard her stifle a sob.

"I better go," he said.

He hung up and went to work.

30 **to stifle** to suppress *(unterdrücken)*

Elevate, he thought. *Elevate, elevate.* Everything had to be brought to the second floor. He recalled the worst of the predictions before the storm: if the levees broke, there would be ten, fifteen feet of water in some places. Methodically, he began to prepare. Everything of value had to be brought higher. The work was simply work, and he went about it calmly and quickly.

He took the TV, the DVD player, the stereo, all the electronics upstairs. He gathered all the kids' games and books and encyclopedias and carried those up next.

Things were tense at the house in Baton Rouge. With the weather windy and grey, and so many people sharing a small house, tempers were flaring. Kathy thought it best to make her family scarce. She and her kids put away their sleeping bags and pillows and left in the Odyssey, intending to drive around most of the day, going to malls or restaurants — anything to kill time. They would return late, after dinner, only to sleep. She prayed that they could return to New Orleans the next day.

Kathy called Zeitoun from the road.

"My jewelry box!" she said.

He found that, and the good china, and he brought it all upstairs. He emptied the refrigerator; he left the freezer full. He put all the chairs on top of the dining room table. Unable to carry a heavy chest, he put it on a mattress and dragged it up the stairs. He placed one couch on top of another, sacrificing one to save the other. Then he got more books. He saved all the books.

1 **to elevate** to lift – 2 **to recall** to remember – 11 **tense** nervous – 13 **tempers were flaring** people were losing their tempers, getting nervous – 13 **to make oneself scarce** *(inf)* to disappear

Kathy called again. "I told you not to cancel the property insurance," she said.

She was right. Just three weeks before, he had chosen not to renew the part of their flood insurance that covered their furniture, everything in the house. He hadn't wanted to spend the money. He admitted she was right, and knew she would remind him of it for years to come.

"Can we talk about it later?" he asked.

Zeitoun went outside, the air humid and gusty. He tied the canoe to the back porch. The water was whispering through the cracks in the back fence, rising up. It was flowing into his yard at an astonishing rate. As he stood, it swallowed his ankles and crawled up his shins.

Back inside, he continued to move everything of value upward. As he did, he watched the water erase the floor and climb the walls. In another hour there was three feet of water indoors. And his house was three feet above street level.

But the water was clean. It was translucent, almost green in tint. He watched it fill his dining room, momentarily struck by the beauty of the sight. It brought forth a vague memory of a storm on Arwad Island, when he was just a boy, when the Mediterranean rose up and swallowed the lower-sitting homes, the blue-green sea sitting inside living rooms and bedrooms and kitchens. The water breached and dodged the Phoenician stones surrounding the island without any difficulty at all.

At that moment, Zeitoun had an idea. He knew the fish in his tank wouldn't survive without filtration or food, so he reached inside and liberated them. He dropped them in the water that filled the house. It was the best chance they had. They swam down and away.

9 **gusty** windy – 12 **at an astonishing rate** very quickly – 15 **to erase** to remove, to destroy – 18 **translucent** [træn'slu:sənt] clear – 24 **to dodge** to move out of the way of

Using his cell phone, he talked to Kathy throughout the day. They reviewed what couldn't be saved, the furniture too large to carry upstairs. There were dressers, armoires. He removed all the drawers he could, carried upstairs everything that could be removed and lifted.

The water devoured the cabinets and windows. Zeitoun watched, dismayed, as it rose four, five, six feet in the house — above the electrical box, the phone box. He would have no access to electricity or a land-line for weeks.

By nightfall the neighborhood was under nine feet of water and Zeitoun could no longer go downstairs. He was spent; he had done all he could. He lay on Nademah's bed on the second floor and called Kathy. She was driving around with the kids, dreading a return to the house in Baton Rouge.

"I saved all I could," he said.

"I'm glad you were there," she said, and meant it. If he hadn't been at home they would have lost everything.

They talked about what would become of the house, of the city. They knew the house would have to be gutted, all the insulation and wiring replaced, the plaster and Sheetrock and paint and wallpaper. Everything, down to the studs, was gone. And if there was this much water Uptown, there was more in other neighborhoods. He thought of them — the houses near the lake and the houses near the levees. They didn't stand a chance.

As they talked, Zeitoun realized his phone was dying. Without electricity, they both knew, when his battery was gone there would be no reliable way to call out.

"Better go," he said.

3 **dresser** chest of drawers *(Kommode)* – 3 **armoire** *(Fr)* large wardrobe – 6 **to devour** [dɪ'vaʊɚ] to eat up – 7 **dismayed** [dɪ'smeɪd] with a sense of horror *(entsetzt)* – 9 **land-line** telephone *(Festnetzverbindung)* – 11 **spent** tired, exhausted – 14 **to dread** to fear – 19 **to gut** to remove the inner parts – 20 **wiring** electricity – 21 **stud** *(AE)* upright post which holds a wall together *(Ständer)*

"Please leave," she said. "Tomorrow."

"No, no," he said, but even as he spoke, he was reconsidering. He had not anticipated being confined to this house for long. He knew there was enough food for a week or more, but now the situation would present a greater strain than he had planned.

"Tell the kids I said goodnight," he said.

She said she would.

He turned off his phone to conserve what power it had left.

Kathy was still driving. She'd exhausted all means of diversion and was about to go back to her brother's house when her phone rang again. It was Adnan. He was in Baton Rouge with his wife Abeer, he said, and they had no place to stay.

"Where'd you stay last night?" Kathy asked.

"In the car," he said, sounding apologetic and ashamed.

"Oh my God," she said. "Let me see what I can do."

She planned to ask Mary Ann and Patty once she got back to the house. It would be crowded, but there was no way a pregnant woman should be sleeping in a car when there was enough room at her family's house.

When Kathy returned to Andy's, it was ten o'clock and the rooms were dark. All the kids, save Nademah, were asleep in the car. She roused them and walked quietly into the house. After the kids were settled in their sleeping bags, Mary Ann appeared and confronted her.

"Where were you all day?"

"Out," Kathy said. "Trying to stay out of the way."

"Do you know how expensive gas is?" Mary Ann said.

2 **to reconsider** to think an idea over, possibly to make a new decision – 3 **confined** kept in, restricted – 10 **to exhaust** to use up – 11 **diversion** distraction *(Ablenkung)*

"Excuse me?" Kathy said. "I didn't know you were paying for my gas."

Kathy was exasperated, defeated. In the house, they were made to feel burdensome; now she was being scolded for leaving. She vowed to herself to get through the night and think of a new plan the next day. Maybe she could drive to Phoenix to stay with Yuko. It was a ludicrous idea, to travel fifteen hundred miles when her blood relatives lived fifty miles from New Orleans, but she'd run to Yuko's house before and could do so again.

The tension was bad enough already, but for Adnan and Abeer's sake, Kathy had to ask. After all, Mary Ann knew them; she'd met Adnan and Abeer many times. Couldn't they stay for one night?

"Absolutely not," Mary Ann said.

On the dark second floor, Zeitoun held a flashlight between his teeth, sifting through the pile of belongings he'd salvaged. He shelved the books he could. He boxed the certificates and pictures. He found pictures of his children when they were smaller, pictures from a vacation they'd all taken to Spain, pictures from their trip to Syria. He organized them, found a plastic bag, put them safely inside and then re-boxed them.

In another, older box he came upon another photo, sepia-toned and in a rickety frame, and paused. He hadn't seen it in years. He and his brother Luay and sister Zakiya were playing with their brother Mohammed, eighteen years older.

3 **exasperated** angry – 7 **ludicrous** ['lu:dɪkrəs] silly – 17 **to sift through** to look through carefully – 17 **to salvage** to save – 23 **sepia** ['si:piə] dark brown – 24 **rickety** almost broken

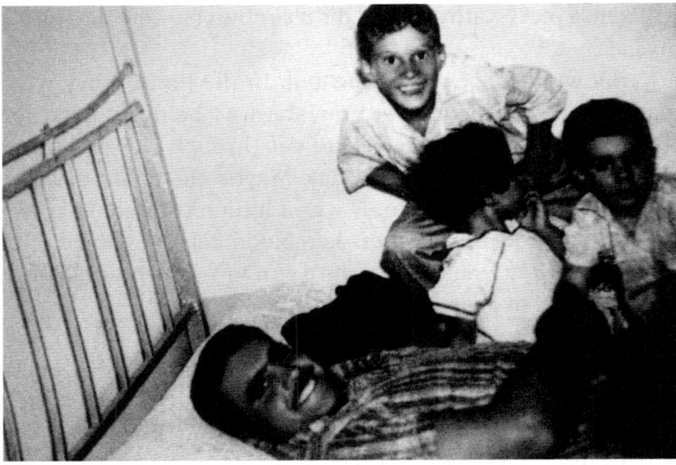

They were all wrestling with him in the bedroom Zeitoun and Ahmad and all the younger boys had shared in Jableh. There little Abdulrahman was, on the far right, maybe five years old, his tiny fingers swallowed by Mohammed's huge hand.

Zeitoun stared at his brother's electric smile. Mohammed had everything then. He *was* everything, the most famous and accomplished athlete in Syrian history. He was a long-distance ocean swimmer, one of the best the world had ever known. That he was from a country not well known for its coast made his achievements all the more remarkable. He had won races in Syria, Lebanon, and Italy. He could swim thirty miles at a stretch, and faster than anyone else. Faster than any Italian, any Englishman or Frenchman or Greek.

Zeitoun examined the picture more closely. Poor Mohammed, he thought, all his brothers and sisters swamping him. They did that to him whenever he was home. The races — in Greece, Italy, the United States — kept him away too long. He was feted by heads of state and featured in newspapers and magazines all over the world. They called him the Human Torpedo, the Nile Alligator, the Miracle. When he was home his siblings went wild, buzzing around him like flies.

And then, at age twenty-four, he was gone. Killed in a car accident in Egypt, just before a race in the Suez Canal. Zeitoun still missed him terribly, though he was only six when it happened. After that, he knew Mohammed only through stories, photos, and tributes, and the monument to him that stood on the waterfront in Jableh, just down the street from their home. Growing up they had to pass it every day, and its presence made forgetting Mohammed, even momentarily, impossible.

Zeitoun sat and stared at the photo for a minute or so before putting it back in the box.

He couldn't sleep inside the house. It was hotter this night, and in New Orleans he had never withstood this kind of heat without air-conditioning. Laying on sweat-soaked sheets, he had a thought. He looked in one of the upstairs closets for the tent he'd bought a few years back. The previous summer, he'd

3 **accomplished** perfect, famous – 11 **to swamp sb** *here:* to climb all over sb – 14 **to fete** to celebrate – 32 **closet** ['klɑːzɪt] *(AE)* cabinet *(Schrank)*

set it up in the backyard, and the kids had slept outside when the heat relented and allowed it.

He found the tent and crawled through the window of Nademah's room and onto the roof. Outside it was cooler, a breeze cutting through the stagnant air. The roof over the garage was flat, and he set up the tent there, securing it with books and a few cinder blocks. He dragged one of the kids' mattresses out and squeezed it through the tent's door. The difference was vast.

Laying on the mattress, he listened for the movement of water. Was it still rising? He wouldn't be surprised. He would not be shocked if, come morning, there was twelve, thirteen feet of water covering the neighborhood.

The darkness around him was complete, the night silent but for the dogs. First a few, then dozens. From all corners of the neighborhood he heard them howling. The neighborhood was full of dogs, so he was accustomed to their barking. On any given night, one would become excited by something and set off the rest, an arrhythmic call-and-response that could last hours until they calmed, one by one, into silence. But this night was different. These dogs had been left behind, and now they knew it. There was a bewilderment, an anger in their cries that cut the night into shards.

WEDNESDAY AUGUST 31

Zeitoun woke with the sun and crawled out of his tent. The day was bright, and as far as he could see in any direction the city was underwater. Though every resident of New Orleans imagines great floods, knows that such a thing is possible in a city surrounded by water and ill-conceived levees, the sight, in the light of day, was beyond anything he had imagined. He

2 **to relent** to stop – 5 **stagnant** still, not moving – 7 **cinder block** *(AE)* breeze block (large, industrially made brick used for building walls) – 14 **but** *here:* except – 22 **bewilderment** confusion – 29 **ill-conceived** poorly planned

could only think of Judgment Day, of Noah and forty days of rain. And yet it was so quiet, so still. Nothing moved. He sat on the roof and scanned the horizon, looking for any person, any animal or machine moving. Nothing.

As he did his morning prayers, a helicopter broke the silence, shooting across the treetops and heading downtown.

Zeitoun looked down from the roof to find the water at the same level as the night before. He felt some relief in knowing that it would likely remain there, or even drop a foot once it reached an equilibrium with Lake Pontchartrain.

Zeitoun sat beside his tent, eating cereal he had salvaged from the kitchen. Even with the water no longer rising, he knew he could do nothing at home. He had saved what he could save, and there was nothing else to do here until the water receded.

When he had eaten, he felt restless, trapped. The water was too deep to wade into, its contents too suspect to swim through. But there was the canoe. He saw it, floating above the yard, tethered to the house. Amid the devastation of the city, standing on the roof of his drowned home, Zeitoun felt something like inspiration. He imagined floating, alone, through the streets of his city. In a way, this was a new world, uncharted. He could be an explorer. He could see things first.

He climbed down the side of the house and lowered himself into the canoe. He untied the rope and set out.

1 **Judgment Day** last day of the world (according to the Bible) *(Jüngstes Gericht)* – 11 **an equilibrium** *here:* the same level – 11 **Lake Pontchartrain** large saltwater lake in New Orleans, connected to the Gulf of Mexico – 17 **trapped** caught – 20 **tethered** tied – 20 **amid** in the middle of – 24 **uncharted** not recorded on a map

He paddled down Dart Street, the water flat and clear. And strangely, almost immediately, Zeitoun felt at peace. The damage to the neighborhood was extraordinary, but there was an odd calm in his heart. So much had been lost, but there was a stillness to the city that was almost hypnotic.

He coasted away from his home, passing over bicycles and cars, their antennae scraping the bottom of his canoe. Every vehicle, old and new, was gone, unsalvageable. The numbers filled his head: there were a hundred thousand cars lost in the flood. Maybe more. What would happen to them? Who would take them once the waters receded? In what hole could they all be buried?

Almost everyone he knew had left for a day or two, expecting little damage. He passed by their homes, so many of which he'd painted and even helped build, calculating how much was lost inside. It made him sick, the anguish this would cause. No one, he knew, had prepared for this, adequately or at all.

He thought of the animals. The squirrels, the mice, rats, frogs, possums, lizards. All gone. Millions of animals drowned. Only birds would survive this sort of apocalypse. Birds, some snakes, any beast that could find higher ground ahead of the rising tide. He looked for fish. If he was floating atop water shared with the lake, surely fish had been swept into the city. And, on cue, he saw a murky form darting between submerged tree branches.

He remembered the dogs. He rested his paddle on his lap, coasting, trying to place the pets he'd heard crying in the dark.

He heard nothing.

4 **odd** strange – 16 **anguish** pain – 20 **possum** opossum – 21 **apocalypse** [ə'pɑ:kəlips] scene of destruction, as at the end of the world – 23 **atop** on top of – 25 **on cue** happening at exactly the right moment – 25 **to dart** to jump – 25 **submerged** lying under the surface

He was conflicted about what he was seeing, a refracted version of his city, one where homes and trees were bisected and mirrored in this oddly calm body of water. The novelty of the new world brought forth the adventurer in him — he wanted to see it all, the whole city, what had become of it. But the builder in him thought of the damage, how long it would take to rebuild. Years, maybe a decade. He wondered if the world at large could already see what he was seeing, a disaster mythical in scale and severity.

In his neighborhood, miles from the closest levee, the water had risen slowly enough that he knew it was unlikely that anyone had died in the flood. But with a shudder he thought of those closer to the breaches. He didn't know where the levees had failed, but he knew anyone living nearby would have been quickly overwhelmed.

He turned on Vincennes Place and headed south. Someone called his name. He looked up to see a client of his, Frank Noland, a fit and robust man of about sixty, leaning out from a second-story window. Zeitoun had done work on his house a few years ago. The Zeitouns would see Frank and his wife occasionally in the neighborhood, and they always exchanged warm greetings.

Zeitoun waved and paddled over.

"You got a cigarette?" Frank asked, looking down.

Zeitoun shook his head no, and coasted closer to the window where Frank had appeared. It was a strange sensation, paddling over the man's yard; the usual barrier that would prevent one from guiding a vehicle up to the house was gone. He could glide directly from the street, diagonally across the lawn, and appear just a few feet below a second-story window. Zeitoun was just getting accustomed to the new physics of this world.

1 **refracted** distorted, changed – 2 **to bisect** to cut in two – 8 **the world at large** the whole world – 9 **scale** size *(Ausmaß)* – 12 **shudder** shiver, shake (from cold, or *(here)* from fear or anguish)

Frank was shirtless, wearing only a pair of tennis shorts. His wife was behind him, and they had a guest in the house, another woman of similar age. Both women were dressed in T-shirts and shorts, suffering in the heat. It was early in the day, but the humidity was already oppressive.

"You think you could take me to where I can buy some smokes?" Frank asked.

Zeitoun told him that he didn't think any store would be open and selling cigarettes this day.

Frank sighed. "See what happened to my motorcycle?" He pointed to the porch next door.

Zeitoun remembered Frank talking about this motorcycle — an antique bike that he had bought, restored, and lavished attention on. Now it was under six feet of water. As the water had risen the day before, Frank had moved it from the driveway up to the porch and then to his next-door neighbor's porch, which was higher. But now it was gone. They could still see the faint, blurred likeness of the machine, like a relic from a previous civilization.

He and Frank talked for a few minutes about the storm, the flood, how Frank had expected it but then hadn't expected it at all.

"Any chance you can take me to check on my truck?" Frank asked. Zeitoun agreed, but told Frank that he'd have to continue on a while longer. Zeitoun was planning to check on one of his rental properties, about two miles away.

Frank agreed to come along for the ride, and climbed down from the window and into the canoe. Zeitoun gave him the extra paddle and they were off.

"Brand new truck," Frank said. He had parked it on Fontainebleau, thinking that because the road was a foot or so higher than Vincennes, the truck would be spared. They

13 **to lavish** to give generously – 18 **blurred** not clear, hazy

made their way up six blocks to where Frank had parked the truck, and then Zeitoun heard Frank's quick intake of breath. The truck was under five feet of water and had migrated half a block. Like his motorcycle, it was gone, a thing of the past.

"You want to get anything out of it?" Zeitoun asked.

Frank shook his head. "I don't want to look at it. Let's go."

They continued on. Soon they saw an older man, a doctor Zeitoun knew, on the second-floor porch of a white house. They paddled into the yard and asked the doctor if he needed help. "No, I've got somebody coming," he said. He had his housekeeper with him, he said, and they were well set up for the time being.

A few doors down, Zeitoun and Frank came upon a house with a large white cloth billowing from the second-floor window. When they got closer, they saw a couple, a husband and wife in their seventies, leaning out of the window.

"You surrender?" Frank asked.

The man smiled.

"You want to get out?" Zeitoun asked.

"Yes, we do," the man said.

They couldn't safely fit anyone else in the canoe, so Zeitoun and Frank promised to send someone back to the house as soon as they got to Claiborne. They assumed there would be activity there, that if anywhere would have a police or military presence, it would be Claiborne, the main thoroughfare nearby.

"We'll be right back," Zeitoun said.

As they were paddling away from the couple's house, they heard a faint female voice. It was a kind of moan, weak and tremulous.

11 **for the time being** so far, at the moment – 14 **to billow** to move in the wind – 25 **thoroughfare** main road – 30 **tremulous** trembling, timid

"You hear that?" Zeitoun asked.

Frank nodded. "It's coming from that direction."

They paddled toward the sound and heard the voice again.

"Help."

It was coming from a one-story house on Nashville.

They coasted toward the front door and heard the voice again: "Help me."

Zeitoun dropped his paddle and jumped into the water. He held his breath and swam to the porch. The steps came quicker than he thought. He jammed his knee against the masonry and let out a gasp. When he stood, the water was up to his neck.

"You okay?" Frank asked.

Zeitoun nodded and made his way up the steps.

"Hello?" the voice said, now hopeful.

He tried the front door. It was stuck. Zeitoun kicked the door. It wouldn't move. He kicked again. No movement. With the water now to his chest, he ran his body against the door. He did it again. And again. Finally it gave.

Inside he found a woman hovering above him. She was in her seventies, a large woman, over two hundred pounds. Her patterned dress was spread out on the surface of the water like a great floating flower. Her legs dangled below. She was holding on to a bookshelf.

"Help me," she said.

Zeitoun talked gently to the woman, assuring her that she would be taken care of. He knew that in all likelihood she had been there, clinging to her furniture, for twenty-four hours or more. An elderly woman like this would have no chance of swimming to safety, much less have the strength to cut a hole through her roof. At least the water was warm. She might not have survived.

20 **to hover** to float – 23 **to dangle** to hang loosely

Zeitoun pulled her out the front door and caught a glimpse of Frank in the canoe. His jaw had gone slack, his eyes disbelieving.

No one knew what to do next. It would be very difficult to fit a woman of her size into the canoe under normal circumstances. And lifting her into it would require more than two men. Even if they could lift her and fit her inside, they couldn't possibly fit all three of them. The canoe would certainly capsize.

He and Frank had a quick whispered conversation. They had no choice but to leave her and find help. They would paddle quickly to Claiborne and flag down a boat. They told the woman the plan. She was unhappy to be left alone again, but there was no choice.

They reached Claiborne in a few minutes and immediately saw what they were looking for: a fan boat. Zeitoun had never seen one in person, but they were familiar from movies. This was a military model, loud, with a great fan anchored perpendicularly to the rear. It was headed directly toward them.

Zeitoun thought it was very lucky to have found another craft so quickly, and he was filled with something like pride, knowing that he had promised help and could now deliver it.

He and Frank positioned their canoe in the path of the boat and waved their arms. The fan boat came straight for them, and when it was close, Zeitoun could see that there were four or five uniformed officers aboard; he wasn't sure if they were police or military, but he was very happy to see them. He waved, and Frank waved, both of them yelling "Stop!" and "Help!"

But the fan boat did not stop. It swung around the canoe holding Zeitoun and Frank, not even slowing down, and continued down Claiborne. The men aboard the fan boat barely glanced at them.

2 **slack** loose – 8 **to capsize** to overturn – 18 **perpendicular** vertical; at right angles to

The fan boat's wake nearly tipped their canoe. Zeitoun and Frank sat still, gripping either side until the waves subsided. They hardly had time to exchange incredulous looks when another boat came their way. Again it was a fan boat, also with four military personnel aboard, and again Zeitoun and Frank waved and called for help. Again the fan boat swung around them and continued without a word.

This happened repeatedly over the next twenty minutes. Ten of these vessels, all staffed by soldiers or police officers, ignored their canoe and their calls for assistance. Where were these boats going, what were they looking for, if not for residents of the city asking for help? It defied belief.

Finally a different sort of boat approached. It was a small fishing boat manned by two young men. Though Zeitoun and Frank were disheartened and unsure if anyone would stop, they gave it a try. They stood in the canoe, they waved, they yelled. This boat stopped.

"We need help," Frank said.

"Okay, let's go," the men on the boat said.

The young men threw a line to Zeitoun, who tied it to the canoe. The motorboat towed Zeitoun and Frank to the woman's house, and once they were close, the young men cut the engine and coasted toward the porch.

Zeitoun jumped into the water again and swam to her door. The woman was exactly as they'd left her, in her foyer, floating near the ceiling.

Now they only had to figure out how to get her into the fishing boat. She couldn't lift herself into the boat; that wasn't an option. She couldn't drop down into the water for leverage. It was too deep and she could not swim.

"You have a ladder, ma'am?" one of the young men asked.

2 **to subside** to become less strong – 15 **disheartened** discouraged – 29 **for leverage** because she had no leverage *(Hebelwirkung)*

She did. She directed them to the detached garage at the end of the driveway. Zeitoun dropped into the water, swam to the garage, and retrieved it.

When he brought it back, he set it on the ground and against the boat. The plan was that the woman would let go of the bookshelf, grab the ladder, put her feet onto it, and climb up until she was above the boat and able to step into the hull.

Zeitoun held the ladder while the two young men steadied it against the boat, ready to receive her. It seemed an ingenious plan.

But she couldn't climb the ladder. She had a bad leg, she said, and couldn't put pressure on it. It took a certain degree of agility, and she was eighty years old, weakened by staying awake for twenty-four hours while floating near her ceiling, thinking only that she might drown in her own home.

"I'm sorry," she said.

There was only one option now, they decided. They would use the ladder as a sort of gurney. They would prop one end on the side of the fishing boat, and one of the young men would stand on the porch, holding the other side. They would then have to lift it high enough to get her over the lip of the boat, and far enough in that she could roll into the hull.

Zeitoun realized that two men, one on either end of the ladder, would not be enough to lift a woman of over two hundred pounds. He knew he would have to push from below. So when the two young men were in position, and the woman was ready, Zeitoun took a deep breath and went under. From below the surface, he could see the woman let go of the bookshelf and grab the ladder. It was awkward, but she managed to place herself atop it, as if it were a kind of raft.

As she put weight on the ladder, Zeitoun positioned his shoulders under it and pushed up. The motion was akin to a shoulder-press machine he'd once used at a gym. He straightened his legs, and as he did, the ladder rose from the

9 **ingenious** [ɪn'dʒiːnjəs] clever – 13 **agility** quickness – 18 **gurney** *(AE)* metal stretcher *(Trage)* – 30 **raft** simple, flat boat *(Floß)* – 32 **akin** [ə'kɪn] similar

water until he saw light breaking the surface, until he felt the air on his face and was finally able to exhale.

The woman rolled into the bed of the boat. It was not a graceful landing, but she managed to sit up. Though she was wet and breathing heavily, she was unhurt.

Zeitoun shuddered as he watched her recover. It was not right to watch a woman of her age suffer like this. The situation had stolen her dignity, and it pained him to bear witness.

Zeitoun climbed back into the canoe. Frank, smiling and shaking his head, stretched out his hand from the fishing boat.

"That was something," Frank said.

Zeitoun shook his hand and smiled.

The men sat in silence, letting the woman determine when it was time to go. They knew it was an impossible thing for her to see her house like this, untold damage and loss within. At her age, and with the years it would take to restore the home, she would likely never return. They gave her a moment. Finally she nodded and they arranged their convoy. Zeitoun was alone in the canoe, being towed behind. He was soaked and exhausted.

With Frank directing the fishing boat, they made their way toward the couple who had been waving the white cloth. On the way there, they heard another cry for help.

It was another older couple in their seventies, waving from their second-story window.

"You ready to leave?" Frank asked.

"We are," the man in the window said.

The young fishermen brought the caravan to the window, and the couple, fit and agile, lowered themselves into it.

With six people now aboard the fishing boat, they arrived at the white-flag house. The couple living there lowered

2 **to exhale** to breathe out – 20 **to tow** [toʊ] to pull

themselves down, making the number in the fishing boat eight. The young men had seen a temporary medical staging ground set up at the intersection of Napoleon and St. Charles, and they agreed that they would deliver the passengers there. It was time for Zeitoun and Frank to part ways with their companions. Frank stepped back into the canoe and said goodbye.

"Good luck with everything," one of the young men said.

"You too," Zeitoun said.

They had never exchanged names.

In Baton Rouge, Kathy was again driving to kill time, her car full of children. Needing distraction from the news on the radio — it was getting worse every hour — she stopped periodically at whatever stores or restaurants were open. Zeitoun had sounded so calm on the phone the previous night, before his phone had given out. But since then conditions in the city had devolved. She was hearing reports of unchecked violence, widespread chaos, thousands presumed dead. What was her lunatic husband doing there? She tried his phone again and again, hoping he had somehow found a way to charge it. She tried the home phone, in case the water had miraculously dropped below the phone box and the wiring was undamaged. She got nothing. The lines were dead.

On the radio, they were reporting that another ten thousand National Guardsmen were being sent to the region, about one-third of them directed to maintain order. There would soon be twenty-one thousand National Guard troops in the area, coming from all over the country — West Virginia, Utah, New Mexico, Missouri. How could her husband be so calm when every branch of the armed forces was scrambling?

3 **intersection** place where two roads cross – 19 **lunatic** ['luːnət̬ɪk] mad – 26 **National Guardsmen** citizen soldiers, reserve of US military – 27 **to maintain** [meɪn'teɪn] to keep – 31 **to scramble** (of soldiers) to hurry into the right strategic positions

She turned off the radio and tried Zeitoun again. Nothing. She knew she shouldn't worry yet, but her mind took dark turns. If she was out of touch with her husband already, how would she know if anything was wrong? How would she know if he was alive, in danger, dead? She was getting ahead of herself. He was in no danger. The winds were gone, and now it was just water, placid water. And troops were on their way. No cause for worry.

Returning to her family's house in Baton Rouge, she found her mother there. She had come to deliver ice. She greeted all the kids and looked at Kathy.

"Why don't you take off that thing and relax?" she said, pointing to Kathy's hijab. "He's not here. Be yourself."

Kathy suppressed a dozen things she wanted to say, and instead channeled her rage into packing. She would take the kids and go to a motel, a shelter. Anywhere. Maybe to Arizona. It just wasn't working in Baton Rouge. And it was all so much worse not knowing where Zeitoun was. Why did that man insist on staying? It was a cruel thing, really. He wanted to make sure that his family was safe, but Kathy, his wife, wasn't afforded the same certainty. When they next spoke, she was determined to get him to leave the city. It didn't matter anymore why he wanted to stay. Forget the house and property. Nothing could be worth it.

In New Orleans, Zeitoun was invigorated. He had never felt such urgency and purpose. In his first day in his flooded city, he had already assisted in the rescue of five elderly residents. There was a reason, he now knew, that he had remained in the city. He had felt compelled to stay by a power beyond his own reckoning. He was needed.

5 **to get ahead of oneself** to move or *(here)* think too fast – 7 **placid** calm – 16 **shelter** place where the homeless can stay – 25 **to invigorate** to give strength – 26 **urgency** importance – 29 **compelled** forced

Zeitoun and Frank's next stop was Zeitoun's property, back on Claiborne at number 5010. He and Kathy had owned the home, a two-story residence, for five years. It was a rental unit, with four to six tenants at any given time.

When they arrived, they found Todd Gambino, one of Zeitoun's tenants, on the front porch, a bottle of beer in his hand. Todd was a stout man in his late thirties, and had lived there as long as the Zeitouns had owned the building. He worked as a mechanic at a SpeeDee Oil Change and Tune-Up franchise most of the week, and had a part-time job delivering lost luggage for the airport. He was a good tenant; they'd never had a late check or any sort of problem from him.

He stood up, incredulous, as Zeitoun approached.

"What're you doing here?" he asked.

"Really? I came to check on the building," Zeitoun said, smiling, knowing how ludicrous it sounded. "I wanted to check on you."

Todd couldn't believe it.

Zeitoun and Frank got out of the canoe and tied it to the porch. They were both happy to stand on solid ground again.

Todd offered them beers. Zeitoun passed. Frank accepted and sat on the porch steps while Zeitoun went inside.

Todd lived in the first-floor unit of the building, and had brought all of his possessions up to the second floor. The front rooms and hallway of the house were full of furniture, chairs and desks stacked on tables and couches. Various electronics saved from the flood were now resting on the dining-room table. It looked like a haphazard estate sale.

The damage to the house was extensive but not irreparable. Zeitoun knew the basement would be a loss, and might not be habitable for some time. But the first and second floors had not been badly harmed, and this gave Zeitoun comfort. There

3 **rental unit** house with tenants *(Mietshaus)* – 7 **stout** corpulent – 12 **they never had a late check** he never paid the rent late – 13 **incredulous** not believing his eyes – 28 **haphazard** [ˌhæpˈhæzɚd] chaotic

was a lot of dirt, mud, grime — much of it from Todd moving things upstairs and rushing in and out of the house — but the damage could have been far worse.

Zeitoun learned from Todd that because the house's phone box was above the water line, the landline was still working. He immediately dialed Kathy's cell phone.

"Hello? I'm here," he said.

She almost screamed. She hadn't realized how worried she'd been. *"Alhamdulilah,"* she said, Arabic for *Praise be to God.* "Now get out."

He told her he would not be leaving. He told her about the woman in the ballooning dress in the foyer, how he had lifted the ladder to save her. He told her about the fishermen, and Frank, and the two elderly couples. He was talking so fast she laughed.

"So when do you plan to leave?" she asked.

"I don't," he said.

He tried to explain. If he left, what would he do? He would be in a home full of women, with nothing to occupy himself. He would eat, watch TV, and be left to worry from afar. Here, in the city, he could stay and monitor developments. He could help where needed. They had a half-dozen properties to look after, he reminded her. He was safe, he had food, he could take care of himself and prevent further damage.

"Really? I want to see this," he said.

He wanted to see everything that had happened and would happen with his own eyes. He cared about this city and believed in his heart he could be of use.

"So you feel safe?" she asked.

"Of course," he said. "This is good."

Kathy knew that she couldn't dissuade him. But how would she explain to her children, as they watched images of the city drowning, that their father was there by choice, paddling

1 **grime** black dirt

around in a secondhand canoe? She tried to reason with him, noting that the TV reports were saying that things were only getting worse, that the water would soon become infected with all manner of pollutants — oil, garbage, animal remains — and that diseases would soon follow.

Zeitoun promised to be careful. He promised to call back at noon the next day, from the house on Claiborne.

"Call every day at noon," she said.

He said he would.

"You better," she said.

They hung up. Kathy turned on the television. The news led with reports of lawlessness and death. The media consensus was that New Orleans had descended into a "third-world" state. Sometimes this comparison was made with regard to the conditions, where hospitals were not open or working, where clean water and other basic services weren't available. In other instances, the words were spoken over images of African American residents wilting in the heat outside the Morial Convention Center or standing on rooftops waving for help. There were unverified reports of roving gangs of armed men, of guns being fired at helicopters trying to rescue patients from the roof of a hospital. Residents were being referred to as refugees.

Kathy was certain Zeitoun was unaware of the level of danger being reported. He may have felt safe where he was in Uptown, but what if there really was chaos, and that chaos was simply making its way to him? She was reluctant to believe the hyperbolic and racially charged news coverage, but still, things were devolving. Most of those left in the city were trying desperately to get out. She couldn't stand it. She called the house on Claiborne again. No answer.

28 **hyperbolic** *here:* exaggerated – 28 **racially charged** racist – 29 **to devolve** to become worse, to deteriorate

He was already gone. Zeitoun and Frank were paddling back to Zeitoun's house on Dart Street. As they made their way home, passing a half-dozen fan boats along the way, it occurred to Zeitoun that he and Frank had heard the people they had helped, in particular the old woman floating inside her home, because they were in a canoe. Had they been in a fan boat, the noise overwhelming, they would have heard nothing. They would have passed by, and the woman likely would not have survived another night. It was the very nature of this small, silent craft that allowed them to hear the quietest cries. The canoe was good, the silence was crucial.

Zeitoun dropped Frank at his house and made for home. His paddle kissed the clean water, his shoulders worked in perfect rhythm. Zeitoun had traveled five, six miles already that day, and he wasn't tired. Night was falling, and he knew he had to be home, safe on his roof. But he was sorry to see the day end.

He tied the canoe to the back porch and climbed up into the house. He retrieved a portable grill and brought it to the roof. He made a small fire and cooked chicken breasts and vegetables he'd thawed that day. The night fell as he ate, and soon the sky was darker than any he'd known in New Orleans. The sole light came from a helicopter circling downtown, looking tiny and powerless in the distance.

Using bottled water, Zeitoun cleaned up and prayed on the roof. He crawled into the tent, his body aching but his mind alive, playing back the events of the day. He and Frank really had saved that woman, hadn't they? They had. It was a fact. They had brought four others to safety, too. And there would be more to do tomorrow. How could he explain to Kathy, to his brother Ahmad, that he was so thankful he had stayed in the city? He was certain he had been called to stay, that God knew he would be of service if he remained. His choice to stay in the city had been God's will.

11 **crucial** essential, very important – 23 **sole** only

Too excited to sleep, he went back through the window and into the house. He wanted to find the photo of Mohammed again. He'd forgotten who was with him in the picture — was it Ahmad? — and he wanted to see the expression on Mohammed's face, that world-conquering smile.

He retrieved the box of pictures, and while looking for that one he found another.

He'd forgotten about this photo. There he was, Mohammed with the vice president of Lebanon. Zeitoun hadn't seen the image for a few years. Mohammed wasn't even twenty, and he'd won a race starting in Saida and ending in Beirut, a distance of twenty-six miles. The crowd was stunned. He had come out of nowhere, Mohammed Zeitoun, a sailor's son from the tiny island of Arwad, and stunned everyone with his strength and endurance. Zeitoun knew his father, Mahmoud, was somewhere in the crowd. He never missed a race. But it had not always been so.

Mahmoud wanted Mohammed, and all of his sons, working on dry land, so Mohammed spent his early teenage years as a craftsman, laying brick and apprenticing for an ironsmith. He was a powerfully built young man, and was finished with school at fourteen. At eighteen he looked much older, with a full mustache and a square jaw. He was both a workhorse and a charmer, admired equally by his elders and the young women in town.

With his father's grudging approval, Mohammed crewed on local fishing boats in the afternoons and evenings, and even at fourteen, after a full day of fishing miles from land, Mohammed insisted on swimming to shore. The other fishermen would have barely pulled in the last net when they would hear a splash and see Mohammed cutting through the sea, racing them to the beach.

15 **endurance** [ɪnˈdjuːrənts] being able to bear stress – 26 **grudging** disapproving, reluctant

Mohammed didn't tell his father about such endeavors, and he certainly didn't tell him when, a few years later, he decided that he was destined to be the world's greatest long-distance swimmer.

It was 1958. Egypt and Syria, reacting to a number of political factors, including growing American influence in the region, merged, creating the United Arab Republic.

The union was meant to create a more powerful bloc, one that might grow to include Jordan, Saudi Arabia, and others. There was wide public support for the alliance, pride bursting from the streets and windows of Syria and Egypt, the citizens of both countries seeing the union as a step along the way to a broader alignment between the Arab states. There were parades and celebrations from Alexandria to Lattakia.

One of the commemorative events was a race between Jableh and Lattakia, in which swimmers from all over the

1 **endeavor** [en'devɚ] effort – 3 **he was destined** he had to; it was his fate *(Schicksal)* – 13 **alignment** connection, agreement – 15 **commemorative** [kə'memərət̬ɪv] in memory of

Arab world would swim thirty kilometers through the Mediterranean. It was the first race of its kind on the Syrian coast, and eighteen-year-old Mohammed followed every step, from the preparations to the race itself. He watched the swimmers train, studying their strokes and regimen, longing to be part of it himself. He managed to be appointed to the crew of the guide boat for one of the competitors, Mouneer Deeb, which would keep pace with him along the race's route.

Along the way, unable to contain himself, Mohammed jumped in and swam alongside Deeb and the other contestants. He not only kept up with the professionals, he impressed one of the judges. "That boy is great," the judge said. "He is going to be a champion." From that day on Mohammed thought of little else but the fulfillment of that prophecy.

Still only eighteen years old, he worked mornings as a mason and ironsmith, afternoons as a fisherman, and at night he began to train for the next year's race. He kept his training secret from his father, even when he undertook two long-distance tests, one between Lattakia and Jableh and another between Jableh and Baniyas. Soon enough, though, Mahmoud learned of his son's aspirations, and, fearing he would lose his son to the unforgiving sea that had almost taken his own life, he forbade him from swimming long distances. He wanted him out of fishing, away from the sea. He wanted his son alive.

But Mohammed could not stop. As difficult as it was to disobey his father, he continued to train. Telling no one in his family, Mohammed entered the next year's race. As he stepped out of the water in Lattakia, the cheers were deafening. He had won handily.

Before Mohammed could return home, an old friend of Mahmoud's, himself a champion swimmer, visited the Zeitoun house, congratulating Mahmoud on his son's victory. This is how Mahmoud learned that Mohammed Zeitoun was the best swimmer in all of Syria.

5 **regimen** ['redʒəmən] *here:* intense physical training – 10 **contestant** competitor (*here:* swimmer) – 21 **aspiration** goal

By the time Mohammed arrived home that night, Mahmoud had given up his resistance. If his son wanted this, and if his son was destined to swim — if God had made him a swimmer — then Mahmoud could not stand in the way. He bought Mohammed a bus ticket to Damascus to train and compete with the best swimmers in the region.

Zeitoun found another photo. Mohammed's first major victory came in that same year, 1959, in a race in Lebanon. The field was crowded, filled with well-known names, but Mohammed not only finished first, he did so in record time: nine hours and fifty-five minutes. This photo, Zeitoun was almost sure, was taken during the celebration afterward. Thousands were there, applauding his brother.

How old was Zeitoun at the time? He did the calculations in his head. Just a year. He was maybe one year old. He remembered nothing of those early wins.

The next year, Mohammed entered the famed race between Capri and Naples, a contest that attracted the best swimmers in the world. The favorite was Alfredo Camarero, an Argentinean, who had placed first or second in the race five years running. Mohammed was an unknown when the race began at six in the morning, and after eight hours, when he was approaching shore, he had no idea that he was in the lead. It wasn't until he stepped out of the sea, hearing shrieks of surprise and the chanting of his name, that he realized he'd won. "Zeitoun the Arab has won!" they cheered. No one could believe it. A Syrian winning the world's greatest long-distance competition? Camarero told everyone that Mohammed was the strongest swimmer he had ever seen.

Mohammed dedicated the victory to President Nasir. In return, Nasir made the twenty-year-old Mohammed an honorary lieutenant in the navy. The prince of Kuwait attended the race and celebrated him at an honorary dinner in Naples. The next year Mohammed won the Capri-to-Naples race again, this time breaking the course record set by

Camarero by fifteen minutes. Mohammed was now indisputably the best ocean swimmer in the world.

As a boy, Abdulrahman was enthralled, proud beyond measure. To grow up in that house, with a brother like that, to bask every day in the glory he'd brought to the family — his siblings' pride in Mohammed fueled how they felt when they awoke each day, how they walked and talked and were perceived in Jableh and Arwad and everywhere across Syria. It changed, permanently, how they saw the world. Mohammed's accomplishments implied — proved, really — that the Zeitouns were extraordinary. It was incumbent, thereafter, on each and every child to live up to that legacy.

It had been forty-one years since Mohammed's death. Mohammed's incredible rise and premature passing had shaped the trajectory of Zeitoun's family in general and of Abdulrahman in particular, but he didn't like to dwell on it. In his less generous moments he believed his brother had been stolen from him, that the unfairness of taking such a beautiful man so young put many things into question. But he knew he was wrong to think this way, and it was unproductive in any case. All he could do now was honor his brother's memory. Be strong, be brave, be true. Endure. Be as good as Mohammed was.

Zeitoun tucked himself into the tent and fell into a fitful sleep. All over the neighborhood, the dogs were mad with hunger. Their barking was wild, unmoored, spiraling.

3 **enthralled** [ɪnˈθrɔːld] captivated, enthusiastic – 5 **to bask** to bathe *(sich aalen)* – 8 **to perceive** to see, to view – 10 **accomplishment** *here:* success – 11 **to be incumbent on sb** *(fml)* to be a duty, obligatory – 12 **to live up to a legacy** *einem Erbe gerecht werden* – 14 **premature passing** death that came too early – 16 **to dwell on sth** to think about sth for a long time – 26 **unmoored** out of control (if a boat is unmoored, it is not tied to anything)

THURSDAY SEPTEMBER 1

By six a.m., Kathy had the Odyssey packed and the kids buckled in. Her sisters were still asleep as she quietly backed out of the driveway, leaving Baton Rouge. It was fifteen hundred miles to Phoenix.

"Are we really leaving Mekay?" Nademah asked.

Even Kathy couldn't believe it, but what else could they do? She had begged Patty to let her leave the dog there for a week; she'd given dog food and money to one of Patty's teenage sons to care for poor Mekay. It was better than putting her in a kennel, and far better than trucking the dog all the way to Phoenix and back. Kathy didn't have the nerves for it. It was hard enough with four kids.

They were beginning what would be a three-day drive, minimum — more likely four or five. What was she doing? It was crazy to drive four days in a car full of kids. And making the decision without her husband! It had been so long since she'd been in such a situation. But she had no choice. She couldn't stay in Baton Rouge for however many weeks it would be before New Orleans was habitable again. She hadn't even begun to think about school, about clothes — they'd only packed for two days — or about what they would do for money while the business was at a standstill.

Heading west on I-10, she felt some measure of relief in knowing that at the very least, on the open road she would have some time to think.

Out on the highway, she dialed the Claiborne house. Though it was hours before their agreed-upon time, she called in case Zeitoun had gotten there first and was waiting to call her. The phone rang three times.

"Hello?" a man said. The voice was an American's, not her husband's. It was gruff, impatient.

"Is Abdulrahman Zeitoun there?" she asked.

11 **kennel** dog shelter

"What? Who?"

She repeated her husband's name.

"No, no one here by that name."

"Is this 5010 Claiborne?" she asked.

"I don't know. I think so," the man said.

"Who is this?" she asked.

There was a pause, then the line went dead.

Kathy drove for a mile before she could even wrap her mind around what had just happened. Who was that voice? It was not one of the tenants; she knew them all. It was a stranger, someone who had found a way into the house and was now answering the phone. Again her mind took quick turns downward. What if the man on the phone had killed her husband and robbed the house and moved in?

She pulled into a McDonald's and parked, calming herself down. She turned on the radio and almost immediately came upon a report from New Orleans. She knew she shouldn't listen, but she couldn't help it. The reports of lawlessness were worse than before, and Governor Blanco, in a statement directed to would-be criminals, warned that war-hardened U.S. soldiers were on the way to New Orleans to restore order at any cost. "I have one message for these hoodlums," she said. "These troops know how to shoot and kill, and they are more than willing to do so if necessary, and I expect they will."

Kathy knew she should turn the dial before the kids heard any of it, but it was too late.

"Did they say the city was flooded, Mama?"

"Is our house under water?"

"Are they shooting people, Mama?"

Kathy turned the radio off. "Please, babies, don't ask me questions."

She steeled herself and got back on the highway, determined to drive straight through to Phoenix. She just had to get to

20 **would-be** possible – 33 **to steel** to harden

Yuko and she would be okay. Yuko would settle her. Of course Zeitoun was okay, she told herself. The man on the phone could have been anyone. There would be nothing unusual about people sharing a phone when most of the city's landlines had ceased to function.

For a few minutes she was calm. But the kids started in with the questions again.

"What happened to our house, Mama?"

"Where's Daddy?"

This got Kathy's mind going again. What if that man *was* her husband's killer? What if she had just spoken to the man who had murdered him? She felt as if she had been watching, from above, the convergence of forces on her husband. Only she knew what was happening in the city, the madness, the suffering and desperation. He had no television, couldn't know the extent of the chaos. She had seen the images from helicopters, the press conferences, she had heard the statistics, the stories of gangs and rampant crime. Kathy bit her lip. "Babies, don't ask me right now. Don't ask me."

"When are we going home?"

"Please!" Kathy snapped. "Just leave it alone for a minute. Let me think!" She couldn't hold it in anymore. She could barely see the road. The lines were disappearing. She felt it coming on and pulled over. She was blind with tears, wiping her nose with the back of her hand, her head against the steering wheel.

"What's wrong, Mama?"

The highway flew beside her.

In a few minutes, she managed to gather herself enough to pull into a rest stop. She called Yuko.

"Don't drive another foot," Yuko said.

5 **to cease** to stop – 13 **convergence** coming together – 18 **rampant** frequent, unchecked

Within twenty minutes a plan was shaped. Kathy stayed put while Yuko's husband Ahmaad looked into flights. Kathy would only have to make it as far as Houston. Yuko would arrange for Kathy and the kids to spend the night at a friend's house there. Ahmaad would fly to Houston immediately, and in the morning he would meet her there and drive the family all the way to Phoenix.

"Are you sure?" Kathy asked.

"I'm your sister. You're my sister. You're all I have," Yuko said. Her mother Kameko had passed away that year. The loss had been devastating to both Yuko and Kathy.

This got Kathy crying all over again.

That morning Zeitoun woke after nine, exhausted from the howling of the dogs. He was determined this day to find them.

After his prayers, he paddled out over his flooded yard. The dogs seemed very near. He crossed the street and went left on Dart. Only a few houses down, he found the source.

It was a house he knew well. He paddled closer, and the dogs went wild, their desperate sounds coming from within. Now he had to find a way inside. The first story was flooded, so he assumed the dogs — two of them, he guessed — were trapped on the second. There was a many-boughed tree near the house. He paddled to it and tied the canoe to the trunk.

He lifted himself into the tree, climbing until he could see through a second-story window. He saw no dogs, but he could hear them. They were in that house, and they knew he was close. The tree where he was standing was about ten feet from the window. He couldn't jump. It was too far.

At that moment, he spotted a plank, a foot wide and sixteen feet long, floating in the sideyard. He climbed down, paddled to the plank, brought it to the house, and leaned it against the tree. He climbed up again and lifted the plank to create a

23 **many-boughed** [ˌmeni.baʊd] with many branches

bridge between the tree and the roof. He was about sixteen feet off the ground, about eight feet above the waterline.

The bridge he created was not so different from the scaffolding he used every day in his work, so after testing it quickly with the weight of one foot, he walked across and onto the roof.

From there he pried a window open and ducked into the house. The barking grew louder and more urgent. He walked through the bedroom he'd arrived in, hearing the dogs grow more hysterical. As he strode through the second-floor hallway he saw them: two dogs, a black Labrador and a smaller mixed breed, in a cage. They had no food, and their water dish was empty. They seemed confused enough to bite him, but he didn't hesitate. He opened the cage and let them out. The Labrador ran past him and out of the room. The smaller dog cowered in the cage. Zeitoun stepped back to give him room, but he stayed where he was.

For the Labrador, there was nowhere to go. He tried the stairs and saw the water reached to just a few inches below the second floor. He returned to Zeitoun, who had a plan.

"Wait here," he told them.

He walked back across the plank bridge, climbed down the tree and into his canoe, and paddled back to his house. He climbed up to the roof, slipped through his window, and went down the few steps not underwater. Knowing Kathy kept the freezer stocked with meat and vegetables, he leaned down and removed two steaks, quickly closing the door to keep the finite cold from escaping. He walked back up to the roof, grabbed two plastic water bottles, and dropped them and the steaks into the canoe below. He shimmied down and returned to the house of the dogs.

Again they sensed him approaching, and this time they were both waiting by the window, their heads peeking over

4 **scaffolding** construction next to a house which is used when e.g. the house is being painted *(Gerüst)*

the sill. When they smelled the meat, frozen though it was, they began barking wildly, their tails wagging. Zeitoun refilled their water dish and they dove for it. After drinking their fill they went to work on the steaks, gnawing on them until the meat thawed. Zeitoun watched for a few minutes, tired and content, until he heard more barking. There were other dogs, and he had a freezer full of food. He went back to his house to prepare.

He stacked more meat into his canoe and went in search of the other animals left behind. Almost immediately after leaving his house he heard a distinct barking, muffled, coming from almost the same location as the dogs he'd just found.

He paddled closer, wondering if there was actually a third dog in the home he'd just been in. He anchored the canoe to the tree again, took two steaks with him, and climbed up. From the middle bough he looked this time to the neighboring house, the one on the left, and saw two more dogs, jumping against the glass.

He pulled the plank away from the first house and arranged it so it extended to the other. The dogs, seeing him coming, went wild, leaping in place.

In a moment, he had opened the window and stepped in, the two dogs jumping at him. He dropped the two steaks and the dogs pounced, forgetting about him entirely. He needed to give them water, too, so he again paddled home and brought more water bottles and a bowl back to them.

Zeitoun left the window open enough to allow the dogs to get fresh air, then walked across the plank again and climbed down the tree to his canoe. He paddled off, thinking it was about time to call Kathy.

As he paddled, he noticed that the water was growing more contaminated. It was darker now, opaque, streaked with oil

1 **sill** horizontal board of a window *(Fensterbank)* – 11 **muffled** low, can barely be heard

and gasoline, polluted with debris, food, garbage, clothing, pieces of homes. But Zeitoun was in high spirits. He felt invigorated by what he'd been able to do for the dogs, that he was there for those animals, and four dogs that almost certainly would have starved would now live because he had stayed behind, and because he had bought that old canoe. He couldn't wait to tell Kathy.

By noon he'd returned to the house on Claiborne. Today Todd was gone and the house was empty. He went inside and called.

"Oh thank God!" Kathy said. "Thank God thank God thank God. Where have you been?" She and the kids were still driving to Houston. She pulled over.

"What're you worried about?" Zeitoun asked. "I said I'd call at noon. It's noon."

"Who was that man?" she asked.

"What man?" he asked.

She explained that when she'd called earlier that day, someone else had answered the phone. This was unsettling to Zeitoun. As they spoke, he looked around the house. There was no sign of theft or crime of any kind. There were no broken locks or windows. Maybe the man had been a friend of Todd's? He promised Kathy it was nothing at all to worry about, that he would get to the bottom of it.

Kathy, calmer now, was glad to hear that he had been able to help the dogs, that he was feeling useful. But she didn't want him in New Orleans anymore, no matter how many dogs he was feeding or how many people he was finding and saving.

"I really want you to leave," she said. "The news coming out of the city, it's so bad. There's looting, killing. Something bad is going to happen to you."

31 **to loot** (during a riot or war) to steal *(plündern)*

Zeitoun could hear how worried she was. But he hadn't seen anything like the chaos she described. If it existed at all — and she knew how the media was — it would be downtown. Where he was, he said, it was so quiet, so calm, so otherworldly and strange, that he couldn't possibly be in danger. Maybe, he said, there was a reason he'd stayed, a reason he'd bought that canoe, a reason he was put in this particular situation at this particular time.

"I feel like I'm supposed to be here," he said.

Kathy was silent.

"It's God's will," he said.

She had no answer to this.

They moved on to practical matters. Her cell phone never worked well at Yuko's house in Phoenix, so she gave Zeitoun the landline there. He wrote it down on a piece of paper and left it by the Claiborne phone.

"Get the kids into school when you get to Phoenix," he said.

Kathy rolled her eyes.

"Of course," she said.

"I love you and them," he said, and they hung up.

He set out again, and immediately saw Charlie Ray, who lived just to the right of the Claiborne house. He was a blue-eyed carpenter in his fifties, a friendly and easygoing native Zeitoun had known for years. He was sitting on his porch like today was a day like any other.

"You stayed too," Zeitoun said.

"I guess I did."

"You need anything? Water?"

Charlie didn't, but said he might soon. Zeitoun promised to check in with him again, and paddled off, curious about how many people had remained in the city. If Frank stayed, and Todd and Charlie had weathered the storm, surely there were tens of thousands more. He was not alone in his defiance.

34 **defiance** [dɪˈfaɪənts] resistance

He continued on, knowing he should feel tired. But he was not at all tired. He had never felt stronger.

This day he ventured closer to downtown, passing families wading through the water, pushing laundry tubs full of their possessions. He paddled by a pair of women pushing an inflatable baby pool, their clothes and food inside. Each time, Zeitoun asked if he could help, and occasionally they would ask for a bottle or two of water. He would hand them whatever he had. He was finding so many things — bottled water, MREs, canned food — and whenever he saw anyone, he gave them whatever was in his canoe. He had plenty for himself at home, and didn't want any more weighing him down.

He paddled up to the I-10 ramp at Claiborne and Poydras, a concrete structure about ten feet above the waterline. Dozens of people were there, waiting for rescue. A helicopter had dropped off water and food, and they seemed to be well provisioned. They asked Zeitoun if he wanted any water, and he said that he had enough, but that he would bring it to those who needed it. They gave him a case. As he turned his canoe around he saw a half-dozen dogs with the group, most of them puppies. They seemed healthy and well-fed, and were keeping cool from the heat under the shade of the cars.

Zeitoun, assuming that whatever was ailing the city was likely worse downtown, chose not to get too close to the epicenter. He turned around and made his way back to Dart Street.

As Kathy was driving to Houston, Yuko was making arrangements for the family to spend the night with a longtime friend of theirs she called Miss Mary. Like Yuko and Kathy, Mary was an American, born into a Christian household,

3 **to venture** to take a risk; to dare – 4 **laundry** wash – 10 MRE *(abb)* Meal, Ready-to-Eat (pre-packaged meal, made by the U.S. military for emergencies) – 23 **to ail** to (make) feel pain or suffering – 25 **epicenter** center of a crisis

who had converted to Islam as an adult. Now her house had become a sanctuary for families fleeing the storm, and when Kathy's Odyssey pulled into the driveway there were already a dozen or more people there, all of them Muslims from New Orleans and other parts of Louisiana and Mississippi.

Mary, a bright-eyed woman in her forties, met Kathy and the kids in the driveway. She took their bags and hugged Kathy so tight that Kathy started crying yet again. Mary took them inside and showed the kids the pool in back, and within minutes the four of them were swimming and happy. Kathy collapsed on the couch and tried not to think of anything.

When he got back to the house on Dart, Zeitoun found his tent in the water below. It had been blown off the roof — probably, Zeitoun guessed, by a helicopter. He retrieved it and set it up again, dried the interior with towels, and then went inside the house to look for ballast. He brought out stacks of books, this time the heaviest ones he could find, and put them in the corners of the tent.

As he was inside stabilizing it, he heard another helicopter approach. The sound was deafening. He expected it to pass over his house on its way elsewhere, but when he poked his head out and looked up he saw that it was hovering over his house, over him. Two men inside were signaling to him.

He waved them off, trying to indicate that he was fine. But this only seemed to intrigue them more. The second man in the helicopter was beginning to lower a cage to him when Zeitoun thought to give the man a thumbs-up. He signaled to his tent and then to himself and gave the helicopter a series of frantic thumbs-ups and *a-okay* signals. Finally understanding Zeitoun's intent to stay, one of the men in the helicopter decided to drop a box of water down to him. Zeitoun tried to wave him off again, to no avail. The box came down, and

25 **to intrigue** to arouse interest – 29 **frantic** excited, desperate – 32 **to no avail** without success

Zeitoun leapt out of the way before it knocked the tent flat and sent plastic bottles bouncing everywhere. Satisfied, the helicopter tilted away and was gone.

Zeitoun returned to restabilizing his shelter, beginning to get ready for bed. But like the night before, he was restless, his mind racing with the events of the day. He sat on the roof, watching the movement of the helicopters circling and swooping over the rest of the city. He made plans for the following day: he would venture farther toward downtown, he would revisit the I-10 overpass, he would check on the state of their office and warehouse over on Dublin Street. On the first floor there they kept their extra supplies — tools, paints, brushes, drop cloths, everything — and on the second floor they had their offices, with their computers, files, maps, invoices, deeds to the properties. He winced, thinking of what had become of the building, a rickety thing to begin with.

All night the helicopters roamed overhead. Besides them it was quiet; he heard no dogs. After his prayers, he fell asleep under a vibrating sky.

<u>FRIDAY SEPTEMBER 2</u>

In the morning Zeitoun rose early, climbed down to his canoe, and paddled across the street to feed the dogs. They whimpered as he approached, and he took it as relief and gratitude. He climbed the tree, stepped carefully across the plank to the house on the right, and crawled through the window. He dropped two large pieces of steak for the dogs and refilled their water dish. As they busied themselves, he climbed out of the window, stepped carefully over to the next-door roof, and made his way into the second house to feed the second pair of dogs. They barked and wagged their tails, and

15 **invoice** bill – 15 **deed** legal document – 15 **to wince** to suddenly change the expression of one's face (in pain) – 16 **rickety** falling apart

he dropped two pieces of lamb between them and refilled their water. He left through the window, climbed down to his canoe, and paddled off.

It was time to see what had become of his office building. It was about a half mile away, just off Carrollton, a nearby road lined with warehouses, chain stores, and gas stations. The water was filthy now, streaked with oil and spotted with detritus. Anyone left to wade through this would become sick, he was sure. But so far this day, he had seen no one in the water. The city was emptying. Every day there were fewer people wading, fewer faces in windows, fewer private watercraft like his.

It had been drizzling throughout the morning but now the rain began to pick up. The wind came on, and the day grew miserable. Zeitoun paddled into the wind, struggling to control the canoe, the wind rippling the brown-blue water.

He took Earhart over to Carrollton, and took Carrollton southwest on his way to Dublin. He expected that there might be people on Carrollton — like Napoleon and St. Charles, it seemed a logical thoroughfare for rescue or military boats — but when he got close, he saw no official personnel at all.

Instead he saw a group of men gathered at the Shell station just across the street from his office. The station was elevated from the main road and was under only a few feet of water. The men, about eight or nine of them, were carrying full garbage bags from the station's office and loading them into a boat. It was the first looting he had seen since the storm, and these men were the first who fit the description of those Kathy had warned him about. This was an organized group of criminal opportunists who were not simply taking what they needed to survive. They were stealing money and goods from the gas station, and they were operating in numbers that

8 **detritus** rubbish, debris

seemed designed to intimidate anyone, like Zeitoun, who might see them or try to impede them.

Zeitoun was far enough away to observe without fear of them reaching him — at least not quickly. Still, he slowed his canoe to keep a safe distance, trying to figure out a way to get to his office without passing directly by them.

But one of the men had already noticed him. He was young, wearing long denim shorts and a white tank top. He squared his shoulders to Zeitoun and made a point of revealing the handle of a gun he had holstered in his belt.

Zeitoun quickly looked away. He did not want to invite confrontation. He turned his canoe around and made his way toward the house on Claiborne. He would not check on the office this day.

He arrived before noon and called Kathy. She was still in Houston at Miss Mary's house.

"Won't be able to check on the office today," he said.

"Why?" she asked.

He didn't want her to worry. He knew he had to lie.

"Rain," he said.

She told him that friends had been calling her, checking in to see where she and Zeitoun were, if they were safe. When she told them that her husband was still in the city, there was always a three-stage response. First they were shocked, then they realized it was Zeitoun they were talking about — a man who did not inspire worry in any situation — and finally they asked that while he was paddling around, would he mind checking on their property?

Zeitoun was all too happy to be given a mission, and Kathy obliged. She had just gotten a call from the Burmidians, friends of theirs for thirteen years. Ali Burmidian was a professor of computer science at Tulane University, and ran

2 to impede to hinder

the Masjid ar-Rahmah, a Muslim student association on campus. They had a building on Burthe Street that housed a resource center and dorm for visiting students from the Arab world.

Delilah Burmidian had just called Kathy, asking if Zeitoun could check on the building, to see what kind of damage it had sustained. Zeitoun said no problem, he would check on it. He knew the building well — he'd been to functions there a few times over the years — and he knew how to get there. He was curious, actually, to see what had become of the campus, given that it was on higher ground.

"Call again at noon," she said.

"Of course," Zeitoun said.

Before he left, Zeitoun called his brother Ahmad. After expressing great relief to hear from him, Ahmad got serious.

"You must leave," Ahmad said.

"No, no. I'm fine. Everything is fine," Zeitoun said.

Ahmad tried playing the big brother. "Go to your family," he said. "I really want you to leave. Your family needs you."

"They need me here more," Zeitoun said, trying not to sound too grandiose. "This is my family, too."

Ahmad had no way to counter such a statement.

"This call is expensive," Zeitoun said. "I'll call you tomorrow."

When he arrived at Tulane, the water was so low there that he easily stepped from the canoe onto dry land. He walked into the tiled courtyard of the Masjid ar-Rahmah and looked around. The grounds were crosshatched with downed branches, but otherwise the property was undamaged. He was about to look inside when he saw a man emerging from the building's side door.

"Nasser?" he said.

3 **dorm** dormitory, student boarding house – 7 **to sustain** *here:* to suffer – 28 **crosshatched** *here:* covered (with branches)

It was Nasser Dayoob. Also from Syria, Nasser had left the country in 1995, traveling first to Lebanon. From Beirut he stowed away on a tanker whose destination he did not know. It turned out it was heading to the United States, and when it made port Nasser jumped off and immediately sought asylum. He was eventually granted sanctuary, and by then he'd moved to New Orleans. He had stayed at the Masjid ar-Rahmah during his legal proceedings.

"Abdulrahman?"

They shook hands and exchanged stories of what they had been doing since the storm. Nasser's home, in the Broadmoor neighborhood adjacent to Uptown, had been flooded, and he'd come to the student association for shelter, knowing it was on higher ground.

"You want to stay here or come with me?" Zeitoun asked.

Nasser knew that he would be safe at the campus, with little possibility of flooding or crime, but still he went with Zeitoun. He too wanted to see what had become of the city and of his home.

He ran back into the building to get his duffel bag and then stepped into the canoe. Zeitoun gave him the other paddle and they were off.

Nasser was thirty-five and tall, with freckles and a thick mess of red hair. He was quiet, with a slightly nervous demeanor; when Kathy met him she'd thought he was a fragile sort of man. He was a sometime housepainter, and had occasionally worked for Zeitoun. They were not close friends, but running into Nasser here, after the flood, gave Zeitoun some comfort. They shared a lot of history — Syria, emigration to America and New Orleans, work in the trades.

As they paddled, they talked about what they had seen so far, what they had been eating, how they had been sleeping.

3 **to stow away** to hide on board a ship – 6 **to grant sanctuary** to give asylum

Both men had heard the dogs barking. Always the dogs barking at night. And Nasser, too, had fed dogs in the empty homes, on the streets, wherever he encountered them. It was one of the strangest aspects of this in-between time — after the storm but before anyone had returned to the city — the presence of these thousands of left-behind animals.

The wind was stronger now. Fighting through an angry horizontal rain, they paddled by the post office near Jefferson Parkway and Lafitte. The parking lot there had become a staging ground for evacuations. Residents who wanted to be airlifted out of the city could come to the post office and helicopters would take them, presumably, to safety.

As they paddled closer, Zeitoun asked Nasser if he wanted to leave. Not yet, Nasser said. He'd been hearing about the New Orleanians stranded under highway overpasses, and he didn't want to be among them. Until he heard more reliable reports of successful evacuations, he would stay in the city. Zeitoun told him he was welcome to stay at the Dart house or the house on Claiborne. He mentioned that there was a working phone on Claiborne, and this was a godsend to Nasser. He needed to call a half-dozen relatives, to let them know he was alive.

They paddled back to Claiborne, passing a full case of bottled water bobbing in the middle of the waterway. They lifted it into the canoe and continued on.

When they arrived at the house, Nasser got out and began tying up the canoe. Zeitoun was stepping out when he heard a voice calling his name.

"Zeitoun!"

He figured it was Charlie Ray, calling from next door. But it was coming from the house behind Charlie's, on Robert Street.

12 **presumably** it is expected

"Over here!"

It was the Williamses, a couple in their seventies. Alvin was a pastor at New Bethlehem Baptist Church and wheelchair bound; Beulah was his wife of forty-five years. Zeitoun and Kathy had known them for almost as long as they'd lived in New Orleans. When the Zeitouns had lived nearby, Pastor Williams's sister used to come to Kathy for meals. Kathy could never remember how it started, but the sister was elderly, and liked Kathy's cooking, so around dinnertime, Kathy always had a plate ready for her. It went on for months, and it warmed Kathy to know someone would go to the trouble to eat what she'd made.

"Hello!" Zeitoun called out, and paddled over.

"You think you could help us get out of here?" Alvin asked.

The pastor and Beulah had waited out the storm but had now exhausted their supply of food and water. Zeitoun had never seen them look so weary.

"It's time to go," Alvin said.

Given the rain and the wind, it was impossible to try to evacuate them in the canoe. Zeitoun told them he would find help.

He paddled up Claiborne, the wind and rain fighting him, to the Memorial Medical Center, where he knew there were police and National Guard soldiers stationed. As he approached, he saw soldiers in the alleyway, on the roof, on the ramps and balconies. It looked like a heavily fortified military base. When he got close enough to see the faces of the soldiers, two of them raised their guns.

"Don't come any closer!" they ordered.

Zeitoun slowed his canoe. The wind picked up. It was impossible to stay in one place, and making himself heard was difficult.

"I'm just looking for help," Zeitoun yelled.

One of the soldiers lowered his gun. The other kept his trained on Zeitoun.

25 **alleyway** back street

"We can't help you," he said. "Go to St. Charles."

Zeitoun assumed the soldier hadn't heard him correctly. The wind was turning his canoe around, veiling his words. "There's an old couple down the road that needs to be evacuated," he clarified, louder this time.

"Not our problem," the soldier said. "Go to St. Charles."

Now both guns were lowered.

"Why not call somebody?" Zeitoun asked. Did the soldier really mean that Zeitoun should paddle all the way to the intersection of Napoleon and St. Charles when the soldier could simply call another unit on his walkie-talkie? What were they doing in the city, if not helping evacuate people?

"We can't call nobody," the other soldier said.

"How come?" Zeitoun asked. "With all this technology, you can't call someone?"

Now the soldier, only a few years older than Zeitoun's son Zachary, seemed afraid. He had no answer, and seemed unsure of what to do next. Finally he turned and walked away. The remaining soldiers stared at Zeitoun, holding their M-16s.

Zeitoun turned his canoe around.

He paddled to the intersection of Napoleon and St. Charles, his shoulders aching. The wind was making the work twice as difficult. The water grew shallow as he approached the intersection. He saw tents there, and military vehicles, and a dozen or so police officers and soldiers. He stepped out of his canoe and walked up to a man, a soldier of some kind, standing on the grassy median — New Orleanians called it the *neutral ground*.

"I have a situation," Zeitoun said. "I have a handicapped man who needs help, medical attention. He needs help now." "Okay, we'll take care of it," the man said. "Do you want the address?" Zeitoun asked.

3 **to veil** [veɪl] to hide, cover the sound of – 20 **M-16** rifle (large gun)

"Yeah, sure, give me that," the man said, opening a small notebook. Zeitoun gave him the exact address.

The man wrote it down and put his notebook back in his pocket.

"So you'll go?" Zeitoun asked.

"Yup," the man said.

"When?" Zeitoun asked.

"About an hour," the man said.

"It's okay. They're on their way," Zeitoun said. "They said one hour." The pastor and his wife thanked Zeitoun and he returned to the Claiborne house. He picked up Nasser, and they set out to see what they could do. It was just after one o'clock.

A thousand miles away, Yuko's husband Ahmaad was driving the Odyssey. Kathy was resting and the kids were in the back as they barreled through New Mexico. Ahmaad had been at the wheel for seven hours without a break. At this pace, they would make it to Phoenix by Saturday afternoon.

Ahmaad discouraged Kathy from listening to any news on the radio, but even on the rock and country stations snippets of information were leaking through: President Bush was visiting New Orleans that day, and had just lamented the loss of Trent Lott's summer home in coastal Mississippi. Heavily armed National Guardsmen had just entered the Convention Center, and though they had been led to believe their entry would be met with something like guerilla warfare, they had found no resistance whatsoever — only exhausted and hungry people who wanted to leave the city. Kathy took comfort in this, thinking that perhaps the city was coming under control. The military presence, one commentator was saying, "would soon be overwhelming."

20 **snippet** small piece

Making their rounds, Zeitoun and Nasser found an abandoned military jeep and in it, a box of meals, ready-to-eat — MREs. Shortly after, they encountered a family of five on an overpass, and gave them some water and the box of MREs. It was a tidy coincidence. Zeitoun didn't like to carry anything of value at all, and welcomed any opportunity to unload anything he'd found.

It was about five o'clock, the sky darkening, when Zeitoun and Nasser made their way back to the Claiborne house.

Zeitoun was sure that the pastor and his wife would have been rescued by that point, but just to be certain, he and Nasser made a detour and paddled over to Robert Street.

Alvin and Beulah were still there, on the porch, their bags still ready, a light rain still falling on them. They had been waiting for four hours.

Zeitoun was furious. He felt helpless, betrayed. He'd made a promise to the pastor and his wife, and because he had been lied to, his promise had not been kept.

He apologized to the couple, explaining that he had first tried the hospital, where he was sent away at gunpoint, and then gone to St. Charles to tell the soldiers and the relief workers about their plight. The pastor expressed confidence that help was still on its way, but Zeitoun didn't want to take any chances.

"I'll figure something out," he said.

When he and Nasser returned to the Claiborne house, they saw a small motorboat tied to the front porch. Inside the house, they found Todd Gambino sitting inside with a new dog. With the boat — which Todd had seen floating under a

2 **to abandon** to give up, to desert – 5 **coincidence** [koʊˈɪntsɪdənts] two things unexpectedly happening at the same time *(Zufall)* – 12 **to make a detour** [ˈdiːtʊr] to go somewhere that is not on the direct route (but not somewhere completely different either) – 16 **to betray** to deceive *(verraten)* – 22 **plight** desperate situation

ruined garage and figured he would put to use — he'd been making his own rounds around the city, plucking people from porches and rooftops and bringing them to the overpasses and other points of rescue. He'd even found this dog, which was now happily eating food at Todd's feet, on a roof and had taken him in.

Again Zeitoun felt the presence of some divine hand. The Williamses needed help immediately, help he had not been able to provide, and here was Todd, with precisely the vehicle they needed, at precisely the right moment.

Todd did not hesitate. Zeitoun agreed to care for the dog while he was gone, and Todd was off. He picked up Alvin and Beulah, cradling them one by one into the motorboat. Then he sped off toward the staging ground at Napoleon and St. Charles.

The mission took all of twenty minutes. Soon Todd was back, drinking a beer and relaxing again on the porch, his hand stroking the rescued dog's matted fur.

"Some things you just have to do yourself," he said with a smile.

Zeitoun had known Todd to be a good tenant, but he didn't know this side of him. They talked for a time on the porch, and Todd told him stories of his own rescues — how he'd picked up dozens of people already, how he'd been shuttling them to hospitals and staging grounds, how easy it was with a motorboat. Todd had always been, to Zeitoun's mind, a bit of a wanderer, something of a playboy. He liked to have a good time, didn't want to be too tied down with rules and responsibilities. He smoked, he drank, he kept irregular hours. But here he was, his eyes alight, talking about carrying people to safety, how his arrival at any given house or overpass was met with cheers and thanks. A time like this could change a man, Zeitoun knew, and he was happy to see it happening here and now to Todd: a good man made better.

7 **divine** from God

That night Nasser came back with Zeitoun to the house on Dart. They removed the last of the lamb from the freezer and barbecued on the roof, recounting what they had seen and what they had heard. But Nasser was exhausted, and faded quickly. He crawled into the tent and was soon fast asleep.

Again Zeitoun was restless. He was still angry about the pastor and his wife. Nothing upset him more than someone breaking a promise. Who had that man been, at Napoleon and St. Charles, who had said he would send help to the Williams couple? Why had he said he would come if he did not plan to come? Zeitoun tried to be generous. Perhaps he had been pulled away to another emergency. Perhaps the man had gotten lost along the way. But it was no use. There was no excuse that could suffice. The man had abrogated a simple agreement. He had promised help and he had not kept that promise.

Unable to sleep, Zeitoun went back inside and sat on the floor of Nademah's room. Her smell, the smell of his girls, was faint now, replaced by rain and the beginnings of mildew. He missed them already. He could not think of more than a few times when he had been apart from them this long. It was always like this: the first day alone afforded a welcome sense of calm and quiet, but slowly the missing would begin. He would miss their voices, their bright dark eyes, the rumble of their feet up and down the stairs, their squeals and constant singing.

He opened one of the photo albums he'd saved and lay down on Nademah's bed, smelling her strawberry shampoo on the pillowcase. He found a picture from his first year at sea,

19 **mildew** ['mɪldjuː] mold *(Schimmel)*

aboard a ship captained by Ahmad. He marveled at his hair, so much of it then, and such vanity. He was about thirty pounds lighter then, a constant grin on his face, a man tasting the full feast of youth. His brother Ahmad had saved him, had opened to him worlds upon worlds.

Ahmad left home a year after their father's death, traveling to Turkey to study medicine. This was the presumption in the house, at least. Though Mahmoud had forbidden his sons from pursuing a life on the sea, Ahmad wanted nothing else. So he took a bus to Istanbul, telling his mother that his intention was to become a doctor. And for a while he did study medicine. But soon Ahmad left college and enrolled in a naval officer's training academy. When his mother learned Ahmad was to become a ship captain, she was surprised, but did not stand in his way. Two years later, Ahmad had graduated and was crisscrossing the Mediterranean and the Black Sea.

Zeitoun found one of Ahmad's photos. He had more pictures of Ahmad than he did of himself—it was almost comical how many photos his brother took and kept and distributed to family members. He documented every port, every ship. In this one, he and his crew were grilling something, some kind of animal. Zeitoun stared at it. It looked like a greyhound. *Could it be?* No. Zeitoun hoped it was not a dog. The banner above the men said EASTER 1978. In another picture, Ahmad was standing in the middle of downtown New Orleans. When he saw this photo, and so many others of Ahmad standing in front of this city or that monument, Zeitoun always thought of the people Ahmad had asked to take the pictures. Ahmad must have met a thousand people during these trips, chiefly in the pursuit of someone to help him document that *Ahmad Zeitoun, of Jableh, Syria, was here.* Here in Tokyo. Here in America. Here in India.

1 **to marvel at** to admire – 2 **vanity** *Eitelkeit* – 29 **in the pursuit** trying to find

1978 New Orleans USA

1978 Greek Pascua , Altamar , M/V Glyfada Spirit

1 9 7 6 Tsukumi - Japan

1 9 7 8 Dubai

While Ahmad was seeing every corner of the world in rapid succession, Zeitoun was back home in Jableh, and he wanted out. It was a hollow home, and Zeitoun couldn't stand it. During the days he worked at his brother Lutfi's construction-materials store, hearing the stories of Ahmad's continuing adventures, his trips to China, Australia, South Africa, Holland. Zeitoun knew his father would not have approved when he was alive, but he was gone now, and Mohammed was gone, too. Zeitoun did not want to be stuck in Jableh.

His mother knew his feelings. She had heard him pace back and forth on the second floor, had seen his eyes' longing look when he talked to Ahmad on the phone. So on her own accord, she called Ahmad one day and asked him to take his younger brother with him. It was time, she said, for Abdulrahman to leave Jableh and get away, if only for a spell, from their home so full of melancholy.

Ahmad called his younger brother and told him he'd be shipping out in a few weeks' time. Zeitoun was speechless. He kissed the phone. He kissed his mother and sisters. And when the time came, he gathered a sackful of things and met Ahmad in Greece.

On his first voyage, he was a deckhand, the youngest man onboard. The other crew members hailed from everywhere — South Africa, Turkey, Nigeria — and welcomed him warmly. Zeitoun was convinced Ahmad was treating him a bit more roughly than the others, to compensate for any suspicions of nepotism, but he didn't mind. He washed and painted and hauled. He did the jobs no one wanted to do.

They sailed from Piraeus to Naxos and back, and Zeitoun was in love with it all. He let his hair grow, he spent his free

3 **hollow** empty – 15 **spell** short time – 27 **nepotism** [ˈnepəṭɪsm] treating your relatives better than others *(Vetternwirtschaft)*

time on deck, looking out, watching the water come at the ship and disappear behind it. Though the schedule was grueling, four hours on and four off, all day and night, he didn't mind. He didn't need to sleep, not yet.

He had not known until then how badly he had needed this kind of freedom. He felt twice as strong, three times as tall. And finally Zeitoun knew Ahmad's secret, why he had become a sailor, why he had risked so much to become a captain. As they passed on deck or on their way to their different quarters, Zeitoun and Ahmad shared knowing glances, sheepish smiles. Only now did Zeitoun know liberation, and it was everything. Ahmad could see that his younger brother would not be returning to Jableh any time soon.

Their lives were at sea, together and apart, as they passed from their twenties to their early thirties. There were cargo ships, passenger ships, combinations of both. They brought Nebraskan wheat to Tokyo, Brazilian bananas to London, American scrap metal to India. They brought Romanian cement to Nigeria, and always in Nigeria there were stowaways; every time they left Lagos they could count on finding two or three men hiding, and always they made the same arrangement: earn your keep onboard, and when we reach the next port you're on your own.

Jobs on general cargo ships were prized most; they usually spent a week or two at port, giving the crew plenty of time to investigate the area. Zeitoun explored dozens of cities, always docking with a pocketful of money and no obligations to anyone. He would rent a car, devour the surrounding towns, explore the coast, visit famed mosques, meet women who would beg him to stay.

3 **grueling** cruel – 19 **stowaway** person who hides on a ship to get free passage – 26 **to investigate** to explore – 29 **famed** famous

But he was a serious young man, perhaps too serious at times. It was no secret that seamen liked to play cards and enjoy a drink or two. Zeitoun didn't gamble and had never had a drop of alcohol, so when his own shifts were over, he went back to work, helping whoever needed it. And when there wasn't work to do, while his crewmates got stoned and took each other's money playing cards, he found a different diversion: he would go to the small pool onboard the ship and tie a rope around his waist. He would tie the other end to the wall, and then he would swim — three hours at a stretch, strengthening his arms and back, testing himself. He was always testing himself, seeing how much his body could do.

In the end, Zeitoun spent ten years as a sailor. Aboard a ship called the *Star Castor* he saw the Persian Gulf, Japan, Australia, and Baltimore. Aboard the *Capitan Elias,* he saw Holland and Norway. He saw herds of humpbacks, breaching grey whales, schools of dolphins leading the ships to port. He saw the aurora borealis, meteor showers over tumbling black waves, night skies so clear the stars seemed within reach, hung from a ceiling by fishing wire. He served on the *Nitsa,* the *Andromeda,* he sailed all the way until 1988, when he landed in Houston and decided to explore inland. That brought him to Baton Rouge, and Baton Rouge brought him to Kathy, and Kathy brought him Zachary and Nademah and Safiya and Aisha.

Zeitoun prayed on the floor in his house, and then lay down on Nademah's bed, wondering where his wife and children were this night, if they had made it to Phoenix yet, thanking God that they were safe, that he was safe, that they would see each other soon.

16 **humpback** type of whale – 18 **aurora borealis** northern lights

SATURDAY SEPTEMBER 3

In the morning Zeitoun rose with the sun, prayed, and then checked the freezer. There wasn't much left, and what was left was thawing. It would be rotten by the following day. He figured it had to be eaten immediately, so he removed some hamburger for the dogs and figured he'd barbecue the rest that night. He'd invite Todd and Nasser and anyone else he could find. They'd cook all the meat that remained, and have some grim semblance of a party on his roof.

He paddled across the street to feed the dogs.

"How are you boys today?" he asked the first two.

They whimpered, and ate, and licked his legs. He was amused by how grateful, how surprised, they were every day.

"Have a little faith," he said.

He climbed across the rickety board to the second pair of dogs. They whined as he climbed through the window.

"What're you so worried about?" he asked them. "Every day I come, same time. Don't worry."

Yuko's husband Ahmaad had driven through the night, stopping only once, and they finally arrived in Arizona midday on Saturday. They were both too dazed, too wired to sleep, and that first day at Yuko and Ahmaad's house was full of welcome distraction. Yuko and Ahmaad's five children loved the Zeitoun kids, and they loved their Aunt Kathy, particularly the boys. She was one of them, effortlessly so, and they treated her like a peer. They played video games and watched TV, and Kathy tried not to think about what had become of their home, where Zeitoun might be at that moment.

9 **grim semblance** dark copy – 21 **dazed** confused – 21 **wired** excited

Zeitoun still feared getting near his office on Dublin — the armed men were likely still nearby — so he and Nasser had no set itinerary this day. They decided to do a thorough check of Uptown, to see if any neighbors were left, if any help was needed.

Paddling south on Octavia Street, Zeitoun noted that with the strength of two, and without rain or wind, they were fast. They sped past homes, over cars, around debris.

Zeitoun had worked on a dozen or so homes on this street, and knew he would return when the waters fell away. With every passing day, the standing water went deeper into the homes, made it less likely anything within would be salvageable.

Nasser saw the helicopter first.

The helicopters were everywhere, but didn't usually hover so low for so long, and rarely in such a densely built neighborhood. Zeitoun could see this one through the trees and over the roofs long before he could see the water below it. Zeitoun and Nasser paddled toward it to find out what was going on. As they got closer, they saw a dark smudge in the water, a log or piece of debris. They continued paddling, now feeling the wind from the rotors, the ripples radiating outward.

The object in the water looked like a tire, shiny and bulbous —

It was a body. They were sure now. It had turned, and now the head was visible. It was a man of average size, wearing a T-shirt and jeans, half-submerged, face-down.

Zeitoun looked up to the helicopter. Was it a rescue in progress? He looked closer. No. A man was pointing a camera at the body. He did so for a few more minutes and then the helicopter rose, tilted, and drifted off.

3 **itinerary** [aɪˈtinərəri] plan where to go – 8 **to speed, sped, sped** to go fast – 22 **ripple** small wave – 25 **bulbous** big, blown up

Zeitoun and Nasser maintained their distance. Zeitoun knew too many people in this neighborhood. If this was a neighbor or friend, he didn't want to see him this way.

Rattled, they paddled silently to the Claiborne house. Zeitoun had never imagined that the day would come that he might see such a thing, a body floating in filthy water, less than a mile from his home. He could not find a place for the sight in the categories of his mind. The image was from another time, a radically different world. It brought to mind photographs of war, bodies decaying on forgotten battlefields. *Who was that man?* Zeitoun thought. *Could we have saved him?* Zeitoun could only think that perhaps the body had traveled far, that the man had been swept from closer to the lake all the way to Uptown. Nothing else seemed to make sense. He did not want to contemplate the possibility that the man had needed help and had not gotten it.

When Zeitoun tied the canoe to the Claiborne porch, the phone was ringing. He picked it up and found his brother Ahmad.

"I wish you would leave," Ahmad said.

"I'm fine. Safer every day," Zeitoun said. He had no plans to tell Ahmad about the body.

"My kids are worried about you." Ahmad's son Lutfi and daughter Laila had been watching CNN since the storm. They saw the images of devastation and desperation, and could not believe that their uncle was living amid all that.

"Tell them not to worry," Zeitoun said. "And hello from me."

4 **rattled** unnerved, shaken – 10 **to decay** to rot

Zeitoun was grateful for his brother's constant concern. The Zeitoun siblings were all close-knit, but no one worried more, and spent more time collecting and updating addresses and phone numbers and photos, than Ahmad. Perhaps it was because he felt disconnected from them, living in Spain, but in any case he liked to know where his siblings were, what they were doing. And he focused on Abdulrahman in particular, so much so that one day, a few years before, Ahmad had called in the middle of the day in New Orleans and made a very strange proposal.

"What are you doing today?" he'd asked.

It was a Saturday, and Zeitoun was about to go to the lake with Kathy and the kids.

"Do you know the corner of Bourbon and St. Peter?"

Zeitoun said he did.

"I have an idea," Ahmad began, and then explained that he had found a website where he could tap into a live webcam at that corner. If Zeitoun went there, Ahmad could watch him, in real time, while sitting at his computer in Spain.

"You up for it?" Ahmad asked.

"Sure," Zeitoun said. "Why not?"

Zeitoun packed the kids up in the van, drove the few miles to the French Quarter, and looked for the corner of St. Peter and Bourbon. Once there, he searched for the camera. He didn't find it, but figured he should at least stand there for a while. He and the kids stood on every corner, in fact, just in case. And when he got home, he called Ahmad, who was just about leaping through the phone.

"I saw you!" he said. "I saw you all! Next to the hot-dog stand!" He had watched them for five minutes, grinning the whole time. He had made a screen capture and emailed it.

2 **close-knit** close

When he saw it, Zeitoun laughed, amazed. There he was, with all four kids. Nademah was just below the streetlight, Zachary was holding Safiya, and Zeitoun was holding Aisha. Ahmad, technophile and deeply protective brother, was, in very real ways, watching over Zeitoun at all times.

On the roof that night, Zeitoun and Todd and Nasser barbecued the remaining meat, noting that it was the first time any of them had been at any sort of social event since the storm. The conversation was awkward, and the humor had a dark edge to it. They talked about FEMA, about the Superdome and the Convention Center. They had been hearing isolated reports from the radio and others who had stayed in the city, and they were all relieved they had eschewed shelter there;

10 **FEMA** Federal Emergency Management Agency – 10 **Superdome** large New Orleans football stadium where many people found refuge during Katrina; due to its bad hygienic conditions it was referred to as a "third world refugee camp" (Focus online, Aug. 31, 2005) – 11 **Convention Center** second most important shelter for survivors after the Louisiana Superdome – 13 **to eschew** [es'tʃuː] *(fml)* to avoid

they had known it would turn out poorly. None among them could live caged like that.

They talked about what the city would look like when the water was gone. There would be trees and trash everywhere — the ground would look like that of a dredged lake. The roads would be impassable for cars and bikes, for almost any kind of vehicle.

"A horse could do it," Zeitoun said. "We'll get some horses. Easy."

Everyone laughed.

As the sky blackened, Zeitoun saw an orange light through the trees, less than a mile away. Soon all three men were watching the light grow, the flames twisting higher. Zeitoun was sure it had engulfed two or three buildings at least. Then he looked closer, realizing that the fire was very close to.—

"My office," he said.

There was paint there, hundreds of gallons. Paint thinner, lumber. So many toxic and flammable things.

"We have to go," he said.

Zeitoun and Todd climbed down the side of the house and into Todd's motorboat. They sped toward the fire until they could see the flames blooming white and orange between buildings and over treetops. When they got close, they saw that the fire encompassed an entire block. There were five houses alight, the flames grasping for a sixth. They had no tools to stanch a fire, and no plan at all for what they might do to put out a chemical inferno.

Zeitoun's office was unharmed, but it was no more than twenty feet from the fire. They tested the winds. It was a still night, with heavy humidity. There was no predicting where the fire would go, but it was certain that nothing could stop its course. There was a fire station four blocks away, but it was

1 **poorly** badly – 5 **dredged** dug out, emptied – 14 **to engulf** to swallow up

empty and flooded; there were no firefighters in sight. And with the phones down, with 911 inoperative, there was virtually no way to alert anyone. They could only watch.

Zeitoun and Todd sat in their boat, the heat of the fire pulsing at them. The smell was musky, acrid, and the flames swallowed the homes with remarkable speed. One was an old Victorian Zeitoun had always admired, and a few doors down was a house he had considered buying when it had been on the market a few years earlier. Both homes were devoured in minute. The pieces disappeared into the dark water, leaving nothing.

The wind was picking up, blowing away from Zeitoun's office. If there had been any gust in the other direction, his building would have succumbed, too. He thanked God for this small mercy.

As they watched, they glimpsed a few other watchers, faces orange and silent. Other than the crackle of the fire and the occasional collapsing wall or floor, the night was quiet. There were no sirens, no authorities of any kind. Just a block of homes burning and sinking into the obsidian sea that had swallowed the city.

Coming back to the house on Dart, Zeitoun and Todd were quiet. The stars were out. Todd steered the boat like he was captaining a great yacht. He dropped Zeitoun at his house, and they said good night. Back on the roof, Nasser was already asleep in the tent.

Zeitoun stood there, watching the fire ebb and flow. The flood, and now the fire: it was difficult not to think of passages in the Qur'an that recounted the flood of Noah, the evidence of God's wrath. And yet despite the devastation visited upon

2 **911 inoperative** the emergency number was not working – 3 **to alert** to warn – 5 **musky** *here:* very bad – 5 **acrid** sharp – 13 **gust** strong wind – 14 **to succumb** to give in; (*here:* to collapse) – 16 **to glimpse** to see – 20 **obsidian** *here:* shiny black – 30 **wrath** [ræθ] anger

New Orleans, there was still a kind of order to the night. Zeitoun was safe on his roof, the city was silent and still, the stars were in their place.

He had been on a tanker once, maybe twenty years earlier, navigating through the Philippines. It was late, after midnight, and Zeitoun was keeping the captain company on the bridge.

To stay awake and alert, the captain, a Greek man of middle age, liked to take up provocative subjects. He knew that Zeitoun was a Muslim and a thoughtful man, so he sparked a debate about the existence of God. The captain began by expressing his utter conviction that there was no God, no deity in the sky watching over the human world.

Zeitoun had been on the bridge with the captain for an hour at that point, watching him pilot the ship through the many islands, avoiding high shelves and sandbars, other ships and countless unseen dangers. The Philippines, with over seven thousand islands but only five hundred lighthouses, was known for its frequency of maritime accidents.

"What would happen," Zeitoun asked the captain, "if you and I went below the deck, and just went to our bedrooms and went to sleep?"

The captain gave him a quizzical look and answered that the ship would most certainly hit something — would run aground or into a reef. In any event, disaster.

"So without a captain, the ship cannot navigate."

"Yes," the captain said, "What's your point?"

Zeitoun smiled. "Look above you, at the stars and moon. How do the stars keep their place in the sky, how does the moon rotate around the earth, the earth around the sun? Who's navigating?"

The captain smiled at Zeitoun. He'd been led into a trap.

10 **to spark** to activate – 23 **quizzical** questioning

"Without someone guiding us," Zeitoun finished, "wouldn't the stars and moon fall to earth, wouldn't the oceans overrun the land? Any vessel, any carrier of humans, needs a captain, yes?"

The captain was taken with the beauty of the metaphor, and let his silence imply surrender.

On his roof, Zeitoun crawled into his tent, trying not to wake Nasser. He turned his back to the fire and slept fitfully, thinking of fires and floods and the power of God.

SUNDAY SEPTEMBER 4

In the morning Zeitoun rose early, climbed down to his canoe, and paddled across the street to feed the dogs. He climbed up the tree, crawled through the windows, and fed them all the last of the meat.

"Like barbecue?" he asked.

They did.

"See you tomorrow," he said, making a mental note to get some dog food from Todd.

He picked up Nasser, dropped him at the house on Claiborne, and went on alone. He wasn't sure where he would go today, so he chose a new route, this time going back to Dart, then east on Earhart, heading to Jefferson Davis Parkway.

This day was quieter than the few before it. There were no helicopters, no military boats. He was seeing far fewer people wading through the water, now green-grey and streaked everywhere with oil.

It smelled dirtier every day, a wretched mélange of fish and mud and chemicals.

5 **to be taken** to be convinced or impressed – 6 **to imply** to mean – 27 **wretched mélange** [meɪ'lɑ̃:dʒ] miserable mixture

As he approached the junction of Earhart, Jefferson Davis, and Washington, the land rose up a bit, and he could see dry grass, a wide intersection with a large green and brown patch in the middle. And on the grass there was an astonishing sight, especially given what he and his guests had been talking about the night before. There were three horses, chewing happily. They were free, with no riders or saddles. The scene was at once idyllic and hallucinatory. He paddled closer. One of the horses lifted its head, noticing Zeitoun. It was a beautiful animal, white and perfectly groomed. Seeing Zeitoun as no threat, the horse returned to its meal. The other two, one black and one grey, continued to eat. How they had gotten there was beyond Zeitoun's imagination, but they seemed ethereally content, luxuriating in their freedom.

Zeitoun watched them for a few minutes, then traveled on.

Zeitoun paddled down Jefferson Davis. He carried his canoe across the bridge over I-10 and continued on, reaching the residential stretch of the road. Near the corner of Banks Street, he heard a female voice.

"Hey there."

He looked up to see a woman on the second-floor balcony of a home. He slowed down and paddled toward her.

"Give me a ride?" she asked.

The woman wore a shimmering blue blouse. Zeitoun told her he would be happy to help, and he steered the canoe to her steps. As she descended from the balcony, Zeitoun noticed her short skirt and high heels, her heavily made-up face, her small glittering purse. And finally he realized what might have been obvious to many: she was a prostitute. He didn't know what he thought about paddling around in his canoe with a prostitute aboard, but he didn't have time to turn her away now.

10 **to groom** to clean and brush – 14 **ethereal** [ɪˈθɪriəl] *here:* extraordinary – 14 **to luxuriate** to enjoy (the luxury)

She was about to step into the canoe when Zeitoun stopped her.

"Can you take off the shoes?" he asked.

He was afraid the high heels might puncture the boat's thin aluminum. She complied. She was going to Canal, she said. Could he drop her off there? Zeitoun said he would.

She sat in front of him, her hands on either side of the canoe. Feeling like a gondolier, Zeitoun paddled steadily and said nothing. He wondered if there was, only a few days after the hurricane, already a market for her services. Could she have been working in the home where he picked her up?

"Where you going?" he asked, unable to quell his curiosity.

"To work," she said.

At the corner of Jefferson Davis and Canal, she pointed to the First United Methodist Church.

"Drop me here," she said.

He paddled to the pink brick building, where the water met the church's higher steps, and she lifted herself out.

"Thank you, honey," she said.

He nodded and paddled on.

Zeitoun came to the I-10/Claiborne overpass again, and even from a distance he could see that the people who he had seen awaiting rescue there a few days ago had been taken away. The cars remained, as did piles of garbage and human waste. As he floated closer, something caught his attention: a patch of fur. In a moment he was close enough to see that it was a dog, lying on its side. He remembered that when he was last here, there had been a half-dozen small dogs, most of them puppies, taking shelter in the shade of the cars. As his canoe tapped against the overpass, he could see that there were ten or more animals, the same ones he'd seen before and a few others, in various positions on the road. He anchored his canoe to the overpass and climbed up onto the pavement. He

12 **to quell** to put down, to suppress

gagged at the sight. They were dead. The dogs had been killed, each of them shot in the head. Some had been shot repeatedly — head, torso, legs.

He paddled quickly back to the house on Claiborne, shaken. He called Kathy. He wanted to hear her voice.

"I saw the most terrible thing," he said. He told her about the dogs. He couldn't understand it.

"I'm so sorry," she said.

"I don't know who would do this."

"I don't know either, honey."

"Why kill them all?"

They tried to make sense of it. Even if they were euthanizing the animals, it didn't add up. There were so many boats in the city. It would only take a moment to take them aboard and set them loose anywhere. But perhaps something had changed irrevocably. That this was considered a sane or even humane option signaled that all reason had left this place.

"How're the kids?" he asked.

"Fine," she said. "They miss you."

"Tomorrow you'll put the kids in school?" he asked.

"I'll try," she said.

He tried to understand, but he was frustrated. The kids needed to be in school. But he was in no mood to argue.

They talked about what he planned to do that afternoon. There was both more and less to see each day. There were fewer people left in the city, even downtown, and yet the horses, the prostitute, the dogs — it was growing ever more apocalyptic and surreal. He thought maybe he would relax this day. Think about it all.

"You should," she said. Any time he stayed home she felt more sure of his safety. "Stay at home today."

He decided he would.

1 **to gag** *here:* to retch *(würgen)*

He tried to, at least. He lay there on Nademah's bed, trying to relax. But he couldn't stop thinking about the dogs. Who could shoot a dog? All those animals, needing, trusting. He tried, as always, to give the benefit of the doubt to whoever had done it. But if they could find their way to the dogs with guns and bullets, wouldn't it be just as easy to feed them?

He got out of bed and looked for his Qur'an. There was a passage he'd been thinking about, *al-Haqqah*, "The Reality." He took the book from Nademah's shelf and found the page. It was as he remembered it.

In the name of God,
The Merciful, The Compassionate,
The Reality!
What is The Reality?
What would cause you to recognize
what The Reality is?
Thamud and Ad denied
the Day of Disaster.
Then as for Thamud,
they were caused to perish
by a storm of thunder and lightning.
As for Ad,
they were caused to perish
by a fierce and roaring, raging wind.
He compelled against them
for seven uninterrupted nights and eight days
so you would have seen the people laid prostrate
as if they were the uprooted fallen-down palm trees.
Then see you any ones who endure among them?
Pharaoh and those who came before him
and the cities overthrown,

12 **compassionate** full of pity (mercy) *(gnädig)* – 17 **Thamud** people from ancient Arabia who according to the Qur'an were destroyed by an earthquake – 20 **to perish** to go under, to die – 27 **prostrate** flat on the ground, face down – 30 **Pharaoh** [ˈferoʊ] king in and of Ancient Egypt

were ones of iniquity;
they rebelled against the Messenger
of their Lord,
so He took them with the mounting taking.
When the waters became turbulent,
we carried you in the floating Ark,
that We might make it a Reminder for you,
and attentive ears would hold onto it.

Zeitoun crawled through the window and onto the roof. The sky was muddy, the wind cool. He sat down and watched the city in the distance.

He was struck by the possibility that those who had killed the dogs might not have been law-enforcement officers at all. Perhaps Kathy was right, and armed gangs were free in the city, shooting whatever they chose to.

He pondered his own possibilities for self-defense. What would he do if men came here, to him? He had seen no robberies in his neighborhood thus far. But what if they came here?

As the night darkened, Zeitoun wished he was not alone. He thought of returning to the other house, to talk to Todd and Nasser about what he'd seen.

But instead, he sat on his roof, pushing away thoughts of the dogs on the overpass. Perhaps he was weak in this way. He had always been soft when it came to animals. As a child, he had kept many. He'd caught lizards and crabs. He'd even kept a stray donkey in the back alley for a few days, wanting it to be his, to take care of it. His father scolded him for that, and for the pigeon-grooming operation he'd run with his brother

1 **iniquity** immorality, injustice – 4 **mounting taking** This must mean "flood", but it is not normal English at all. – 13 **law-enforcement officer** policeman or woman – 16 **to ponder** to think about

Ahmad. It was Ahmad's idea, really — another scheme into which he had enticed his little brother.

"Want to see something?" Ahmad had said one day. Ahmad was sixteen, and Abdulrahman would follow him anywhere.

After swearing Abdulrahman to secrecy, Ahmad brought him up to the roof and showed him a cage he had built from scrap wood and chicken wire. Inside was a nest of straw and newsprint, and inside the nest was a bird — something, Abdulrahman thought, between a pigeon and a dove. Ahmad planned to keep dozens like this one on the roof, to feed and care for them, to try to train them to deliver messages. Ahmad asked if Abdulrahman wanted to help. Abdulrahman did indeed, and they agreed to care for the birds together. Abdulrahman, being younger, would clean the cages when necessary, and Ahmad, being older and more experienced in these matters, would find new birds, feed those who lived there, and train them when the time came.

And so they spent hours there, watching the birds come and go, feeding them from their palms, exulting in the familiarity that allowed the birds to land on their arms and shoulders.

Soon there were thirty or more birds living on their roof. Ahmad and Abdulrahman built more homes for them, until they had assembled a complex that looked not unlike the stone and adobe structures in their neighborhood, homes stacked upon each other, rising up from the ocean, interlocking like a crude mosaic, extending inland.

All was good until their father Mahmoud discovered their hobby. He considered the keeping of birds a terrible and unsanitary waste of time. Since Mohammed's death, Mahmoud had been impatient, irritable, and so the kids had tried to find diversions outside their grieving home. This hobby, Mahmoud insisted, was taking them away from their

1 **scheme** (business) plan – 2 **to entice** to attract, tempt – 19 **to exult** to enjoy greatly – 24 **adobe** [ə'doʊbi] clay brick – 25 **to stack** to pile – 26 **crude** primitive, natural – 29 **unsanitary** unhealthy – 31 **to grieve** to mourn *(trauern)*

schoolwork, and if they forsook their education for pigeons, he would be stuck with not only the birds but two illiterate sons.

He demanded that they free the birds and dismantle the cages. The boys were despondent, and argued their case to their mother. She deferred to her husband, and he was unbending. Abdulrahman and Ahmad refused to do it themselves, so one day, as the boys were leaving for school, Mahmoud said he would do it himself while they were gone.

The boys returned that afternoon and ran straight to the roof to see what had been done. They found the birds still there, their homes untouched. Amazed, they ran down to the kitchen, where they found their mother beaming. Apparently when Mahmoud had gone up to the roof, the birds had flocked to him, alighting on his shoulders and arms, and he was so charmed that he couldn't send them away. He allowed the birds to stay.

Mahmoud died a few years later. The cause was heart disease, but the talk in Jableh was that it was simple heartache. He had never gotten over the death of his golden son, the glory of the family and all of Syria, Mohammed.

Zeitoun assumed Nasser was staying at the other house. If he wanted to be here, he could. Todd had a boat. So Zeitoun settled into the tent and went to sleep alone.

MONDAY SEPTEMBER 5

In the morning Zeitoun rose early, said his prayers, and paddled across the street to feed the dogs. He'd gotten a bag of dog food from Todd.

"No more steak, guys," he said. "I'm out."

1 **to forsake, forsook, forsaken** to give up – 4 **to dismantle** to take apart, to tear down – 15 **to alight** to land

They didn't seem to mind. They devoured what he poured. They seemed to be doing well now, and were no longer in the same state of shock as a few days before.

"See? I come every day," he said. "I always come."

He climbed down from the roof and paddled away.

He went by the Claiborne house and found Todd and Nasser on the porch, eating breakfast. He went inside and called Kathy.

"The cops are killing themselves," she said.

Two different officers, overcome by the storm and its aftermath, had taken their own lives. Sergeant Paul Accardo, a prominent spokesman for the department, was found in nearby Luling, in his squad car; he'd shot himself. Officer Lawrence Celestine had committed suicide on Friday, in front of another police officer.

This hit Zeitoun hard. He'd always had good relations with the police in the city. He knew the face of Sergeant Accardo well; the man was frequently on television, and projected an air of reason and calm.

Kathy mentioned the roving gangs, the toxic chemicals, the diseases that were being unearthed and spread. She was trying, again, to convince her husband to leave.

"I'll call you later," he said.

Rob, Walt's husband, called Kathy to check on the Zeitouns, to see where they were staying and if they needed any help. When Kathy told him that Zeitoun was still in New Orleans, Rob was incredulous.

"What's he doing there?" he asked.

"Oh, he's got his little canoe," Kathy said. "He's paddling around the city." She tried to sound nonchalant.

"He's got to get out," Rob said.

"I know," Kathy said. "That's what I tell him every day."

13 **squad car** police car – 20 **to rove** to move about in a threatening and dangerous way

As they talked, Rob mentioned that he and Walt had left their cat when they fled the storm. They had tried to find her before they left, but she was an outdoor cat, given to roaming, and hadn't been in or near the house. Now he was hoping that if Zeitoun found himself in their neighborhood, he could look for any sign of her. If Zeitoun happened to make it over there, there was a generator in the garage that he was welcome to if he needed it.

She called the house on Claiborne. Zeitoun was still there, about to leave. Kathy told him about Rob's hope that he could check on the house. It was a good three miles away, and would require a portage over the highway, but Zeitoun was happy to have a clear-cut task. Kathy mentioned the possibility of the generator, but Zeitoun dismissed it. He preferred not to travel with any possessions at all. Besides being doubtful he'd be able to get the generator into the canoe, he was wary of picking up anything of value. He knew the police were looking for looters.

He and Nasser made their way to Walt and Rob's house. The day was warm and white. They decided to check on Nasser's house along the way, so they went up Fontainebleau to Napoleon. Nasser's house was at the corner of Napoleon and Galvez, and he wanted to see if anything could be salvaged.

When they got there, the water had reached the eaves of the roof. There was no way to get into the house, and nothing inside would be worth it. Nasser had prepared himself for this sight, and it was exactly as he'd expected.

"Let's go," he said.

They took Jefferson Davis Parkway to Walt and Rob's. The water at the house was far lower, only about eighteen inches.

3 **to roam** to wander about – 12 **to require a portage** to have to be carried – 16 **wary** watchful – 24 **eaves** overhanging part of a roof *(Dachvorprung)*

Zeitoun got out of the canoe and walked up to the front door. The house would be fine. But he saw no sign of the cat. He considered jumping the fence to get to the backyard, but it was this kind of suspicious activity that police and neighbors would be looking for.

They turned the canoe around and left. On the way home, they passed the post office at Jefferson Davis and Lafitte, the staging ground for helicopter rescues. They saw no helicopters, but there were rescue workers milling in the parking lot.

"You want to go?" Zeitoun asked Nasser.

"Not today," he said.

That night Zeitoun and Nasser prayed together on the roof of the house on Dart and barbecued hamburger meat on the grill. The night was humid and quiet. There was the occasional sound of breaking glass, the growl of a low-flying helicopter. But overall the city seemed to have reached a new equilibrium. Zeitoun fell asleep missing Kathy and the children, wondering if it was time to leave.

TUESDAY SEPTEMBER 6

In the morning, after his prayers, Zeitoun made his way to the dogs across the street and fed them more of the dog food Todd had acquired for his rescued pet. When he paddled back to the house to pick up Nasser, he noticed Nasser was carrying his black duffel bag.

Zeitoun nodded at it. "You're ready to go?"

Nasser said he was. He was ready to be evacuated. Zeitoun would be sad to see him go, but he was happy to know that his friend would be safe, and that, even better, Zeitoun would no longer have to share his tent. Nasser got in the canoe and they were off.

9 **to mill** to move around in confusion – 16 **equilibrium** balance

They made their way to the post-office parking lot. They had passed it together a half-dozen times, and always Zeitoun had asked Nasser if he was prepared to leave, but he had not been ready, not until now.

"There's your ride," Zeitoun said, pointing to an orange helicopter in the distance, resting on the ground.

They paddled closer and realized there was something strange about the helicopter. It was resting on its side.

"Oh no," Nasser said.

Its rotor was broken, the grass blackened all around it.

"It crashed," Zeitoun said, awed.

"It crashed," Nasser repeated, in a whisper.

They coasted toward it. There was no one near it, no sign that anyone had been hurt. There was no smoke, no rescue crew. The crash must have been the day before. All there was now was a mound of orange steel. Nasser would not fly out this day.

They returned to the Claiborne house, dazed. Zeitoun called Kathy. He couldn't decide if he should tell her about the helicopter. He knew it would upset her, so he chose not to.

"You put the kids in school yet?"

Kathy said she was trying, but it wasn't easy.

Zeitoun exhaled loudly.

"You're like the man who lost his camel and is looking for the rope," she said. It was one of his favorite expressions, and she relished using it against him. He would often say it when he felt Kathy was focusing on irrelevant details while ignoring the crux of a problem.

He wasn't amused.

"C'mon honey," she said.

School wasn't the first thing on Kathy's mind. She had been determined, the night before and all morning, to convince her

26 **to relish** to enjoy

husband to leave the city. Mayor Nagin had ordered a forced evacuation of everyone remaining.

"A forced evacuation," she repeated.

Officials were concerned about the spread of E. coli, the risk of typhoid fever, cholera, dysentery. Unsanitary conditions would threaten the health of anyone still in the area.

"I'm not drinking the water," he said.

"What about the toxic waste?" she asked. "You know the crap buried underground there." She reminded him that parts of the city had been built on landfills containing arsenic, lead, mercury, barium, and other carcinogens. "What if that stuff leaches through?"

Zeitoun didn't know what to say.

"I'll be careful," he said.

What he didn't say was that he was considering leaving. Everything was becoming more difficult, and there was less for him to do. Fewer people were left in the city, and fewer still needed help. There was only the matter of his properties, looking after them, and of course the dogs. Who would feed the dogs, if not him? For now, he told her it would be fine, that he would be careful. That he loved her and would call her in a few hours.

He set out alone for a while and before long, at the corner of Canal and Scott, he encountered a small boat. It was a military craft, with three men aboard: a soldier, a man with a video camera, and one holding a microphone and a notebook. They waved Zeitoun down and one of the men identified himself as a reporter.

"What are you doing?" the reporter asked.

"Just checking on friends' houses. Trying to help," Zeitoun said.

4 **E. coli** bacteria that causes problems in the colon *(Darm)* – 5 **dysentery** ['dɪsəntəri] disorder of the colon *(chronischer Durchfall)* – 11 **carcinogen** [kɑːr'sinədʒən] substances causing cancer – 12 **to leach** to dissolve

"Who are you working with?" the reporter asked.

"Anybody," Zeitoun said. "I work with anybody."

As he paddled back to Claiborne, a hope flickered within Zeitoun that his siblings might see him on TV. Perhaps they would see what he was doing, that he had done something good by staying in his adopted city. The Zeitouns were proud, and there was plenty of sibling rivalry that had pushed them all to an array of achievements — all of them measured against the deeds of Mohammed. None of them had ever done something like that, none had achieved on his level. But Zeitoun felt again that perhaps this was his calling, that God had waited to put him here and now to test him in this way. And so he hoped, as silly as it seemed, that his siblings might see him like this, on the water, a sailor again, being useful, serving God.

When Zeitoun got back to 5010 Claiborne, he saw a blue-and-white motorboat tied to the porch.

When he entered the house, there was a man inside, a man he had never seen before.

"Who are you?" Zeitoun asked.

"Who are *you?*" the man asked.

"This is my house," Zeitoun said.

The man apologized. He introduced himself. His name was Ronnie, and he'd passed by the house one day, looking for a place that might have a working phone. He'd seen the phone box above the waterline and walked into the house. Since then, he'd been coming in periodically to make calls to his brother, a helicopter pilot. Ronnie was white, about thirty-five, six feet, two hundred pounds. He told Zeitoun that he worked for a tree company.

Zeitoun couldn't think of a good reason to ask Ronnie to leave. Zeitoun was happy to see anyone alive and well in the city, so he left Ronnie in the house and went upstairs to see if the water worked. He found Nasser on the second floor.

"You meet this man Ronnie?" Zeitoun asked.

Nasser had, and had found him to be agreeable enough. They both felt there was a certain strength in numbers, and again, if the man wanted to use the phone occasionally, who were they to prevent him from communicating with the outside world?

Impossibly, the water in the bathroom was still functioning. Zeitoun hadn't even thought to check it sooner. It was a miracle. He told Nasser he was going to take a shower.

"Be quick," Nasser said. "I'm next."

No shower had ever felt better. Zeitoun washed away all the sweat and grime, and what he assumed was a fair amount of oil and raw sewage. Afterward, he came downstairs.

"All yours," he told Nasser.

He picked up the phone and called his brother in Spain. He wanted to check in with him quickly before calling Kathy.

Again Ahmad tried to convince him to leave.

"Do you realize the images we're seeing on TV?" he asked.

Zeitoun assured him that he was far away from that kind of chaos. Not counting the armed man at the Shell station, Zeitoun had seen almost no danger in all the time he had been canoeing around the city.

"Hey," he said, excited, "I might be on TV. Someone just interviewed me. Look for it. Tell Kathy."

Ahmad sighed. "So you won't go."

"Not yet."

Ahmad knew better than to argue. But he did want to remind his brother that even if he felt safe now, danger could come at any time. There were roving gangs of armed men, he said. That's all the media could talk about — that it was the Wild West out there. Ahmad felt powerless, and he hated the

13 **raw sewage** human waste and dirt that has not been treated *(Abwasser)*

feeling. He knew his little brother considered him overly cautious. "Won't you please consider leaving, for the sake of your beautiful family, before something happens?"

Zeitoun was holding the piece of paper with Kathy's Phoenix number on it. He needed to call her before she started worrying. He was already ten minutes late. He was about to get off the phone with Ahmad when he heard Nasser's voice from the porch. He was talking to someone outside.

"Zeitoun!" Nasser called.

"What?" Zeitoun said.

"Come here," Nasser said. "These guys want to know if we need water."

Zeitoun assumed it was more men like himself and Nasser — people with boats who were roaming around, trying to help.

When he put the phone down and looked toward the front porch, he saw a group of men, all of them armed, bursting into the house. Zeitoun hung up the phone and walked toward the door.

2 **for the sake of** because of; because you love

PART III

WEDNESDAY SEPTEMBER 7

Kathy woke up tense. She fed and dressed the kids, trying not to think about the fact that her husband hadn't called the afternoon before. He had promised to call. Yuko told her not to worry. It was silly to worry. It had barely been a day, and even the regular contact Zeitoun had maintained so far was remarkable. Kathy agreed, but she knew she would be anxious until he called again.

After Yuko took her own kids to school, she helped keep Kathy's children occupied while Kathy paced, phone in her hand.

At nine, Ahmad called from Spain.

"You hear from Abdulrahman today?" he asked.

"No. You?"

"Not since yesterday."

"So you talked to him?" she asked.

"I did."

"He called you and not me."

"He was about to call you. But he got off the phone quickly. There was someone at the door."

"Who was it?" Kathy asked. Her stomach dropped.

"I have no idea."

She called the Claiborne house and let it ring a dozen times before hanging up.

Now she was a wreck. *He must call today,* she thought. *I'll kill him if he doesn't call at noon.*

At ten o'clock Phoenix time it was noon in New Orleans. Kathy waited. The phone did not ring at ten, ten-thirty, eleven — one o'clock New Orleans time. By noon in Phoenix she was frantic.

She called the Claiborne house again. No answer.

Yuko tried to put it in context. It was miraculous that the phone line at the Claiborne house was working at all. Chances

33 **chances were that** possibly

were that it finally gave way and died. He'll find a way to call, she said. He's in an underwater city, she said. Cut the man some slack.

Kathy was calmer now, but still she paced the living room.

Yuko took the kids to the mall. She didn't want to leave Kathy alone, but the pacing was worrying the kids. Yuko was sure Zeitoun would call while they were gone, so why not let the kids enjoy themselves? The mall had a food court, an arcade for Zach. They planned to be back at three.

Kathy called the Claiborne house again. No answer.

Walt called. "You hear anything from Zeitoun?"

Kathy told him she hadn't.

She called Adnan, Zeitoun's cousin.

"I'm still ashamed," she said. Last they had spoken, Kathy had had to tell him that her sister would not allow Adnan and Abeer to stay with them. It had been painful.

"Don't worry. We're fine," he said.

He was still in Baton Rouge with Abeer and his parents. After spending two nights in their car, they had returned to the mosque, and had been sleeping on the floor there for the past week.

"How is Abdulrahman?" he asked.

"I haven't heard from him. Have you?"

Adnan had not.

Alone and seeking distraction, Kathy turned on the TV, avoiding the news, finding Oprah Winfrey. Or she thought it was Oprah's show. But soon she realized it was a news report replaying portions of the previous day's show, with New Orleans police chief Eddie Compass and Mayor Nagin as Oprah's guests.

Compass was lamenting the extent of the crime in the Superdome. "We had babies in there. Little babies getting

2 **Cut the man some slack** "Give him a chance!" – 9 **arcade** game hall – 26 **Oprah Winfrey** famous African-American talk show host

raped," he said, weeping. From Mayor Nagin: "About three days we were basically rationing, fighting, people were — that's why the people, in my opinion, they got to this almost animalistic state, because they didn't have the resources. They were trapped. You get ready to see something that I'm not sure you're ready to see. We have people standing out there that have been in that frickin' Superdome for five days watching dead bodies, watching hooligans killing people, raping people. That's the tragedy. People are trying to give us babies that were dying."

Kathy turned the TV off again, this time for good. She called the house on Claiborne. The phone rang and rang. She paced. She walked outside, into the assaulting Phoenix heat, then went back inside. She called again. The rings began to sound hollow, desolate.

Four o'clock arrived and he hadn't called.

She called Ahmad in Spain. He hadn't heard from Zeitoun either. He had been calling the Claiborne house all day, to no avail.

In the late afternoon, the kids returned. "Did Dad call?" Nademah asked. "Not yet," Kathy said, "still waiting."

She held herself together for a few seconds but then imploded. She excused herself and ran to the guest room. She did not want her girls to see her this way.

Yuko came in and sat on the bed with Kathy. It's been just one day, she said. Just one day in the life of a man in a city with no services. He would call tomorrow. Kathy pulled herself together, and together they prayed. Yuko was right. It was one day. Of course he would call tomorrow.

7 **frickin'** *(inf)* damned – 11 **for good** forever – 23 **to implode** to collapse violently

THURSDAY SEPTEMBER 8

Kathy woke up with a better outlook. Maybe her husband didn't even realize he'd forgotten to call. He was likely saving any number of new people and animals and homes, and in the midst of it all he'd gotten overwhelmed. In any case, Kathy was determined to put on a brave face for the kids. She cooked their breakfast and pretended she was sane and content. She played GameCube with Zachary and killed the morning with diversions.

Periodically she pushed the redial button on Yuko's phone. The phone at Claiborne rang in an infinite loop.

Noon came and went.

Kathy was losing her grip again.

"I need to go to New Orleans," she told Yuko.

"No you don't," Yuko said. She peppered Kathy with logistical questions. How would she get into the city? Did she plan to buy a boat and dodge the authorities and find her husband on her own? Yuko dismissed the notion.

"We don't want to have to worry about you, too."

Ahmad called Kathy. His tone had been neutral the day before, but now he sounded worried. This unnerved Kathy. If Ahmad, made of the same stuff her husband was — and both of them made of the stuff of their father Mahmoud, who could survive two days at sea tethered to a barrel — felt this to be a dire situation, then if anything, Kathy was underreacting.

Ahmad said he would try to contact the TV station that had interviewed Zeitoun. He would contact all the agencies that tracked missing persons in New Orleans. He would contact the Coast Guard. They agreed to call each other as soon they heard something.

17 **to dodge** *(inf)* to avoid – 18 **notion** idea – 24 **to tether** to fasten with a rope or chain

Date: Thu, 8 Sep 2005 19:08:04 +0200
To: SATERNKatrinaReliefUpdates@csc.com
Subject: Ref. AMER-6G2TNL
Dear Sires,
Many thanks for your answering.
Kindly please do your best to give us any good news about him.
He's my brother, he leave many years ago in New Orleans:
4649 Dart St. New Orleans
New Orleans, LA
70125-2716
Actually I'm at Spain, but her wife and children they left a day before Katrina hit to ARIZONA, his wife: Mrs. Kathy Zeitoun actual contact: 408-[number omitted]
More information:
He remained at home without phone, but he've a small boat and he went daily to: Mr. TODD at:
5010 S. Claiborne Ave 70125-4941 New Orleans
Last calling was on Sept 6 at 14:30 local time, after that till now no calls, no news. The phone which he used is ringing but no answering. Here I including his pictures maybe can help.
Many thanks.
Sincerely,
Ahmad Zeton

In the afternoon, Zeitoun's family began calling from Syria. First it was Fahzia. A secondary-school teacher in Jableh, she spoke fluent English.

"Have you heard from Abdulrahman?" Kathy told her she had not for two days. There was a long silence on the line. "You have not heard from Abdulrahman?"

Kathy explained that the phones were down, that it was likely that her husband was just trying to reach a working phone. This did not sit well with Fahzia.

32 **this did not sit well with her** this did not please her

"Again, please — you have not heard from Abdulrahman?" Kathy loved the Zeitouns of Syria, but she did not need this extra burden. She excused herself and hung up.

Kathy did not attempt to sit at dinner. She paced the rooms, the phone an extension of her arm. She thought through the possibilities — who she knew and what they could do to help. She didn't know a soul still in the city, she realized. It was paralyzing. It seemed impossible that in 2005, in the United States, there was an entire city cut off from all communication, all contact.

Later, thinking the kids were asleep, she passed one of the bedrooms and heard Aisha talking to one of Yuko's kids.

"Our house is under ten feet of water," Aisha said.

Kathy held her breath at the door.

"And we can't find my dad."

In the bathroom, Kathy covered her face in a towel and bawled. Her body convulsed, but she tried not to make a sound.

FRIDAY SEPTEMBER 9

Kathy had no choice but to lie. She had never told a bald-faced lie to her children before, but now it seemed necessary. Otherwise they would all lose their composure. She planned to enroll them in school on Monday, and to have the strength to be thrown into such a situation they had to believe that their father was healthy and in contact. So at breakfast, when Aisha asked if she had heard from Dad, Kathy did not hesitate.

"Yup, heard from him last night," she said.

"On what phone?" Nademah asked. They hadn't heard a ring.

17 **to bawl** to cry – 17 **to convulse** to shake – 22 **composure** [kəmˈpoʊʒɚ] calm state of mind, self-possession

"Yuko's phone," Kathy said. "I got it on the first ring."

"So he's at the house?" Nademah asked.

Kathy nodded. And as smart and skeptical as her kids were, they believed her. Especially Nademah and Zachary. Whether or not they sensed the lie, they *wanted* to believe it. Safiya and Aisha were harder to read, but for the time being her kids' fears had been assuaged and now Kathy only had to worry about her own.

Just after breakfast, the phone did ring. Kathy leapt to it.

It was Aisha, another sister of Zeitoun's. She was the director of an elementary school in Jableh, and also spoke English.

"Where is Abdulrahman?" she asked.

"He's in New Orleans," Kathy answered calmly.

Aisha explained that no one had heard from him in days. He had been in touch a few times after the storm, and then nothing. She was calling on behalf of all the siblings, and she was worried.

"He's fine," Kathy said.

"How do you know?" Aisha asked.

Kathy had no answer.

Kathy got online. Immediately she was swamped with horrific news from the city. Officials were reporting the death toll in and around New Orleans at 118. But Mayor Nagin estimated that the final number might climb as high as ten thousand. She checked her email. Her husband had never sent an email in his life, but she couldn't rule it out. She found an email from Zeitoun's brother Ahmad. He had cc'ed her on an email to another aid agency.

7 **to assuage** [ə'sweɪdʒ] to relieve – 16 **on behalf of** *here:* as a representative of – 22 **death toll** the number of people who had died

From: CapZeton
Date: Fri, 9 Sep 2005 22:12:05 +0200
To: [name omitted]@arcno.org
Subject: Looking for my brother /Abdulrahman Zeitoun

Dear sires,
Kindly, would you please if it's possible to know from you about the persons which they forced to leave houses from New Orleans last Tue. Sept 6th, where they are now?
I would like to have any news about my brother, which we lost the contact with him from Tue. Sept. 6th after 14:30 hrs, while he was at (5010 S. Claiborne Ave. 70125-4941 New Orleans) using a small boat. Moving to 4649 Dart St. where he stay.
My brother's details:
Name: Abdulrahman Zeitoun
Age: 47 years
Address: 4649 Dart St. -New Orleans, LA 70125-2716
From that time till now we haven't any news about him, Kindly please do your best to help us.
Thanking you indeed,
Ahmad Zeton
Malaga-Spain

When it was noon in New Orleans Kathy called the Claiborne house. She let the phone ring, willing it to stop, to be interrupted by her husband's voice. She called all day, but the ringing had no end.

Walt and Rob called. Kathy told them she had not heard from Zeitoun, and asked if Walt knew anyone who could help. Walt knew everyone, it seemed, and always had a solution. He said he would call a friend, a U.S. marshal, who he knew was near the city. Maybe he could get inside and get to the house on Claiborne.

As Kathy put the kids to bed that night, she forced herself to present a face of confidence. They asked if their house was underwater, and Kathy admitted that yes, there was some damage, but that lucky them, their father was a contractor, and that any damage could be quickly fixed.

"And guess what?" she told them. "Now you'll all get new bedroom sets!"

SATURDAY SEPTEMBER 10

Walt called. He had spoken to his friend, the U.S. marshal. The marshal had driven toward the house on Dart Street, but he couldn't get close. The water was still too high.

Walt said he would call a friend he knew who had a helicopter. He hadn't thought it through beyond that — where the helicopter would go or how they would scout for Zeitoun — but he said he would make more calls and call Kathy back soon.

Just as she had the day before, when it was noon in New Orleans she called the Claiborne house. Again the ringing had no end.

Zeitoun's family called.

"Kathy, where's Abdulrahman?" they said. It was Lucy, one of his nieces. All of Zeitoun's nieces and nephews were fluent in English, and were translating for the rest of the family. "I don't know," Kathy said. Another cousin got on the phone. "You need to go find him!" she insisted.

Throughout the morning Zeitoun's sisters and brothers called from Lattakia, from Saudi Arabia. Had Kathy heard from him yet? Why wasn't she in New Orleans looking for him? Hadn't she been watching the TV? She told them she hadn't, that she couldn't bear it.

They filled her in. There had been looting, rapes, murders. It was chaos, anarchy. They repeated Mayor Nagin's assertion

32 **assertion** statement, belief

that the city had devolved into an "animalistic state." And in this way she got the media's funhouse picture of the state of the city via her husband's relatives halfway around the world. God knows, she thought, what kind of spin the media was putting on things out there.

Twenty-five thousand body bags have been brought to the area, they noted. How can you live in that country? they asked. You need to move back here. Syria is so much safer, they said.

Kathy couldn't deal with the questions and the pressure. She was overcome, helpless, trembling. She got off the phone as politely as she could.

She went to the bathroom and for the first time in days looked at her face. There were blue rings around her eyes. She removed her hijab and took in a quick breath. Her hair. She had had no more than ten grey hairs before all of this. Now there was a stripe of white hair rising from her forehead, as wide as her hand.

Yuko forbade Kathy to answer the phone when anyone called from Syria. Yuko fielded all the calls, telling them that Kathy was doing everything she could, everything humanly possible.

Yuko and her husband Ahmaad took Kathy and the kids to Veterans Memorial Coliseum, where the Red Cross had set up a shelter and triage unit for New Orleanians. Various missing-persons agencies were collecting information and trying to connect those separated from their families. Kathy brought a photo of Zeitoun and every piece of information she could find.

25 **triage** ['tri:ɑ:ʒ] *(AE)* process for deciding which injured people should be treated first

At the gym, it was a grim scene. There were dozens of people from New Orleans there, looking like they had fled that very day. Injuries were being treated, families sleeping on cots, piles of clothing everywhere. Kathy's girls clung to her.

The Red Cross took down all of Zeitoun's information and scanned the photo Kathy had brought. They were efficient and kind, and told Kathy that thousands of people had been located, that they were scattered all over the country and every story was stranger than the last. They told Kathy not to worry, that each day brought more order to the world.

Kathy left with some renewed hope. Perhaps he had been injured. He could be in a hospital somewhere, heavily sedated. He could have been found somewhere, unconscious and without identification. Now it was just a matter of time before the doctors and nurses looked through the missing-persons database to find him.

But now the kids were confused. Was their father safe or not? The signals were mixed. Kathy had told them he was fine, he was safe, he was in his canoe. But then why report him to the Red Cross? Why the missing-persons files, why the mentions of police and Coast Guard? Kathy tried to shield them from all this but it was impossible. She wasn't strong enough. She felt weak, porous.

When they got home again Kathy called the Claiborne house. The phone rang and rang. Until now she had been telling herself that the phone might have been out of service, but this day she checked with the phone company. If the phone was not working at all, they told her, she would have gotten something like a busy signal, a particular sound to indicate that the lines were down. But the ringing persisted, and the ringing meant that the phone worked, but no one was there to answer it.

12 **sedated** calmed by tranquilizers – 21 **to shield** to protect – 23 **porous** ['pɔ:rəs] *here:* fragile – 30 **to persist** to stay, to remain

Aisha was taking it the hardest. She seemed to swing between worry and fatalistic resignation. She was irritable. She couldn't concentrate. She withdrew and wept alone.

That night, after the other kids had fallen asleep, Kathy sat behind Aisha on her bed. She took her daughter's thick black hair in her hands and kneaded it with one hand, brushing it with the other. It was something she had done with Nademah to calm her before bed, and Yuko's mom had done the same with Kathy after their baths. It was soothing, meditative for both mother and daughter. In this case Kathy was humming a tune she couldn't even remember the name of, and Aisha was sitting, tense but accepting. Kathy was confident that this would ease her worry, would end with Aisha dropping back into Kathy's lap, contented and sleepy.

"You hear from him?" Aisha asked.

"No, baby, not yet."

"Is he dead?"

"No, baby, he's not dead."

"Did he drown?"

"No."

"Did they find his body?"

"Honey, stop."

But after a half-dozen strokes of her brush, Kathy took in a quick breath. Aisha's hair was coming out in clumps. The brush was full of it.

Aisha's eyes welled. Kathy bawled.

There is nothing worse than this, Kathy thought. *There can be nothing worse than this.*

SUNDAY SEPTEMBER 11

It had been six days since Kathy had spoken to Zeitoun. She could no longer explain his absence. It didn't make sense. The city was overrun with help. The National Guard was

3 **to withdraw, withdrew, withdrawn** to go away – 6 **to knead** [ni:d] to fold and press – 26 **to well** to fill with tears

everywhere, and officials were insisting that the city was virtually empty.

She ran the possibilities through her mind again. If he was still there, canoeing around New Orleans, he would have called again from the Claiborne house. If the Claiborne phone no longer worked, by now he would have found another working phone. Or he would have encountered one of the soldiers and asked for help in contacting Kathy. There seemed to be no way that he was in the city and unable to call.

Which meant that he had left the city. He might have been running low on water or food. He might have accepted a ride out of the city from one of the helicopters or rescue boats. But if he had left, and had been brought to a shelter, he would have called immediately.

She knew that bodies had been found floating, unclaimed and uncovered in the water. *He could be dead,* she told herself. *Your husband could be gone.* There had been murders, she knew. She did not truly believe the accounts of untethered mayhem, but she knew that some murders would have occurred. *It could have been a robbery,* she thought. *Someone had come to steal from one of our properties, he had been there, he had fought back—*

He could not have drowned. He could not have fallen victim to any other sort of calamity. She knew her husband too well. She could not picture any accident taking him. He was too smart, too wary, and even if he had had some kind of incident, he was indestructible. He would have survived, he would have gotten help.

15 **to claim** to take as one's own – 24 **calamity** disaster

When it was noon in New Orleans Kathy called the Claiborne house. She let it ring, needing to hear her husband's voice, but still the ringing had no end.

She had to think of life insurance. She had to think about how she would support her four children. Would she be able to run the business on her own? Of course not. But some semblance of it? She would have to sell the rental properties. Or maybe the rental properties would be something she could manage on her own. Too many questions. No, she would sell the painting and contracting business and hold on to the rentals. Or she could sell a few of the buildings, bring it down to a number she could manage on her own. Should she stay in New Orleans, or move the family to Baton Rouge? To Phoenix? It would have to be Phoenix.

And how long would anyone wait before assuming the worst? One week? Two weeks, three?

She got online and found another email from Ahmad. This one was sent to the TV station that had broadcast the brief interview with Zeitoun. From his office in Spain, Ahmad had found out which station it had been, and had found the name of one of the producers.

From: CapZeton
Date: Sun, 11 Sep 2005 02:01:34 +0200
To: [name omitted]@wafb.com
Subject: New Orleans Hurricane-impacted areas
Dear Sires,
As I informed from some friends in Baton Rouge, that you have on Sept. 5th a meeting with my brother:
Name Abdulrahman Zeitoun, 47 years old, at New Orleans effected zone 4649 Dart St. LA 70125-2716 where he stay, our friend saw him on your TV WAFB CH9 on Sept. 6th.

From that time till this moment we lost the contact with him. Kindly would you please can you give me any information about the day and time when you met him? Or if you have any other information?
Thanking you indeed,
Ahmad Zeton
Malaga-Spain

Kathy found a website with current photos of New Orleans from the air. She searched until she found Uptown, and zoomed in until she saw what was left of her home and neighborhood. The water was filthier than she could have imagined. It looked like the entire city was bathing in oil and tar.

She called every number of every person she knew who might still be in New Orleans. Nothing.

Yuko and Ahmaad consoled her.

"He's old school," Ahmaad said. It was normal for a man like Zeitoun, rugged and independent, to be out of contact for a few days. "They don't make guys like that anymore."

Yuko kept Kathy away from the phones and the news. Still, Kathy caught snippets in the car. In the Odyssey, she heard President Bush's weekly radio address. The president compared the storm to 9/11 and the War on Terror. "America is confronting another disaster that has caused destruction and loss of life," he said. "America will overcome this ordeal, and we will be stronger for it."

13 **tar** thick, black, oily mass *(Teer)* – 16 **to console** to calm *(trösten)* – 17 **old school** *(inf)* *here:* like men used to be: tough and fighting for themselves – 18 **rugged** ['rʌgɪd] strong, tough – 25 **ordeal** [ɔ:r'di:l] difficult and painful situation

MONDAY SEPTEMBER 12

It was time for the girls to start school. They had been out for almost two weeks now, and no matter how awkward it might be to start classes in the middle of September, they needed some semblance of routine. Kathy made the calls. The closest public school was Dr. Howard K. Conley Elementary School. "Bring them right away," Kathy was told. Zach, as a high schooler, would have a more difficult entry.

5 **semblance** sth that seemed like

The girls were nervous. They were not happy to be brought to a new school, where they knew no one and where they would be branded as refugees. Why couldn't they just wait until they returned to New Orleans? What would they study? The books and lesson plans would be different. What was the point? The point, Kathy said, was that their father wanted them in school, and that was enough.

Yuko and Ahmaad bought the girls a new set of school supplies, binders and notebooks and pens and pencils, and Pokemon and Hello Kitty backpacks to carry all of it. This gave the girls some measure of comfort, but when Kathy dropped them off, leaving them all in the office of the Conley principal, she was devastated. She couldn't look at Aisha. Everything was in that girl's wet black eyes, every worry Kathy shared — that these were the first days of their new life together, living in Phoenix, living without their father.

Driving away from the school, Kathy caught the news on the radio. The official death toll in New Orleans was now 279. It seemed to be leaping by a hundred a day, and the search for bodies had only just begun.

Did she have to prepare for a funeral? It had been seven days now. How long could she explain away his absence? President Bush had come to New Orleans two or three times at that point. If the president could make his way to Jackson Square for a press conference, her husband, if alive, could find a phone and call out.

TUESDAY SEPTEMBER 13

With the kids at school during the day, Kathy spiraled downward. She had more time to herself and more time to worry, more time to plan a wretched new life.

13 **devastated** destroyed (*here:* extremely sad) – 28 **to spiral downward** to get worse – 30 **wretched** ['retʃɪd] miserable

She called the house on Claiborne every hour. She called Zeitoun's cell phone in case he had found some place to charge it.

The death toll jumped to 423.

She found Todd Gambino's girlfriend's number and called her. She was in Mississippi, and hadn't heard from Todd in a week. This meant something. Perhaps something had happened to both of them? This was good news. It had to be. The two women agreed to stay in touch.

From Spain, Ahmad called Kathy every day. He called the Coast Guard and the Navy. He wrote to the Syrian Embassy in Washington. Nothing from anyone. He looked into flights to New Orleans. What could it hurt to have him searching for his brother on the ground? He worried that his siblings expected him to go, given that he was the only one who might have any chance at all of entering the United States; getting a visa from Syria was hopeless. His wife ruled out the notion, but still, the idea burrowed into him.

WEDNESDAY SEPTEMBER 14

The death toll was at 648 and climbing.

Kathy checked in with the Red Cross every day. She soon had Zeitoun registered at half a dozen agencies dealing with missing persons. His photo was everywhere.

The girls went to school, came home, watched TV. They found momentary distraction with Yuko and Ahmaad's kids, but their eyes were hollow. They too were planning lives without their father. Did they want to move to Phoenix?

11 **embassy** office which represents one nation in another one *(Botschaft)* – 18 **to burrow** to dig

Would there be a funeral? When would they know what had happened?

In the countless hours of darkening thoughts, Kathy imagined again where she would live. Could she live in Arizona? She would have to find a house near Yuko's. Ahmaad would have to be a father figure. Kathy had already leaned so heavily on Yuko and Ahmaad, she couldn't imagine permanently thrusting her entire family onto them.

She thought of Zeitoun's family in Syria. There was such a support network there, a vast and tight fabric of family. She and Zeitoun had brought the kids there in 2003 for two weeks to visit, and it had been unlike anything she'd expected. First there was the snow. Snow in Damascus! They'd taken a bus north to Jableh, and all along she'd been shocked at what she saw. She'd had, she later admitted, an antique idea of Syria. She'd pictured deserts, donkeys, and carts — not so many busy, cosmopolitan cities, not so many Mercedes and BMW dealerships lining the highway heading north, not so many women in tight clothes and uncovered hair. But there were vestiges of a less modern life, too — merchants selling sardines and cabbage by the roadside, crude homes of brick and mud. As they drove north to Jableh, the road soon met the coastline, and they traveled along a beautiful seaside stretch, hills cascading to the sea, mosques perched above the road, side by side with churches, dozens of them. She'd assumed Syria was entirely Muslim, but she was wrong about this, and about so many things. She loved being surprised, coming to realize that in many ways Syria was a quintessentially Mediterranean country, connected to the sea and in love with food and new ideas and reflecting the influence of Greece, Italy, so many cultures. Kathy devoured it all — the fresh vegetables and fish, the yogurts, the lamb! The lamb was the

8 **to thrust** to throw, force – 10 **fabric** knitted or woven cloth – 20 **vestige** [ˈvestɪdʒ] sign – 28 **quintessential** [ˌkwɪntəˈsenʃəl] typical

best she'd had anywhere, and she ate it whenever she had the opportunity. In beautiful seaside Jableh she'd seen the homes that Zeitoun's grandfather had built, saw the monument to his brother Mohammed. They stayed with Kousay, Abdulrahman's wonderfully life-loving and gregarious brother, who still lived in their childhood home. It was a gorgeous old place on the water, with high ceilings and windows always open to the sea breezes. There was family everywhere within walking distance, so many cousins, so much history. While Zeitoun darted around town, reconnecting with old friends, Kathy had spent an afternoon cooking with Zeitoun's sister Fahzia, and she'd done something wrong with the propane and almost burned down the kitchen. It was terrifying at the time but made for much hilarity in the coming days. They were such good people, her husband's family, everyone so well educated, so open and hospitable, each of their houses full of constant laughter. Would it be impossible to think that Kathy could take the kids and live there, in Jableh? It was a radical idea, but one that would put her in a place of such comfort, embraced by family; the girls would be surrounded by so many relatives that perhaps they wouldn't be quite so devastated at the loss of their dad.

Zeitoun's family in Syria became increasingly despondent and resigned to the loss of Abdulrahman. There were so many bodies being found. Almost seven hundred in New Orleans. Their brother was surely one of them; to believe otherwise was folly. Now they just wanted the peace of mind of knowing how he had died. They wanted his body. To cleanse it, to bury him.

5 **gregarious** social, sociable (loving the company of others) – 14 **hilarity** great fun – 16 **hospitable** ['hɑːspɪt̬əbəl] welcoming – 23 **despondent** negative, without hope – 27 **folly** foolishness – 28 **to cleanse** to clean, purify

SATURDAY SEPTEMBER 17

Yuko had forbidden her to watch TV or get on the internet, but Kathy couldn't resist. She searched for her husband's name. She searched for their address, their company. She searched for any sign that her husband had been found.

She found nothing about him, but found other, terrible things. All over the web she found news of the violence and evidence of its overstatement. One page would report hundreds of murders, crocodiles in the water, gangs of men rampaging. Another page would report that no babies had been raped. That there had been no murders in the Superdome, no deaths in the Convention Center. There was no end to the fear and confusion, the racist assumptions and the rumor-mongering.

No one debated that the city was in chaos, but now there was debate over where that chaos had originated. Was it the residents or was it those sent to bring order? Kathy's mind spun as she read about the unprecedented concentration of armed men and women in the city.

First she read about the mercenaries. Immediately after the storm, wealthy businesses and individuals had called in private-security firms from all over the world. At least five different organizations had sent soldiers-for-hire into the city, including Israeli mercenaries from a firm called Instinctive Shooting International. Kathy took in a quick breath. Israeli commandos in New Orleans? That was it, she realized. Her husband was an Arab, and there were Israeli paramilitaries on the ground in the city. She leapt to conclusions.

And the Blackwater soldiers. Blackwater USA, a private-security firm that employed former soldiers from the U.S. and elsewhere, had sent hundreds of personnel to the region. They

8 **overstatement** exaggeration – 10 **to rampage** ['ræmpeɪdʒ] to move about wildly and violently, often stealing, too – 13 **rumor-mongering** spreading rumors *(Gerüchte verbreitend)* – 18 **unprecedented** [ʌn'presədentɪd] never seen before – 20 **mercenary** ['mɚːsənəri] professional soldier hired by and for a foreign army – 28 **to leap to conclusions** to assume things that are most likely not true *(vorschnell Schlussfolgerungen ziehen)*

were there in an official capacity, hired by the Department of Homeland Security to help maintain order. They arrived in full battle dress. Some carried badges as deputies of the Louisiana State Police.

Kathy became obsessed with all the guns. Her brother had been in the National Guard, and she knew how they were armed. She started doing the math. If all the Blackwater mercenaries were carrying at least two guns each, that would mean hundreds of 9mm Heckler and Koch sidearms, hundreds of M-16 rifles and M-4 machine guns.

She felt as if she had stumbled upon the answer to her husband's disappearance. Nothing else made sense. This seemed the most logical thing. One of these mercenaries, responsible to no one, had shot Zeitoun. Now they were covering it up. This is why she had heard nothing. The whole thing would be covered up.

But there were also so many American troops. Surely they had things under control. As well as she could surmise, there were at least twenty thousand National Guard troops in New Orleans, with more arriving every day. But then she thought of the guns again. If each one of those soldiers had at least one M-16 assault rifle, there were about twenty thousand automatic rifles in the city. Too many. And if Governor Blanco was right, that these were vets coming straight from Afghanistan and Iraq, it could not bode well for her husband.

She searched more websites, went deeper. There were 5,750 Army soldiers in the New Orleans area. Almost a thousand

1 **Department of Homeland Security** *Ministerium für innere Sicherheit* In existence since 2002, it was meant to protect the population against terror attacks. – 3 **in full battle dress** in uniforms that they wear when fighting a real war – 3 **badge** sign of rank *(Abzeichen)* – 3 **deputy** ['depjəti] representative – 11 **to stumble** to trip, to almost fall – 18 **to surmise** [sə'maɪz] to guess, work out – 22 **assault rifle** *Angriffswaffe, Sturmgewehr* – 24 **vet** veteran soldier – 25 **to bode well** to be a good sign

state police officers, many of them there with SWAT teams, armed for urban combat. Four hundred Customs and Border Protection agents and officers deputized for local law enforcement. This included more than one hundred men from Border Patrol Tactical Units — men usually armed with grenade launchers, shotguns, battering rams and assault rifles. There were four Maritime Security and Safety Teams, the new Coast Guard tactical units that Homeland Security had formed as part of the War on Terror. Each MSST carried M-16s, shotguns, and .45 caliber handguns. There were five hundred FBI special agents and a U.S. marshals special-ops team. And snipers. They were sending snipers into the city to shoot looters and gunmen. Kathy added it up. There were at least twenty-eight thousand guns in New Orleans. That would be the low number, counting rifles, handguns, shotguns.

She couldn't look anymore. She turned off the computer and paced. She lay in bed, staring at the wall. She got up, went to the bathroom, inspecting the new swath of white hair on her head.

Again she returned to the computer in search of her husband. She was furious with him, with his stubbornness. If he had just gotten in the Odyssey with them! Why could he not simply surrender to the same logic hundreds of thousands of people had recognized? He had to be apart from that. He had to do more. He had to do something else.

She found an email Ahmad had sent to one of the missing-persons agencies. The pictures he had attached were now the only ones she had of her husband — the only ones she had in Phoenix, anyway. They had been taken a year before, in

1 **SWAT** Special Weapons and Tactics units, trained to perform high-risk operations – 2 **urban combat** fighting in cities – 3 **to deputize** to replace, take the place of – 3 **law enforcement** *Strafverfolgung* – 6 **grenade launcher** weapon that sets a grenade in motion with great accuracy – 6 **battering ram** machine designed to break fortified brick walls – 12 **sniper** soldier who shoots to kill from a hidden place

Malaga. They'd gone, the whole family, and the picture was taken on the beach near Ahmad's house. When Kathy saw that beach, she could only think of the hike, that insane hike her husband had insisted they take. If ever there was a totemic memory that encompassed the man, it was that day.

They had been in Malaga for a few days when the older kids felt comfortable enough in Ahmad and Antonia's house to be left for the morning. Zeitoun wanted to take Kathy and Safiya for a walk on the beach, to be alone for a bit. Zachary and Nademah and Aisha, entertained with Lutfi and Laila and the pool in the backyard, barely noticed when they left.

Kathy and Zeitoun walked down to the beach, Zeitoun carrying Safiya. They walked for a mile or so down the shore, the water cool and calm. Kathy was as content as she had been in years. It was almost like a real holiday, and her husband actually seemed relaxed, like a regular person on an actual vacation. To have him this way, just walking on a beach for no real reason, just to feel the water between his toes — it was a side of him she rarely saw.

But it didn't last long. Almost as soon as she took notice of his sense of peace and leisure, his eyes focused on something in the distance.

4 **totemic** [toʊ'temɪk] symbolic – 5 **to encompass** [en'kʌmpəs] to sum up, be typical of

"See that?" he asked.

She shook her head. She didn't want to see what he saw.

"That rock. See it?"

He had taken notice of a small rock formation in the distance, jutting into the sea a few miles down the shore. Kathy held her breath, afraid of whatever notion was brewing in his mind.

"Let's walk there," he said, his face bright, his eyes alive.

Kathy did not want to walk to a particular destination. She wanted to stroll. She wanted to stroll, then sit on the beach and play with their daughter, then go back to Ahmad's. She wanted a vacation — idleness, frivolity even.

"C'mon," he said. "Such a nice day. And it's not so far."

They walked toward the rock, and the water was pleasant, the sun gentle. But after another thirty minutes, they had not gotten noticeably closer. And they had come upon a low promontory that separated one part of the beach from the next. It seemed a perfect place to turn around. Kathy suggested this, but Zeitoun dismissed it out of hand.

"We're so close!" he said.

They were not so close, but she followed her husband as he climbed over the rock, holding Safiya with one hand, over the jagged ridge and down again to the next stretch of beach.

"See?" he said when they landed on the wet sand. "So close."

They walked on, Zeitoun transferring Safiya to his shoulders. They continued another mile, and again the beach was interrupted by a ridge. They climbed over this one, too. When they were again on level ground, the rock in the distance seemed no closer than when they'd set out. Zeitoun wasn't fazed.

10 **to stroll** to walk for enjoyment – 12 **idleness** leisure, doing nothing – 12 **frivolity** silliness – 17 **promontory** *(AE)* piece of land sticking out towards the sea – 23 **jagged ridge** unevenly cut sequence of rocks – 31 **fazed** angry

They had been walking two hours when the beach was interrupted by another, much larger promontory, this one big enough that homes and shops had been built atop it. They had to climb up a set of steps, through the roads of this small town. Kathy insisted they stop for water, for ice cream. She drank her fill, but they did not pause for long. Soon he was off again, and she had no choice but to follow. They jogged down the steps on the other side to continue on the beach. Zeitoun never broke pace. He was barely sweating.

"So close, Kathy!" he said, pointing to the rock in the distance, which looked no closer than before.

"We should turn around," she said. "What's the point?"

"No, no, Kathy!" he said. "We can't turn around till we touch it." And she knew that he would insist she do it, too. He always wanted his family along for his quests.

Zeitoun showed no signs of fatigue. He switched Safiya, now sleeping, from one arm to the other, and kept going.

They walked for four hours in all, up and over three hillside towns, across fifteen miles of beach, before they were finally close enough to the rock to touch it.

It was nothing much to see. Just a boulder jutting out into the sea. When they were finally upon it, Kathy laughed, and Zeitoun laughed too. She rolled her eyes, and he smiled at her mischievously. He knew it was absurd.

"C'mon, Kathy, let's touch the rock," he said.

They walked out to it and quickly climbed to its peak. They sat there for a few minutes, resting, watching the waves crash against the rocks below. And as ridiculous as it had seemed en route, Kathy felt good. She had married a bullheaded man, a sometimes ridiculously stubborn man. He could be exasperating in his sense of destiny. Whatever he set his mind to, even a crackpot idea of touching some random rock miles in the distance, she knew he would not rest until he had done

16 **fatigue** losing strength – 21 **boulder** big rock – 24 **mischievous** ['mɪstʃəvəs] playful in a teasing way – 32 **crackpot** crazy

it. It was maddening. It was strange, even. But then again, she thought, it gave their marriage a certain epic scope. It was silly to think that way, she knew, but they were on a journey that did sometimes seem grand. She had grown up in a small Baton Rouge house with nine siblings, and now she and her husband had four thriving kids, had been to Spain, to Syria, could seemingly achieve any of the goals they conjured.

"C'mon, touch it," he said again.

They were sitting on it, but she hadn't yet officially touched it.

Now she did. He smiled and held her hand.

"It's nice, right?" he asked.

After that, it became a joke between them. Any time something seemed difficult and Kathy was ready to give up, Zeitoun would say, "Touch the rock, Kathy! Touch the rock!"

And they would laugh, and she would find the strength to continue, partly out of a strange sort of logic: wasn't it more absurd to give up? Wasn't it more absurd to fail, to turn back, than to continue?

MONDAY SEPTEMBER 19

Kathy woke up having reached a new kind of peace. She felt strong, and was ready to start planning. She had been paralyzed for almost two weeks now, waiting for word about her husband, but this was folly. She needed to go home, to the house on Dart. She was suddenly sure that she would find her husband there. His family in Syria was right. The most dangerous thing was these roving gangs of men. That made the most sense. As the city emptied out, the looting likely grew more brazen and engulfed neighborhoods like Uptown. The thieves had come to the house on Dart, and, not expecting to find anyone there, had killed her husband.

2 **epic scope** extraordinary dimension – 7 **to conjure** to bring forth – 29 **brazen** shameless

She needed to get back to New Orleans, hire a boat of some kind, and return to the house on Dart. She needed to see him, wherever he was. She needed to find him and bury him. She needed all of this to end.

All morning she felt a new serenity. It was time to get serious, to stop hoping, and to start working toward whatever came next.

Midday, Kathy heard that another hurricane, this one called Rita, was bearing down on New Orleans. Mayor Nagin, who had planned to reopen the city, now canceled those plans. The storm, being tracked over the Gulf with winds above 150 miles per hour, was expected to hit September 21. Even if she could make it near New Orleans, the winds would again push her back.

Nademah came in the living room.

"Should we pray?" she asked.

Kathy almost said no — all she did was pray — but she didn't want to disappoint her daughter.

"Sure. Let's."

And they prayed on the living room floor. Afterward, she kissed Nademah's forehead and held her close. *I will rely on you so much,* she thought. *Poor Demah,* she thought, *you have no idea.*

And then Kathy's cell phone rang. She picked it up. "Hello?"

"Is this Mrs. Zeitoun?" a voice asked. The man seemed nervous. He pronounced *Zeitoun* wrong. Kathy's stomach dropped. She managed to say yes.

"I saw your husband," the man said.

Kathy sat down. An image of his body floating in the filth—

5 **serenity** [səˈrenət̬i] calm

"He's okay," the voice said. "He's in prison. I'm a missionary. I was at Hunt, the prison up in St. Gabriel. He's there. He gave me your number."

Kathy asked him a dozen questions in one breath.

"Sorry, that's all I know. I can't tell you anything else."

She asked him how she could get hold of Zeitoun, if he was being well cared for—

"Look, I can't talk to you anymore. I could get in trouble. He's okay, he's in there. That's it, I've got to go." And he hung up.

PART IV

TUESDAY SEPTEMBER 6

Zeitoun was enjoying the cool water of his first shower in over a week. The water might shut off for good at any time, he knew, so he lingered for a few seconds longer than he should have.

But he was ready to go. The neighborhoods were emptying out, and it wouldn't be long before there was no one else to help and little left to see. He wondered when and how he might leave. Maybe in a few days. He could head up to Napoleon and St. Charles and ask the officers and aid workers there how he could get out. He would only need to get to the airport in New Orleans or Baton Rouge, and then fly to Phoenix. There wasn't much left to do here, he was running low on food, and he missed Kathy and the kids. It was time.

He walked downstairs.

"Shower's all yours," he told Nasser.

Zeitoun called his brother Ahmad in Spain.

"Do you realize the images we're seeing on TV?" Ahmad asked.

As they were talking, he heard Nasser's voice from the porch. He was talking to someone outside.

"Zeitoun!" Nasser called.

"What?" Zeitoun said.

"Come here," Nasser said. "These guys want to know if we need water."

Zeitoun hung up the phone and walked toward the door.

The men met Zeitoun in the foyer. They were wearing mismatched police and military uniforms. Fatigues. Bulletproof vests. Most were wearing sunglasses. All had M-16s and pistols. They quickly filled the hallway. There were at least ten guns visible.

"Who are you?" one of them asked.

"I'm the landlord. I own this house," Zeitoun said.

28 **fatigues** uniform worn by soldiers when they go into battle

Now he saw that there were six of them — five white men and one African American woman. Under their vests it was hard to see their uniforms. Were they local cops? The woman, very tall, wore camouflage fatigues. She was probably National Guard. They were all looking around the house as if they were finally seeing the inside of a building they had long been watching from afar. They were tense, each of them with their fingers on their triggers. In the foyer, one officer was frisking Ronnie. Another officer had Nasser against the wall by the stairway.

"Give me your ID," one man said to Zeitoun.

Zeitoun complied. The man took the ID and gave it back to Zeitoun without looking at it.

"Get in the boat," he said.

"You didn't look at it," Zeitoun protested.

"Move!" another man barked.

Zeitoun was pushed toward the front door. The other officers had already gathered Ronnie and Nasser onto an enormous fan boat. It was a military craft, far bigger than any other boat Zeitoun had seen since the storm. There were at least two officers pointing automatic rifles at them.

At that moment, another boat arrived. It was Todd, coming home from his rescue rounds.

"What's happening here?" he asked.

"Who are you?" one of the officers demanded.

"I live here," Todd said. "I have proof. It's inside the house."

"Get in the boat," the officer said.

Zeitoun was not panicking. He knew there had been a mandatory evacuation in effect, and he assumed this had something to do with that. He knew it would all get straightened out wherever they were being taken. All he needed was to call Kathy, who would call a lawyer.

8 **to frisk** to search – 12 **to comply** to obey – 29 **mandatory** ['mændətɔ:ri] forced, obligatory – 30 **to straighten out** to clarify

But Yuko's number was in the house, by the phone, on the hall table. If he didn't get it now, he would have no way to reach Kathy. He hadn't memorized it.

"Excuse me," he said to one of the soldiers. "I left a piece of paper on that table. It's my wife's phone number. She's in Arizona. It's the only way—" He moved toward the house, smiling politely. It was everything, that number. The piece of paper was fifteen feet away.

"No!" the soldier yelled. He grabbed the back of Zeitoun's shirt, turned him around, and shoved him onto the boat.

The four captives rode standing, surrounded by the six military personnel. Zeitoun tried to figure out who they were, but there were few clues. Two or three of the men were dressed in black, with no visible patches or insignia.

No one spoke. Zeitoun knew not to exacerbate the situation, and assumed that when they were interviewed by a superior, everything would be explained. They would be scolded for staying in the city when there was a mandatory evacuation in effect, and they would be sent north on a bus or helicopter. Kathy would be relieved, he thought, when she heard he was finally on his way out.

They sped down Claiborne and then Napoleon, until the water grew shallow at the intersection of Napoleon and St. Charles.

The boat cut its engine and coasted toward the intersection. There were a dozen men in National Guard uniforms there, and they all took notice. A smattering of other men in bulletproof vests, sunglasses, and black caps all looked up. They were waiting for them.

The moment Zeitoun and the three other men were led off the boat, a dozen soldiers descended upon them. Two men in

11 **captive** prisoner – 14 **patch** *(AE)* small piece of cloth fixed to a uniform *(Abzeichen aus Stoff)* – 15 **to exacerbate** [ɪgˈzæsɚbeɪt] to aggravate *(verschlimmern)* – 27 **smattering** *here:* small number

bulletproof vests leapt on Zeitoun, tackling him to the ground. His face was pushed into the wet grass. He spat out mud. There was a knee in his back, hands on his legs. It felt like there were at least three men keeping him down with all their force, though he had not moved or struggled. His arms were pulled behind his back and he was handcuffed with plastic ties. His legs were tied together. All the while the men were barking orders: "Hold still!" "Stay there, motherfucker." "Don't move, asshole." Out of the corner of his eye he could see the other three men, Nasser, Todd, and Ronnie, all on the ground, face down, with knees on their backs, hands on their necks. Photographers were taking pictures. Soldiers were watching, their fingers ready on the triggers of their guns.

Struggling to gain their balance with their legs tied, the four men were lifted up. They were shuffled into a large white van. They sat on two benches inside, opposite each other. No one spoke. A young soldier stepped into the driver's seat. His face seemed open; Zeitoun took a chance.

"What's happening here?" Zeitoun asked him.

"I don't know," the soldier said. "I'm from Indiana."

They waited for thirty minutes in the van. Zeitoun could see the activity outside — soldiers talking urgently to each other and on radios. This was a busy intersection that he passed every day. He could see Copeland's restaurant, where he'd often eaten with his family, right there on the corner. Now it was a military post, and he was a captive. He and Todd exchanged looks. Todd was a joker, and he'd had a run-in or two with the law, so even in the back of a military van he seemed amused. He shook his head and rolled his eyes.

Zeitoun thought of the dogs he had been feeding. He caught the attention of one of the soldiers passing by the open back of the van.

27 **to have a run-in with the law** *(inf)* to be in conflict with the police

"I've been feeding dogs," Zeitoun said. "Can I give you the address, and you can take them out, bring them somewhere?"

"Sure," the soldier said. "We'll take care of them."

"You want the address?" Zeitoun asked.

"No, I know where they are," the soldier said, and walked away.

The van drove toward downtown.

"We're going to the Superdome?" Todd wondered aloud.

A few blocks from the stadium, they pulled into the crescent-shaped driveway of the New Orleans Union Passenger Terminal, where incoming and outgoing Amtrak trains and Greyhound buses docked. Zeitoun's earlier assumption — that they were being evacuated by force — seemed to be confirmed. He was relieved, and sat back on the bench. It was wrong that he hadn't been allowed to retrieve any possessions, and he felt that the treatment by the cops and soldiers had been rough. But the result was going to be simple and fair enough: they were being put on a bus or train and sent out of the city.

Zeitoun had picked up and dropped off friends and relatives at the station a handful of times over the years. Fronted by a lush lawn and palm trees, the Union Passenger Terminal had opened in 1954, an art deco-style building once aspiring to grandness but since overtaken by a certain grey municipal malaise. There was a whimsical candy-colored sculpture on the lawn that looked like a bunch of child's toys glued together without reason or order. A few blocks beyond, the Superdome loomed.

11 **crescent-shaped** ['kresənt] shaped like a fairly new moon *(mondsichelförmig)* – 12 **Amtrak** U.S. railroad company – 24 **art-deco** architectural / artistic style of the 1930s – 24 **to aspire to** to aim for – 26 **malaise** *here:* financial problems – 26 **whimsical** strange and often amusing

As they pulled to the side of the building, Zeitoun saw police cars and military vehicles. National Guardsmen patrolled the grounds. The station had become a kind of military base. A few personnel were casual, talking idly against a Humvee, smoking. Others were on guard, as if expecting a siege at any moment.

The van stopped at the station's side door, and the captives were taken out of the van and led inside. When Zeitoun and the others entered the main room of the station, immediately fifty pairs of eyes, those of soldiers and police officers and military personnel, were upon them. There were no other civilians inside. It was as if the entire operation, this bus station-turned-military base, had been arranged for them.

Zeitoun's heart was thrumming. They saw no civilians, no hospital or humanitarian-aid workers, as had been common in areas like the Napoleon-St. Charles staging ground. This was different. This was entirely martial, and the mood was tense.

"Are you kidding me?" Todd said. "What the hell is going on?"

The four men were seated in folding chairs near the Greyhound ticket desk. With every passing minute, everyone in the bus station seemed to take more interest in Zeitoun, Nasser, Todd, and Ronnie.

All around there were men in uniform — New Orleans police, National Guard soldiers, prison guards with the words LOUISIANA DEPARTMENT OF CORRECTIONS on their uniforms. Zeitoun counted about eighty personnel and at least a dozen assault rifles within a thirty-foot radius. Two officers with dogs kept watch, leashes wrapped tight around their fists.

4 **Humvee** 4-wheel drive military vehicle – 5 **siege** [si:dʒ] blockade – 17 **martial** military, war-like – 30 **leash** piece of leather, chain or rope fixed to a dog so it can be held and controlled

Todd was lifted from his chair and brought to the Amtrak ticket counter against the wall. As two officers flanked him, a third officer on the other side of the counter began to question him. The other three men remained seated. Zeitoun could not hear the interrogation.

The soldiers and guards nearby were on edge. When Nasser shifted in his seat, there were immediate rebukes.

"Sit still. Go back to your position."

Nasser at first resisted.

"Stop moving!" they said. "Hands where I can see them."

Zeitoun examined his surroundings. In essential ways, the station was still the same. There was a Subway franchise, various ticket counters, an information kiosk. But there were no travelers. There were only men and women with guns, hundreds of boxes of water and other supplies stacked in the hallways, and Zeitoun and his fellow prisoners.

Todd was arguing with his interrogators. Zeitoun could hear occasional bursts as the questioning at the Amtrak desk continued. Todd was hotheaded on a normal day, so it didn't surprise Zeitoun that he was agitated during the processing.

"Are we going to get a phone call?" Todd asked.

"No," the officer said.

"You have to give us a phone call."

There was no answer.

Todd raised his voice, rolled his eyes. The soldiers around him stood closer, barking admonitions and threats back at him.

"Why are we here?" he asked a passing soldier.

"You guys are al Qaeda," the soldier said.

Todd laughed derisively, but Zeitoun was startled. He could not have heard right.

6 **on edge** tense, nervous – 7 **rebuke** harsh criticism – 17 **interrogator** [ɪnˈterəgeɪt̬ɚ] person who questions sb in an aggressive and threatening way

Zeitoun had long feared this day would come. Each of the few times he had been pulled over for a traffic violation, he knew the possibility existed that he would be harassed, misunderstood, suspected of shadowy dealings that might bloom in the imagination of any given police officer. After 9/11, he and Kathy knew that many imaginations had run amok, that the introduction of the idea of "sleeper cells" — groups of would-be terrorists living in the U.S. and waiting, for years or decades, to strike — meant that everyone at their mosque, or the entire mosque itself, might be waiting for instructions from their presumed leaders in the hills of Afghanistan or Pakistan.

He and Kathy worried about the reach of the Department of Homeland Security, its willingness to contact anyone born in or with a connection to the Middle East. So many of their Muslim friends had been interviewed, forced to send in documents and hire lawyers. But until now Zeitoun had been fortunate. He had had no experience with profiling, hadn't been suspected of anything by anyone with real authority. There were the occasional looks askance, of course, sneers from people upon hearing his accent. Maybe, he thought, this was just one soldier, ignorant or cruel, wanting to stir things up. Zeitoun decided to ignore it.

Still, Zeitoun's senses were awakened. He scanned the room for more signals. He and the three others were still being watched by dozens of soldiers and cops. He felt like an exotic beast, a hunter's prize.

Moments later, another passing soldier looked at Zeitoun and muttered "Taliban."

And as much as he wanted to dismiss both comments, he couldn't. Now he was sure that there was a grave misunderstanding taking place, and that unraveling it,

18 **to profile** to give or write the most important details of a person – 20 **askance** [ə'skænts] with disapproval, distrust – 20 **sneer** scornful comment – 32 **to unravel** to explain, to solve

disproving it, was going to take days. Todd ranted, but Zeitoun knew it would do no good. The question of their innocence or guilt would not be answered in this room, not any time soon.

He sat back and waited.

Before them was an alcove housing a bank of vending machines and video games. Above the machines, wrapping around the interior of the entire station, was a vast mural that occupied, in four long segments, the upper half of the station's main walls.

In all, the mural was about 120 feet long, and it sought to depict the entire history of Louisiana in particular and the United States generally.

Zeitoun looked up at it, and though he had been in the terminal before, he had never really seen this mural. Now that he did, it was a startling thing, a dark catalog of subjugation and struggle. The colors were nightmarish, the lines jagged, the images disturbing. He saw Ku Klux Klan hoods, skeletons, harlequins in garish colors, painted faces. Just above him there was a lion being attacked by a giant eagle made of gold. There were images of blue-clad soldiers marching off to war next to mass graves. There were many depictions of the suppression or elimination of peoples — Native Americans, slaves, immigrants — and always, nearby, was the artist's idea of the instigators: wealthy aristocrats in powdered wigs, generals in gleaming uniforms, businessmen with bags of money. In one segment, oil derricks stood below a flooded landscape, water engulfing a city.

1 **to rant** to speak angrily – 5 **alcove** place in the wall that is built farther back – 5 **vending machine** machine selling candy or drinks – 11 **to depict** to show in pictures – 15 **subjugation** oppression *(Unterwerfung)* – 18 **garish** bright *(grell)* – 24 **instigator** person that initiates (starts) an action or sequence of events or movement – 24 **wig** *Perücke* – 26 **derrick** platform

Nasser was processed next. He was brought to the Amtrak ticket counter, and now Zeitoun saw that they were fingerprinting and photographing each of them.

Soon after Nasser's interrogation began, his duffel bag created a stir. A female officer was removing stacks of American money from the bag.

"This isn't from here," she said.

Nasser argued with her, but this discovery only got the building more excited.

"That *ain't* from here," she said, now more certain.

The money was laid out on a nearby table and soon there was a crowd around it. Someone counted it. Ten thousand dollars.

This was the first Zeitoun knew of the contents of Nasser's bag. When Nasser had brought it into the canoe, Zeitoun had assumed it contained clothes, a few valuables. He never would have guessed it contained $10,000 in cash.

Soon there were more discoveries. Todd had been carrying $2,400 of his own. The officers stacked it on the table in its own pile next to Nasser's. In Todd's pockets they found MapQuest printouts.

"I deliver lost luggage," Todd tried to explain.

This didn't satisfy the officers.

In one of Todd's pockets they discovered a small memory chip, the kind used for digital cameras. Todd laughed, explaining that on it were only photos he'd taken of the flood damage. But the authorities were seeing something more.

Watching the evidence on the table mount, Zeitoun's shoulders slackened. Most municipal systems were not functioning. There were no lawyers in the station, no judges. They would not talk their way out of this. The police and

5 **to create a stir** to excite interest – 28 **evidence** sth that proves sth *(Beweismaterial)* – 29 **to slacken** to relax

soldiers in the room were too worked up, and the evidence was too intriguing. Zeitoun settled in for a long wait.

Todd grew more exasperated. He would calm down for a time, then explode again. Finally one of the soldiers raised his arm, as if to strike him down with the back of his hand. Todd went quiet.

Then it was Zeitoun's turn for processing. He was brought to the Amtrak counter and fingerprinted. He was pushed against a nearby wall on which height markers had been written by hand, from five to seven feet. Zeitoun had stood in this exact place before while waiting to buy train tickets for friends or employees. Now, while handcuffed and guarded by two soldiers with M-16s, his photograph was being taken.

At the ticket counter, he surrendered his wallet and was frisked for any other possessions. He was asked basic questions: name, address, occupation, country of origin. He was not told of the charges against him.

Eventually he was brought back to the row of chairs and was seated again with Todd and Nasser, while Ronnie was processed.

Moments later, Zeitoun was grabbed roughly under the arm. "Stand up," a soldier said.

Zeitoun stood and was led by three soldiers into a small room — some kind of utility closet. Inside there were bare walls and a small folding table.

The door closed behind him. He was alone with two soldiers.

"Remove your clothes," one said.

"Here?" he asked.

The soldier nodded.

Until this point, Zeitoun had not been charged with a crime. He had not been read his rights. He did not know why he was being held. Now he was in a small white room being

1 **worked up** tired – 2 **intriguing** *belastend* – 24 **utility** sth that is supplied by a city which you use at home (e.g. electricity, water, gas)

asked by two soldiers, each of them in full camouflage and holding automatic rifles, to remove his clothes.

"Now!" one of the soldiers barked.

Zeitoun took off his T-shirt and shorts and, after a pause, stepped out of his sandals.

"And the undershorts," the same soldier said.

Zeitoun paused. If he did this, he would live with it always. The shame would never leave him. But there was no alternative. He could refuse, but if he did, there would be a fight. More soldiers. Some sort of retribution.

"Do it!" the soldier ordered.

Zeitoun removed his underwear.

One of the soldiers circled him, lifting Zeitoun's arms as he passed. The soldier held a baton, and when he reached Zeitoun's back, he tapped Zeitoun's inner thigh.

"Spread your legs," the soldier said.

Zeitoun did so.

"Elbows on the table."

Zeitoun couldn't understand the meaning of the words.

The soldier repeated the directive, his voice more agitated. "Put your elbows on the table."

He had no options. Zeitoun knew that the soldiers would get what they wanted. They were likely looking for any contraband, but he also knew that anything was possible. Nothing on this day had conformed to any precedent.

Zeitoun bent over. He heard the sounds of the soldier pulling plastic gloves onto his hands. Zeitoun felt fingers quickly exploring his rectum. The pain was extreme but brief.

"Stand up," the soldier said, removing the glove with a snap. "Get dressed."

10 **retribution** punishment – 14 **baton** [bə'tɑ:n] large stick used by police to threaten to hit (and sometimes actually hit) sb with – 20 **directive** order – 24 **contraband** stolen or smuggled goods – 25 **Nothing on this day had conformed to any precedent.** Nothing of this kind had ever happened to him before. – 28 **rectum** *After*

Zeitoun put on his shorts and shirt. He was led out of the room, where he saw Todd. He was arguing already, threatening lawsuits, the loss of all their jobs. Soon Todd was pushed into the room, the door was closed, and his protestations were muffled behind the steel door.

When Todd's search was complete, the two of them were led back through the bus station. Zeitoun was certain that he saw a handful of looks of recognition, soldiers and police officers who knew what had happened in the room.

Zeitoun and Todd were brought to the back of the station and toward the doors that led to the buses and trains. Zeitoun's thoughts were a jumble. Could it be that after all that, they *were* being evacuated? Perhaps they had been stripped to ensure that they hadn't stolen anything, and now, deemed clean, they were being sent away on a bus? It was bizarre, but not out of the realm of possibility.

But when the guards pushed open the doors, Zeitoun took a quick breath. The parking lot, where a dozen buses might normally be parked, had been transformed into a vast outdoor prison.

Chain-link fences, topped by razor wire, had been erected into a long, sixteen-foot-high cage extending about a hundred yards into the lot. Above the cage was a roof, a freestanding shelter like those at gas stations. The barbed wire extended to meet it.

Zeitoun and Todd were brought to the front of the cage, a few feet from the back of the bus station, and a different guard opened the door. They were pushed inside. The cage was closed, then locked with chain and a padlock. Down the way, there were two other prisoners, each alone in their own enclosure.

"Holy shit," Todd said.

12 **jumble** confused mixture – 15 **to deem** to think – 16 **not out of the realm of possibility** not impossible – 21 **chain-link** metal – 21 **razor wire** similar to barbed wire *(Stacheldraht)*

Zeitoun was in disbelief. It had been a dizzying series of events — arrested at gunpoint in a home he owned, brought to an impromptu military base built inside a bus station, accused of terrorism, and locked in an outdoor cage. It surpassed the most surreal accounts he'd heard of third-world law enforcement.

Inside the cage, Todd ranted and swore. He couldn't believe it. But then again, he noted, it was not unprecedented. During Mardi Gras, when the local jails were full, the New Orleans police often housed drunks and thieves in temporary jails set up in tents.

This one, though, was far more elaborate, and had been built since the storm. Looking at it, Zeitoun realized that it was not one long cage, but a series of smaller, divided cages. He had seen similar structures before, on the properties of his clients who kept dogs. This cage, like those, was a single-fenced enclosure divided into smaller ones. He counted sixteen. It looked like a giant kennel, and yet it looked even more familiar than that.

It looked precisely like the pictures he'd seen of Guantanamo Bay. Like that complex, it was a vast grid of chain-link fencing with few walls, so the prisoners were visible to the guards and each other. Like Guantanamo, it was outdoors, and there appeared to be nowhere to sit or sleep. There were simply cages and the pavement beneath them.

The space inside Zeitoun and Todd's cage was approximately fifteen by fifteen feet, and was empty but for a portable toilet without a door. The only other object in the cage was a steel bar in the shape of an upside-down U, cemented into the pavement like a bike rack. It normally served as a guide for the buses parking in the lot and for passengers forming lines. It was about thirty inches high, forty inches long.

3 **impromptu** makeshift, temporary – 5 **to surpass** to go beyond – 5 **account** report – 12 **elaborate** carefully built – 20 **Guantanamo Bay** outdoor prison for presumed terrorists set up at a U.S. military base in Cuba

Across from Zeitoun's cage was a two-story building, some kind of Amtrak office structure. It was now occupied by soldiers. Two soldiers stood on the roof, holding M-16s and staring down at Zeitoun and Todd.

Todd raged, wild-eyed and protesting. But the guards could hear little of what he said. Even Zeitoun, standing near him, could hear only muffled fragments. It was then that Zeitoun realized that there was a sound, a heavy mechanical drone, cloaking the air around them. It was so steady and unchanging that he had failed to notice it.

Zeitoun turned around and realized the source of the noise. The back of their cage nearly abutted the train tracks, and on the tracks directly behind them stood an Amtrak train engine. The engine was operating at full power on diesel fuel, and, Zeitoun realized in an instant, was generating all the electricity used for the station and the makeshift jail. He looked up at the monstrous grey machine, easily a hundred tons, adorned with a small red, white, and blue logo, and knew that it would be with them, loud and unceasing, as long as they were held there.

One guard was assigned to them. He sat on a folding chair about ten feet in front of the cage. He stared at Zeitoun and Todd, his face curious and disdainful.

Zeitoun was determined to get a phone call. He reached for the chain-link fence in front of him, intending to get the attention of an officer of some kind he saw near the back door of the station. Todd did so, too, and was immediately set straight by the guard who had been assigned to watch them.

"Don't touch the fence!" the guard snapped.

"Don't touch the fence? Are you kidding?" Todd asked.

But the soldier was not joking. "You touch the fence again I'll fuck you up."

7 **muffled** not clear – 12 **to abut** [əˈbʌt] *(AE)* to border on – 17 **to adorn** to decorate – 19 **unceasing** never stopping – 23 **disdain** contempt *(Verachtung)*

Todd asked where they were supposed to stand. He was told they could stand in the middle of the cage. They could sit on the steel rack. They could sit on the ground. But if they touched the fence again there would be consequences.

There were a dozen other guards roaming behind the terminal. One walked by, led by a German shepherd. He made sure to pause meaningfully at their cage, giving Zeitoun and Todd a look of warning before moving on.

Zeitoun could barely stand. There was a stabbing pain in his foot he had ignored until now. He took off his shoe to find his instep discolored. There was something wedged under his skin — some kind of metal splinter, he thought, though he couldn't remember where or when he'd gotten it. The area was purple in the center, ringed by white. He needed to clear out the splinter or the foot would get worse, and quickly.

Zeitoun and Todd took turns sitting on the steel rack. It was only wide enough for one person, so they traded ten-minute shifts.

After an hour, the doors to the station burst open. Nasser and Ronnie appeared, escorted by three officers. Zeitoun and Todd's cage was opened, and Nasser and Ronnie were pushed inside. The cage was locked again. The four men were reunited.

Under the rumble of the engine, the men compared their experiences thus far. All four had been strip-searched. Only Todd had been told why they were being held — possession of stolen goods was the only charge mentioned — and none had been read their rights. None had been allowed to make a phone call.

11 **instep** middle part of the top of the foot

Nasser had tried to explain the cash he had in his knapsack. The police and soldiers were in the city to prevent the widespread looting everyone had heard about. Nasser, being equally concerned about the looting, had decided to keep his money, his life savings, with him.

His interrogators did not accept this. Nasser had had no luck explaining that legions of immigrants kept their money in cash, that trust in banks was tenuous. He explained that one reason a person in his position kept his money in cash was for the possibility, however remote, that he would be stopped, questioned, detained — or deported. With cash he could hide it, keep it, direct its retrieval if he was sent away.

The four men didn't know what would happen to them, but they knew they would spend the night in the cage.

The Syrian names of Zeitoun and Dayoob, their Middle Eastern accents, the ten thousand dollars cash, Todd's cash and MapQuest printouts — it all added up to enough evidence that the four of them knew that their predicament would not be straightened out anytime soon.

"We're screwed, friends," Todd said.

In the cage, the men had few options: they could stand in the center, they could sit on the cement, or they could lean against the steel rack. No one wanted to sit on the ground. The cement beneath them was filthy with dirt and grease. If they made a move toward the fence, the guards would yell obscenities and threaten retribution.

For the first hours in the cage, Zeitoun's overriding goal was to be granted a phone call. All the men had made the request repeatedly during processing, and had been told that there were no phones functioning.

8 **tenuous** *opp of* strong; thin – 20 **screwed** *(inf)* messed up, in a bad situation – 25 **to yell obscenities** to curse

This seemed to be fact. They saw no one talking on cell phones or landlines. There was a rumor that satellite phones were working and that there was one phone, connected to a fax line, in the upstairs office of the bus station.

Every time a guard passed, they begged for access to this or any phone. At best they got shrugs and glib answers.

"Phones don't work," a guard told them. "You guys are terrorists. You're Taliban."

The day's light was dimming. Processing had taken three hours, and the four men had been in the cage for three more. They were each given small cardboard boxes with the words BARBECUE PORK RIB printed on the side. Inside was a set of plastic cutlery, a packet of cheese spread, two crackers, a packet of orange-drink crystals, and a bag of pork ribs. These were military-style meals, ready to eat.

Zeitoun told the guard that he and Nasser were Muslims and could not eat pork.

The guard shrugged. "Then don't eat it."

Zeitoun and Nasser ate the crackers and cheese and gave the rest to Todd and Ronnie.

With the darkness coming, the sound behind them seemed to grow louder. Already he was tired, but Zeitoun knew that the engine would ensure that none of them slept. He had worked on ships before, in engine rooms, but this was louder than that, louder than anything he had ever known. In the glare of the floodlights, it resembled a great furnace, moaning and ravenous.

"We can pray," Zeitoun said to Nasser.

He had caught Nasser's eye, and he knew what he was thinking. They needed to pray, were urged to do so five times

6 **glib** superficial, meaningless – 26 **furnace** large container for a very hot fire – 27 **ravenous** ['rævənəs] extremely hungry

a day, but Nasser was nervous. Would this arouse more suspicion? Would they be mocked or even punished for worshiping?

Zeitoun saw no reason not to do so, even while being held in an outdoor cage. "We must," he said. If anything, he thought, they needed to pray more often, and with great fervor.

"What about *wuduu*?" Nasser asked.

The Qur'an asked that Muslims wash themselves before their prayers, and there was no means of doing so here. But Zeitoun knew that the Qur'an allowed that if there was no water available, Muslims could use dust to cleanse themselves, even if only ceremoniously. And so they did so. They took gravel from the ground and rubbed it over their hands and arms, their heads and feet, and they knelt and performed *salaat*. Zeitoun knew their prayers were arousing interest from the guards, but he and Nasser did not pause.

As the night went black, the lights came on. Floodlights from above and from the building opposite. The night grew darker and cooler, but the lights stayed on, brighter than day. The men were not given sheets, blankets, or pillows. Soon there was a new guard on duty, sitting on the chair opposite them, and they asked him where they were supposed to sleep. He told them that he didn't care where they slept, as long as it was on the pavement, where he could see them.

Zeitoun didn't care about sleep this night. He wanted to stay awake in case a supervisor of some sort, a lawyer, any civilian at all, happened by. The other men tried to rest their heads on the pavement, in the crooks of their arms. No one slept. Even when someone would find themselves in a place where they might be able to rest, the sound of the engine, its

7 **fervor** passion

vibrations in the ground, took over. There could be no sleep in this place.

Somewhere in the small hours, Zeitoun tried to drape himself over the steel rack, stomach-down. He found a minute or so of rest this way, but it was a position he could not maintain. He tried to lean his back against it, arms crossed. It could not be done.

Other guards occasionally walked by with their German shepherds, but the night was otherwise uneventful. There was only the face of the guard, his M-16 by his side, the floodlights coming from every angle, illuminating the faces of Zeitoun's fellow prisoners, all drawn, exhausted, half-mad with fatigue and confusion.

WEDNESDAY SEPTEMBER 7

When the sky began to pale into dawn, Zeitoun realized he had not slept at all. He had closed his eyes for a few minutes at a time, but had not found sleep. He'd refused to lie on the pavement, but even if he could have brought himself to do so, even if he could quell the panic about his situation, his family, his home, the uninterrupted drone of the engine would have kept him awake.

He watched as the night guard left and was replaced by a new man. The new guard's expression was the same as his predecessor's, seeming to take for granted the guilt of the men in the cage.

Zeitoun and Nasser performed their *wuduu* and their *salaat,* and when they were done, they stared at the guard, who was staring at them.

3 **in the small hours** very early in the morning – 3 **to drape** to wrap, hang

Zeitoun became more alert, even optimistic, as the sky brightened. He assumed that with each day since the hurricane, the city would find its way toward some kind of stability, and that the government would soon send help. With that help, the chaos that had brought him to this cage would be reined in and the misunderstanding manifested here would be mitigated.

Zeitoun convinced himself that the previous day had been an aberration, that today would bring a return to reason and procedure. He would be allowed a phone call, would learn about the charges against him, might even see a public defender or a judge. He would call Kathy and she would hire the best lawyer she could find, and this would be over in hours.

The other men in the cage, all of whom had finally found some rest during the night, woke one by one, and stood to stretch. Breakfast was brought. Again it was MREs, this time including ham slices. Zeitoun and Nasser ate what they could and gave the rest to Todd and Ronnie.

As the prison awoke, Zeitoun examined the chainlink structure closely. It was about 150 feet long. The razor wire was new, the portable toilets new. The fencing was new and of high quality. He knew that none of this had existed before the storm. New Orleans Union Passenger Terminal had never before been used as a prison. He did some rough calculations in his mind.

It would have taken maybe six flatbed trucks to get all the fencing to the station. He saw no forklifts or heavy machinery; the cages must have been assembled by hand. It was an impressive feat, to get such a construction project completed so soon after the storm. But when had they done it?

6 **to rein in** to limit – 7 **to mitigate** to become milder – 9 **aberration** mistake, sth that went wrong *(Irrtum)* – 11 **public defender** lawyer for the defence of an accused person

Zeitoun had been brought into the station on September 6, seven and a half days after the hurricane passed through the city. Even under the best of circumstances, building a prison like this would have taken four or five days. That meant that within a day of the storm's eye passing over the region, officials were making plans for the building of a makeshift outdoor prison. Fencing and razor wire would have had to be located or ordered. The toilets and floodlights and all other equipment would have had to be borrowed or requisitioned.

It was a vast amount of planning and execution. A regular contractor would have wanted weeks to complete the task, and would have used heavy machinery. Without machines, dozens of men would be needed. To do it as quickly as they had, fifty men would be needed. Maybe more. And who were these men? Who did this work? Were there contractors and laborers working around the clock on a prison days after the hurricane? It was mind-boggling. It was all the more remarkable given that while the construction was taking place, on September 2, 3, and 4, thousands of residents were being plucked from rooftops, were being discovered alive and dead in attics.

At midday, Zeitoun heard something strange: the sound of buses at the bus station. He looked up to see a school bus arriving at the far end of the lot. From it descended thirty or more prisoners, one woman among them, in orange jumpsuits.

They were the incarcerated from the Jefferson Parish and Kenner jails — those who had been in jail before the storm. Within the hour, the long row of cages began to fill. And again, just like Guantanamo, all prisoners could be seen by anyone, from any angle. Now, with the orange uniforms completing the picture, the similarities were too strong to ignore.

9 **to requisition** to request, to ask for formally – 17 **mind-boggling** *(inf)* too much to think

Quickly after each group was locked into a cage, they were warned about touching the fence. Any touching of any fence would result in severe consequences. And so they came to know the strange rules of their incarceration. The pavement would be their bed, the open-door toilet would be their bathroom, and the steel rack would be the seat they could share. But for the first hour, while the new prisoners got acquainted with their new cells, there was much yelling from the guards about where and how to stand and sit, what not to touch.

A man and a woman were housed one cage away from Zeitoun, and soon a rumor abounded that the man was a sniper, that it had been he who had been shooting at the helicopters that had tried to land on the roof of a hospital.

Lunch was different than previous meals. This time the guards brought ham sandwiches to the cages and then stuffed them through the holes in the wire.

Again Zeitoun and Nasser did not eat.

The presence of dogs was constant. There were at least two always visible, their handlers sure to parade them past the cages in close proximity. occasionally one would explode into barking at some prisoner. Someone in Zeitoun's cage mentioned Abu Ghraib, wondering at what point they'd be asked to pose naked, in a vertical pyramid, and which guard would lean into the picture, grinning.

By two o'clock there were about fifty prisoners at the bus station, but Zeitoun's cage was still the only one with its own dedicated guard.

"You really think they consider us terrorists?" Nasser asked.

23 **Abu Ghraib** place in Iraq where prisoners were tortured cruelly by US soldiers

Todd rolled his eyes. "Why else would we be alone in this cell while everyone else is crammed together? We're the big fish here. We're the big catch."

Throughout the day, a half-dozen more prisoners came through the station and were brought to the cages. These men were dressed in their civilian clothes; they must have been picked up after the storm, as Zeitoun and his companions had been. The pattern was clear now: the prisoners who were being transferred from other prisons came by bus and weren't processed, while those arrested after the storm were processed inside and brought through the back door.

By overhearing the guards and prisoners talking, Zeitoun realized the prison had been given at least two nicknames by the guards and soldiers. A few referred to it as Angola South, but far more were calling it Camp Greyhound.

In the afternoon, one of the guards approached a man in the cage next to Zeitoun's. He talked to an orange-clad prisoner for a few moments, gave him a cigarette, and then returned to the bus station.

Moments later, the guard reappeared, leading a small television crew. The guard led them straight to the man he'd given a cigarette to. The reporter — Zeitoun could see now the crew was from Spain — conducted an interview with the prisoner, and then, after a few minutes, he approached Zeitoun with the microphone and began to ask a question.

"No!" the guard yelled. "Not that one."

The crew was ushered back into the station.

"Holy shit," Todd said. "They bribed that dude."

As they were leaving, the cameraman swept his lens over the whole outdoor jail, Zeitoun included. There was a bright

10 **to process** to examine – 27 **to usher** to lead quickly – 28 **to bribe** to give sb money to say or do sth *(bestechen)*

light attached to the camera, and being viewed that way, in the glare of a floodlight and shown to the world as a criminal in a cage, made Zeitoun furious. It was a lie.

But Zeitoun had a sudden hope, given that the crew was Spanish, that the footage might be broadcast to his brother in Malaga. Ahmad would see it — he saw everything — and he would tell Kathy, and Kathy would know where he was.

At the same time, Zeitoun couldn't bear the thought of his family in Syria knowing he was being kept like this. No matter what happened, if and when he was released, he could not let them know that this had happened to him. He did not belong here. He was not this. He was in a cage, being viewed, gaped at, seen as visitors to the zoo see exotic animals — kangaroos and baboons. The shame was greater than any his family had ever known.

In the late afternoon a new prisoner was brought through the bus-station doors. He was white, about fifty, thin and of average height, with dark hair and tanned skin. Zeitoun thought little of him until his own cage was opened and the man was pushed inside. There were now five prisoners in their cage. No one knew why.

The man was dressed in jeans and a short-sleeved shirt, and seemed to have stayed clean during and after the storm. His hands, face, and clothing were all without dirt or stain. His attitude, too, bore no shadow of the suffering of the city at large.

He introduced himself to Zeitoun and the three others, shaking each of their hands like a conventioneer. He said his name was Jerry. He was gregarious, full of energy, and made jokes about his predicament. The four men had spent a sleepless night in an outdoor cage and did not have the energy to make much conversation, but this new prisoner more than filled the silence.

14 **baboon** African monkey *(Pavian)* – 28 **conventioneer** sb who attends a convention (an official meeting for business people, etc.) – 30 **predicament** situation

He laughed at his own jokes, and about the bizarre situation they found themselves in. Without prompting, Jerry told the story of how he had come to be arrested. He had stayed behind during the storm, just as he always did during hurricanes. He wanted to protect his house, and after Katrina passed, he realized he needed food, and couldn't walk to any stores nearby. His car was on high ground and was undamaged, but he was out of gas. So he found a length of tubing in his garage and was in the middle of siphoning gasoline from a neighbor's car — he planned to tell his neighbor, who would have understood, he said — when he was discovered by a National Guard flatboat. He was arrested for theft. It was an honest misunderstanding, he said, one that would be straightened out soon enough.

Zeitoun pondered the many puzzling aspects to Jerry's presence. First, he seemed to be the only prisoner in the complex entertained by the state of affairs — being held at Camp Greyhound. Second, why had he been put in their cage? There were fifteen other cages, many of them empty. There didn't seem to be any logic to taking a man brought in for gasoline-siphoning and placing him with four men suspected of working together on crimes varying from looting to terrorism.

Jerry asked how the rest of them had come to be in Camp Greyhound. Todd told the story for the four of them. Jerry said something about how badly the four of them had gotten screwed. It was all common small talk, and Zeitoun was tuning out when Jerry changed his tone and line of questioning.

He began to direct his efforts toward Zeitoun and Nasser. He asked questions that didn't flow from the conversational strands he had begun. He made disparaging remarks about the United States. He joked about George W. Bush, about the administration's dismal response to the disaster so far. He

8 **tubing** rubber pipe – 32 **strand** subject, part – 32 **to disparage** to speak in a disrespectful way – 34 **dismal** bad, lazy

questioned the competence of the U.S. military, the wisdom of U.S. foreign policy around the world and in the Middle East in particular.

Todd engaged with him, but Zeitoun and Nasser chose to remain quiet. Zeitoun was deeply suspicious, still trying to parse how this man had ended up in their cage, and what his intentions might be.

"Be nice to your mom!"

While Jerry talked, Zeitoun turned to see a prisoner a few cages away from him. He was white, in his mid-twenties, thin, with long brown hair. He was sitting on the ground, his knees drawn up to his chest, and he was chanting the statement like a mantra, but loudly.

"Be nice to your mom! Treat her kind!"

The other three detainees in the young man's cage were visibly annoyed by him. He had apparently been repeating these strange directives for some time, and Zeitoun had only begun to hear them.

"Don't play with matches! Fire is dangerous!" he said, rocking back and forth.

The man was disabled in some way. Zeitoun watched him carefully. He was not right in the head. He seemed to have been stunted, mentally, at no more than five or six years of age. He recited basic rules and warnings that a very small child might be asked to memorize in kindergarten.

"Don't hurt your mom! Be nice to your mom!"

He went on like this. His cage mates hushed him and even nudged him with their feet, but he took no notice. He was in something like a trance state.

Because the train engine was so loud, his chanting wasn't much of a nuisance for anyone else. But his child's mind could not seem to understand where he was or why.

6 to parse *here:* to analyze – 15 **detainee** prisoner – 31 **nuisance** ['nu:sənts] disturbance

One of the guards, sitting a few yards away from the man's cage, kept insisting that he stay in the middle of the enclosure, where he could be easily seen. Any movement left or right was forbidden. But the man in the cage didn't understand this. He would simply get up and move over to another side. What motivated the man to decide it was time to move from here to there was unclear. But the unprovoked and unsanctioned movement enraged the guard.

"Get back there! Where I can see you!" he yelled.

The man didn't know he was being addressed. "Brush your teeth before bed," he was saying. "Wash your arms and hands. Go pee-pee now so you don't wet the bed."

The guard stood. "Get back over there or I'm gonna come down on you, motherfucker!"

The man remained where he was, in an unsanctioned part of the cage. There he continued to rock, squatting, focused on the space between his feet.

"I'm going to count to three," the guard yelled.

The man, in an almost deliberate provocation, reached out and touched the fence.

That was it. The guard got up and a few seconds later returned with another guard. The second guard was carrying something that looked like a fire extinguisher.

They opened the cage. As they did, the man looked up, suddenly afraid. His eyes were wide with wonder and surprise as they lifted him to his feet and dragged him out of the cage.

A few feet away, they dropped him on the pavement, and with the help of two more guards, they tied his hands and feet with plastic handcuffs. He did not resist.

Then they stepped away, and the first guard, the one who had warned him, aimed the hose and sprayed him, head to toe, with a substance Zeitoun could not immediately discern.

34 **to discern** to recognize

"Pepper spray," Todd said.

The man disappeared in the haze and screamed like a scalded child. When the smoke cleared, he was cowering in a fetal position, wailing like an animal, trying to reach his eyes with his hands.

"Get the bucket!" the guard said.

Another guard came over and dumped a bucket of water on the screaming man. They didn't say another word. They left him screaming, and soon moaning, soaked and gassed, on the pavement behind the Greyhound station. After a few minutes, they dragged him to his feet and returned him to the cage.

"You have to wash the pepper spray off," Todd explained. "Otherwise you get burned, blistered."

This night's MRE was beef stew. Zeitoun ate. The smell of pepper spray hung in the air.

The previous night had been calm compared to the day, but this night brought more fury, more violence. Other prisoners had been added to the cages throughout the evening, and now there were more than seventy at Camp Greyhound; they were angry. There was less space, more agitation. There were challenges issued by the prisoners to the guards, and soon more pepper-sprayings.

Always the procedure was the same: a prisoner would be removed from his cage and dragged to the ground nearby, in full view of the rest of the prisoners. His hands and feet would be tied, and then, sometimes with a guard's knee on his back, he would be sprayed directly in the face. If the prisoner protested, the knee would dig deeper into his back. The spraying would continue until his spirit was broken. Then he would be doused with the bucket and returned to his cage.

3 **to scald** to burn – 4 **fetal** ['fiːt̬əl] like a foetus (i.e. curled up tight) – 31 **to douse** to wet

Zeitoun had watched elephants as a boy, when a Lebanese circus passed through Jableh. Their trainers used large steel hooks to pull the beasts one way or the other, to prod or punish them. The hooks looked like crowbars or ice picks, and the trainers would grab the elephants between the folds of their hide and then pull or twist. Zeitoun thought of the trainers now, how these guards too had been trained to deal with a certain kind of animal. They were accustomed to hardened maximum-security prisoners, and their tools were too severe to work with these men, so many of them guilty of the smallest of crimes — curfew violations, trespassing, public drunkenness.

The night dragged on. There were bursts of screaming, wailing. Arguments broke out among prisoners. Guards would leap up, remove a man, put him in a new cage. But the fighting continued. The prisoners this night were wired, agitated.

Zeitoun and Nasser brushed whatever dust they could over their hands and arms and neck to cleanse themselves, and they prayed.

The guilt Zeitoun now felt was profound and growing. Kathy had been right. He should not have stayed in the city, and he certainly should not have stayed when she asked him, every day after the storm, to get out. *I'm so sorry, Kathy,* he thought. He could not imagine the suffering Kathy was enduring now. She had said every day that something bad could happen, something unexpected, and now she had been proven right. She did not know if he was alive or dead, and every indication would point to the latter.

3 **to prod** to touch with an object – 4 **crowbar** bar of iron or steel crooked at one end – 11 **curfew** when people are not allowed to be outside after a certain time *(Ausgangssperre)* – 11 **violation** breach – 11 **to trespass** to illegally enter sb's private property

Anything in this prison would be tolerable if he could only call her. He did not want to imagine what she was telling the kids, what kinds of questions they would be asking.

But why not allow the prisoners their phone call? Any way he approached the question, he couldn't see the logic in prohibiting calls. It was troublesome, maybe, to escort the prisoners into the station to make the calls, but wouldn't the calls end up relieving the prison of at least some of the jailed? Any municipal jail, he figured, expects many of their prisoners to leave within a day or two, through bonds or dropped charges or any number of outcomes for the small-time offender.

The ban on phone calls was, then, purely punitive, just as the pepper-spraying of the child-man had been born of a combination of opportunity, cruelty, ambivalence, and sport. There was no utility in that, just as there was no utility in barring all prisoners from contacting the outside world.

Oh Kathy, he thought. *Kathy, I am so sorry. Zachary, Nademah, Aisha, Safiya, I am so very sorry tonight that I was not and am not with you.*

By two or three in the morning, most of the prisoners were asleep, and those who remained awake with Zeitoun were quiet. Again Zeitoun refused to sleep on the pavement, and caught only occasional rest by draping himself over the steel rack.

He knew the conditions had begun to take a very real toll on his psyche. He had been angry until now, but he had been thinking clearly. Now the connections were more tenuous. He had wild thoughts of escape. He pondered whether something very bad might happen to him here. And throughout the night

9 **municipal** *(adj)* city – 10 **bond** *(AE)* money that sb pays to get a prisoner out of jail on bail *(Kaution)* – 11 **dropped charges** end of legal accusations – 12 **small-time offender** person who is charged with petty (small) crimes – 13 **punitive** *(adj)* used as a punishment – 26 **to take a toll on** *here:* to cause damage to

he thought of the child-man, and heard his screams. Under any normal circumstances he would have leapt to the defense of a man victimized as that man had been. But that he had to watch, helpless, knowing how depraved it was — this was punishment for the other prisoners, too. It diminished the humanity of them all.

THURSDAY SEPTEMBER 8

Zeitoun woke to screams and curses. He had somehow managed to doze off in the early hours, while draped over the steel rack. He stood and saw that down the line of cages, more prisoners were being sprayed.

Now the guards were shooting the pepper spray through the fencing. They didn't bother removing the prisoners from their cages. The tactic lessened the individual dosages, but spread the gas all over the complex. After Zeitoun and Nasser prayed, they and the rest of the prisoners spent the morning shielding their eyes and mouths with their shirts, coughing through the poison.

The splinter in Zeitoun's foot was now infected. It had darkened to a dull blue overnight, and he could no longer put any weight on it. He had seen his workers, most of whom were uninsured and afraid to register at a hospital, ignore their injuries. Broken fingers went unset, horrible cuts went untreated and led to all manner of sickness. Zeitoun had no idea what kind of object was lodged inside him, but knew he needed to take it out as soon as possible. All he needed was a moment of attention, a sterile needle, a knife even. Anything to carve into the foot and remove whatever was lodged inside.

The pain was intense, and Zeitoun's cage mates tried to help, to come up with a solution — anything sharp to use on it. But none of them had even a set of keys.

4 **depraved** immoral, unjust, terrible – 5 **to diminish** to reduce

Minutes later, a man emerged from the station and came toward him. He was wearing green hospital scrubs and had a stethoscope around his neck. He was portly, with a kind face and a ducklike walk. The relief Zeitoun felt in the seconds he saw him approach was beyond measure.

"Doctor!" Zeitoun called.

The man did not break stride. "I'm not a doctor," he said, and continued on.

Breakfast again was MREs, an omelet filled with bacon, and again Zeitoun and Nasser gave their pork to Todd and Ronnie. But there was something new to the breakfast this day, Tabasco, and Zeitoun had an idea. He took the small bottle and slammed it on the cement, breaking it into shards and blades. He took the sharpest piece and cut into the swollen area of his foot, releasing far more fluid — clear, then white, then red — than he thought possible. Then he cut through to the dark object lodged inside, and after soaking his foot in blood, he pried it out. It was a metal sliver, the size of a toothpick.

He wrapped his foot in all the extra paper napkins in the cage, and the relief was immediate.

Throughout the day there were more pepper sprayings, both individual treatments and more indiscriminate ones. In the late afternoon one of the guards brought out a thick-barreled gun and shot it into one of the cages. Zeitoun thought a man had been killed until he saw that the gun was shooting not bullets but beanbags. The victim writhed on the ground, holding his stomach. From then on, the beanbag gun became a favorite weapon for submission. The guards alternated between the pepper spray and the beanbag gun, shooting the men and women in the cages.

2 **scrubs** clothing that a surgeon wears during an operation – 3 **portly** corpulent – 7 **to break stride** to stop walking – 12 **Tabasco** hot, spicy sauce – 23 **indiscriminate** general, random

Jerry continued to engage Zeitoun and Nasser in conversation. He was pointedly uninterested in Todd and Ronnie. He asked Zeitoun more about his heritage, about Syria, about his career, about his visits back home. He churned through the same line of questioning with Nasser, always disguising it with good cheer and innocent curiosity. Nasser, reticent by nature, withdrew almost completely. Zeitoun tried to brush off the questions, feigning exhaustion. The presence of Jerry grew more unsettling by the day.

Who was he? Why, when there were almost one hundred prisoners elsewhere in the complex, was he in their cage? Todd would later insist that he had been a spy, a plant — meant to glean information from the Syrians in the cage. Of course he was undercover, Todd said. But if this were true, Zeitoun thought, he was a very dedicated public servant. He ate outside in the cage, and when night fell and the air cooled, he slept as Zeitoun's cage mates slept, without blankets or pillows, on the filthy ground.

That night, when it was his turn to lie over the guardrail in the cage, Zeitoun tried to do so comfortably but could not. There was a new pain in his side, coming from the area of his right kidney. The pain was sharp when he tried to drape himself over the steel rail, and when he stood in place it dulled but remained. It was yet another thing to think about, another reason he would not find rest this night.

FRIDAY SEPTEMBER 9

At midday, Zeitoun and the cage mates were told they would be moving out of Camp Greyhound. A series of school buses pulled into the far area of the lot.

Zeitoun was removed from his cage, handcuffed, and pushed toward one of the buses. He was lined up and then

7 **reticent** ['reţɪsənt] reserved – 8 **to feign** [feɪn] to pretend – 22 **kidney** inner organ *(Niere)*

handcuffed to another prisoner, a man in his sixties. It was a simple school bus, decades old. Zeitoun and his companion were told to board. They shuffled up the steps, past the armed driver and a handful of armed guards, and sat down. Todd, Nasser, and Ronnie, all paired with new men, were brought onto the bus. None of the fifty prisoners onboard were told where they were going. Zeitoun looked for Jerry, but he was no longer with them. He was gone.

They drove out of the city, heading north. Zeitoun and the man to whom he was handcuffed did not talk. Few prisoners spoke. Some seemed to know where the bus was heading. Others could not imagine what was next. Still others seemed content that finally they were out of the bus station, that it could not possibly get worse.

They left the city and Zeitoun saw the first expanse of dry land he'd witnessed since the storm. It reminded him of reaching port after a long trip at sea; the temptation was to leap from the ship and dance and run on the solid and limitless earth.

Forty miles on, Zeitoun saw a sign on the highway indicating that they were approaching the town of St. Gabriel. He took this as a positive sign, or a darkly comic one. In Islam, the archangel Gabriel, the same Gabriel who in the Bible spoke to the Virgin Mary and foretold the birth of Jesus, is believed to be the messenger who revealed the Qur'an to the Prophet Muhammad. In the Qur'an, Gabriel is described as having six hundred wings, and is assumed to have accompanied Muhammad when he ascended to the heavens.

The bus slowed at what at first looked like a country club. There was a vast green lawn enclosed by a white fence, the kind typically surrounding a horse ranch. The bus turned and passed through a gate of red brick. On the entranceway Zeitoun saw a sign confirming where they were: the ELAYN

Hunt Correctional Center. It was a maximum security prison. Most of the men on the bus seemed unsurprised. The silence was absolute.

They made their way down a long driveway lined with tidy trees. White birds scattered as they approached another gate, this one resembling a highway tollbooth. A guard waved the bus through, and soon they arrived within the prison grounds.

Hunt Correctional Center was a complex of one-story red-brick buildings laid out across an immaculate green campus. Everything was arranged in orderly grids. The fences, and the barbed wire atop them, gleamed in the sun. The grass was bright and newly cut. Sprinklers ticked and spun in the distance.

The prisoners were processed one by one, at tables placed outside. Zeitoun's entrance interview was brief and his hosts were polite. Two women asked him about his health, any medications he was using, his food restrictions. He was struck by how professional and respectful they were. It occurred to him that this level of professionalism might mean that standard procedure — a phone call for the accused — would be observed, and he would be free within a day or two. At the very least, Kathy would know he was alive. That was all that mattered.

They were brought into a changing room and told to strip naked. Zeitoun did so, in the company of a dozen other men, and with such numbers he did not fear strip searches or violence. He removed his shirt, shorts, and underwear, and they were taken away by prison workers.

1 **correctional center** prison

He and the other prisoners were given orange short-sleeved jumpsuits. They were not given underwear. Zeitoun stepped into the jumpsuit, zipped it up, and put his shoes back on.

They were put back on a bus and driven through the prison complex — an array of geometrically arranged buildings with blue roofs. The bus stopped at what seemed to be the last prison block, in what was evidently the highest-security section of the prison.

Zeitoun and the others on the bus were led into one of the long cell-blocks. He was brought down a long concrete hallway and then directed into a cell. It was no more than six feet by eight feet, meant for one prisoner. Nasser was inside already. The door closed. The bars were baby blue.

The cell was constructed entirely from cement. The toilet was molded from cement and placed in the center of the cell. The bed, on the side of the room, was made of cement, with a rubber mattress atop it. On the back wall there was a small window covered in thick Plexiglas. A vague white square was visible, presumably the sky.

Zeitoun and Nasser barely spoke. There was nothing to say. They both knew their predicament had just taken a far more serious turn. The two Syrian Americans had been isolated. When they had been caged with Todd and Ronnie, it seemed possible that the charges against them — whenever they were actually leveled — might be limited to looting. But now the two Syrians had been separated from the Americans, and there was no predicting where this would go.

Zeitoun remained certain that one phone call would free him. He was a successful and well-known man. His name was known all over the city of New Orleans. He only needed to reach Kathy and she would knock down every wall to get to him.

All day Zeitoun made it his business to sit by the bars, waving a napkin, pleading with the guards to grant him a call.

The guards seemed to relish concocting variations of their denials.

"Phone's broken," they would say.

"Not today."

"Lines are down."

"Maybe tomorrow."

"What'll you do for me?"

"Not my problem. You're not our prisoner."

This was the first but not the last time Zeitoun would hear this. He had not been processed in a traditional way, and was not assigned to Hunt for the long term. Therefore he was not technically a Hunt prisoner, and so was not bound by the institution's standard operating procedure. This was what Zeitoun was told many times by the guards:

"You're FEMA's problem."

FEMA was footing the bill for his incarceration, they said, and that of all the other prisoners from New Orleans. The Elayn Hunt Correctional Center was renting space to warehouse these men, but otherwise made no claims to their welfare or rights.

The night came but was barely distinguishable from the day. The lights were out by ten, but the prison was full of voices. Prisoners talked, laughed, screamed. There were various unidentifiable sounds coming from all corners. Smacking, grunting. The smoke seemed to increase as the night went on. The smells were rancid—cigarettes, marijuana, old food, sweat, decay.

The pain in Zeitoun's side had gotten worse. It was a throbbing ache, as if his kidney were inflamed. He never overworried about any such problems, but what if Kathy had been right, that toxins in New Orleans had found their way

1 **to relish** to enjoy – 1 **to concoct** *here:* to produce, invent – 2 **denial** [dɪˈnaɪəl] refusal – 16 **to foot the bill** to be responsible; to pay – 27 **decay** *here*: rotting

into his body? Or perhaps it was the pepper spray at Greyhound — he had surely inhaled enough of the gas to cause some internal reaction.

But he dismissed the pain. He could think only of Kathy. It had now been four days since she had heard from him. He could not imagine her suffering. Where would his mind be if she went missing for four days? He hoped she had not told the children. He hoped she had not told anyone. He hoped she had found comfort in God. God had a plan, he was certain.

In the early hours, Zeitoun, weakened by lack of sleep and food and the grim nothingness of his surroundings, recalled the passage of the Qur'an called *al-Takwir*, or "The Darkening":

In the Name of God
The Merciful, The Compassionate
When the sun is darkening,
when the stars plunge down,
when the mountains have been set in motion,
when the pregnant camels have been ignored,
when the savage beasts
have been assembled together,
when the seas have been caused to overflow,
when the souls have been mated,
when the buried infant girl has been asked
for what impiety she was slain,
when the scrolls have been unfolded
when the heaven has been stripped off,
when hellfire has been caused to burn fiercely,
when the Garden has been brought close,
every soul shall know to what it is prone.
So no! I swear an oath by the stars that recede,

25 **impiety** lack of respect and belief – 25 **to slay, slew, slain** to kill – 26 **scroll** roll of papyrus (old form of paper) – 30 **to what it is prone** *(old)* what it deserves – 31 **to recede** to go back *(zurückweichen)*

by the ones that run, the setting stars
by the night, when it swarms,
by the morning, when it sighs,
truly that is the saying of a generous Messenger,
possessed of strength,
secure with the Possessor of the Throne,
one who is obeyed and trustworthy.
Your companion is not one who is possessed.

SATURDAY SEPTEMBER 10

Again Zeitoun had not slept. The night before, the fluorescent lights above had been turned off at ten p.m., and had come on at three in the morning. In this prison, three o'clock was considered the beginning of the day.

After he and Nasser prayed, Zeitoun tried to exercise inside the cell. His foot was still raw, but he jogged in place. He did push-ups, jumping jacks. The pain in his side, though, only increased with the activity. He stopped.

Breakfast was sausage, which he could not eat, and scrambled eggs, which were nearly inedible. He took a few bites and drank the juice provided. He and Nasser sat on the bed, side by side, barely talking. The only thing on Zeitoun's mind was making a phone call. There was nothing else in the world.

He heard the guard coming down the hallway, picking up the breakfast trays. As soon as the footsteps were close enough, Zeitoun leapt up to the front gate. The guard jumped back a step, startled by Zeitoun's sudden appearance.

"Please," he said, "one phone call?"

The guard ignored the question and instead looked around Zeitoun to Nasser, who was still sitting on the bed. The guard gave Zeitoun a quizzical eye and moved on to the next cell.

27 **startled** suprised

An hour later, Zeitoun heard the guard's footsteps again, and again Zeitoun rose up to meet him as he passed the gate. "Please, can I make a call?" he asked. "Just to my wife."

This time the guard issued a cursory shake of the head before peering around Zeitoun to see Nasser, who again was sitting on the bed. Now the look the guard gave Zeitoun was suggestive, even lewd. He raised his eyebrows and nodded over to Nasser. He was implying that Zeitoun and Nasser were romantically engaged, and that Zeitoun, fearing detection, had leapt from the bed when he heard the guard approaching.

By the time Zeitoun realized what the guard was implying, it was too late to argue. The guard was gone, down the hall. But this implication, that Zeitoun was bisexual, that he would betray his wife, so enraged him that he could barely contain himself.

At midday, Zeitoun was taken out of his cell. He was brought to a small office, where a prison guard stood next to a digital camera. He instructed Zeitoun to sit down on a plastic chair. As Zeitoun waited for the next command, the photographer squinted at him and cocked his head.

"You eyeballing me?" he yelled.

Zeitoun said nothing.

"Why the fuck you eyeballing me?"the photographer yelled. He went on about how difficult he could make Zeitoun's stay at Hunt, that a man with an attitude like that would not last long. Zeitoun had no idea what he had done to provoke the man. He was still cursing as Zeitoun was led out of the room and returned to his cell.

In the late afternoon, Zeitoun again heard footsteps coming down the hallway. He went to the front of the cell and there he

7 **suggestive** *here:* suggesting sex – 7 **lewd** suggesting lust – 22 **to eyeball** to stare

saw the same guard. "What are you two doing in there?" the guard asked. "What are you saying?" Zeitoun hissed. He had never been so angry. "You can't do that kind of thing in your cell, buddy," the guard said. "I thought that was against your religion anyway."

That was it for Zeitoun. He let loose a barrage of expletives and threats to the guard. He didn't care what happened.

The guard seemed shocked. "You really talking to me that way? You know what I can do to you?"

Zeitoun was finished. He went to the back of the cell and folded his arms. If he were any closer, he would be too tempted to throw himself against the bars, grabbing for any part of the guard's flesh.

SUNDAY SEPTEMBER 11

In the morning the door was opened and four men were added to their cell. All four were African American, between thirty and forty-five. Zeitoun and Nasser nodded to them in greeting, and with a quick choreography about who would sit where, the new residents found places in the tiny cell. Three men sat width-wise on the bed, and three on the floor, against the wall. Cramped and soaked in sweat, they rotated every hour.

Zeitoun no longer harbored any expectations of being granted a phone call from any of the guards he had seen thus far. He pinned his hopes on seeing a new guard, a new employee of the prison, some visitor. He had no idea how the prison worked, how any prison worked. But he had seen movies where lawyers walked the cellblocks, where visitors passed through. He needed to find someone like that. Any one person from the world outside — someone who might grant one small mercy.

6 **barrage of expletives** [bəˈrɑːʒ] a number of vulgar curses – 20 **width-wise** along the width of the bed (therefore very squashed together, because there was no room in there)

The men in the cell told each other how they had ended up at Hunt. All had been picked up in New Orleans after the storm. This entire wing of the prison, they said, held Katrina prisoners. "We're all FEMA," one said. Two of the men had been arrested for moving furniture, in situations not unlike Zeitoun's.

One man said he was a sanitation worker from Houston. His company had been contracted shortly after the storm to come in and begin the cleanup. One morning he was walking from the hotel to his truck when a National Guard truck pulled up. He was arrested on the spot, handcuffed, and brought to Camp Greyhound.

It was his first time behind bars, and of all the prisoners doing "Katrina time," as they'd termed it, he was the most perplexed by it all. He had, after all, come to New Orleans at the behest of his company. He usually picked up garbage in Houston, but after the hurricane, his supervisor said they had taken a contract in New Orleans. This prisoner, thinking it would be interesting to see what had become of the city and wanting to help in its cleanup, went willingly. He was in uniform, and had identification, the keys to his truck, everything. But nothing worked. He was charged with looting and put in the cages behind the bus station.

Another of the cellmates said he was a fireman in New Orleans. He stayed after the storm, just as he had been asked to stay. He was in his yard when he was picked up by a passing Humvee. They charged him with looting, loaded him into the back, and brought him to Greyhound.

Zeitoun learned that most of those brought to Camp Greyhound had been arraigned in a more or less standard

13 **to do time** *(inf)* to be in prison – 15 **at the behest** on behalf of *(im Auftrag von)* – 30 **to arraign** to take sb to court and formally accuse them of a crime

fashion. Most had been brought inside the bus station the morning after their arrest, and in an upstairs office, a makeshift court had been arranged. There had been a judge, and at least one lawyer. The arrestees were told their charges, and most of them were offered a deal: if they didn't contest the charges, they would be given a misdemeanor conviction and would be required to perform community-service hours, starting immediately. Some of those who took the bargain — thus accepting the permanent strike on their record — were promptly brought to the police station downtown, where they began repairing and repainting the damaged offices.

The stabbing pain in his side, which Zeitoun had first felt at Greyhound, had now amplified tenfold. It felt like a long screw was being twisted, slowly, into his kidney. It was difficult to sit, to stand, to lay down. Whenever he switched positions, he would find relief for five minutes before the pain returned. He was not one to worry about such things. He had had so many injuries over the years and rarely sought treatment. But this felt different. He thought of infections, the many diseases Kathy had mentioned when trying to get him to leave the city. He needed to find help.

There was a nurse who came through the cellblock once a day, pushing a cart full of medicine, handing pills to the prisoners.

Zeitoun stopped her as she wheeled by. He told her about the pain.

"Do you have a prescription?" she asked.

He told her no, that the pain was new.

"Then you need to see the doctor," she said.

He asked how he could see the doctor.

3 **makeshift** temporary – 5 **to contest** to question, deny, fight against – 6 **misdemeanor** [ˌmɪsdɪˈmiːnɚ] a less serious offense, not a crime *(Vergehen)* – 9 **strike on their record** i.e. they would forever be a "criminal" *(Eintrag in die Akte)* – 13 **to amplify tenfold** to increase ten times

She told him to fill out a form describing his pain. The doctor would look at the form and then decide if Zeitoun needed attention. The nurse handed him the form and wheeled her cart down the hall.

Zeitoun filled out the form, and when she came back on her way out, he handed it to her.

After dinner Zeitoun's cellmates shared the stories they had heard from the other prisoners they'd encountered. The prisoners who had arrived at Hunt during the first days after the storm had lived through conditions beyond comprehension.

The thousands from Orleans Parish Prison, including those who were in jail for public intoxication, shoplifting, and other misdemeanors, had been left on the city's Broad Street overpass for three days. They'd been on television, a sea of men in orange sitting on a roadway filthy with feces and garbage, surrounded by guards with automatic rifles.

When buses finally arrived, the prisoners were taken to Hunt. Instead of being housed inside the prison, they were brought to the football stadium on the property. There they were held for days more, outside, without any kind of shelter. Thousands of prisoners, from murderers and rapists to DUIs and petty thieves, were thrown together on the stadium grass.

There were no bathrooms. The prisoners urinated and defecated wherever they could. There were no pillows, sheets, sleeping bags, or dry clothing. The men were given one thin blanket each. The area on which Hunt had been built was marshland, and the ground grew wet during the night. The men slept on the mud, with no protection against the elements, bugs, or each other. There were multiple stabbings. Men fought over blankets.

16 **feces** excrement – 22 **DUI** person who drives under the influence (of alcohol or drugs) – 23 **petty thief** sb who commits small crimes of theft *(kleinkrimineller Dieb)*

Water was received through two small pipes extending from the grass. The men had to wait their turn and then drink from their hands. For sustenance, prison guards took sandwiches, fashioned them into balls, and threw them over the wall of the stadium and onto the field. Whoever caught one ate. Whoever could defend themselves ate. Many did not eat at all.

None of the men in Zeitoun's cell knew whether or not these prisoners were still on the football field, or what had become of them.

MONDAY SEPTEMBER 12

In the morning, the other four men were removed from the cell, and Zeitoun and Nasser were alone again. They had nothing to do but wait for any new face, anyone who might lead to recognition from the outside world that they existed here.

The boredom was profound. They had been given no books, no paper, no radio. The two men could only stare at the grey walls, the black floor, at the baby blue bars, or at each other. But they feared talking too much.

They assumed they were being monitored in some way. If a spy, Jerry, could be planted with them in an outdoor cage, it would be unsurprising if their conversations were being monitored here, in a maximum security prison.

Zeitoun sat against the bed and closed his eyes. He wanted only to pass these days.

He recounted their arrest, and the hours and days before it, countless times, trying to figure out what had brought such attention to them. Was it simply that four men were occupying one house? Such a thing, after a hurricane, when most of the

3 **sustenance** food – 17 **profound** deep

city had been evacuated, was worthy of investigation, he conceded. But there had been no investigation. There had been no questions, no evidence seized, no charges leveled.

Kathy often worried about the National Guard and other soldiers returning to the United States after time in Iraq and Afghanistan. She warned him about passing groups of soldiers in airports, about walking near National Guard offices. "They're trained to kill people like you," she would say to Zeitoun, only half-joking. She had not wanted their family to become collateral damage in a war that had no discernible fronts, no real shape, and no rules.

Almost twenty years earlier, he had been working on a tanker called the *Andromeda*. They had just brought Kuwaiti oil to Japan, and were returning to Kuwait for more. This was 1987, and Iran and Iraq were in the midst of their long and crippling war. Most of their own refineries had been destroyed during the fighting, so both nations had come to rely on imported oil, and routinely tried to blockade or damage any ships bringing oil to their enemy via the Straight of Hormuz. Zeitoun and his shipmates knew that entering the Gulf of Oman, en route to the Persian Gulf, meant risking the wrath of Iraqi or Iranian submarines and warships. The seamen were paid extra for the risk.

Zeitoun's bunk was over the fuel tanks, and he was asleep one early morning when he was jolted by an explosion below. He didn't know if it was one of the tanks, or if the ship had struck something. He quickly realized that if the tank had exploded, he would be dead, so they must have hit something, or had something hit them. He was rushing to the bridge to find out when another explosion shook the ship.

2 **to concede** to acknowledge reluctantly *(zugeben)* – 10 **collateral damage** damage that happens by chance (in the crossfire of another situation) – 10 **discernible** recognizable – 16 **refinery** industrial plant where crude oil is turned into petrol – 24 **bunk** bed in a ship

They had been struck twice by Iranian torpedoes. Together they created a hole big enough to drive a small motorboat through. But it was clear the Iranians didn't mean to sink the tanker. If they had wanted to, that would have been quite easy. They wanted only to send a warning, and to cripple the ship.

They managed to make it to Addan, and there they spent a month repairing the hull. While waiting to ship out again, Zeitoun decided that perhaps his father Mahmoud had been right. It was time to settle somewhere, time to build a family, to remain safe and constant, on land. A few months later, he got off the *Andromeda* in Houston and began searching for Kathy.

TUESDAY SEPTEMBER 13

Zeitoun and Nasser did not discuss the possibility that they would not be released from this prison for many months, or even years. But they were both thinking it — that no one knew where they were, which afforded the authorities, whoever it was who wanted them kept here, complete and unchecked power to keep them detained and hidden indefinitely.

Zeitoun could think of no indication so far that any measure could be taken to advance his case. He had not been allowed to make a phone call, and there was no hint that he would ever be allowed to do so. He'd had no contact with anyone from outside. There was the nurse, but she was a full-time employee of the prison. Professing his innocence to her was futile, as professions of innocence were likely all she heard all day. In fact, he knew that his very presence in a maximum-security prison likely proved his guilt in the minds of all who worked at the facility. The guards were used to overseeing men who had been convicted at trial.

Further, the prison was so isolated that there was no oversight whatsoever, no civilians who came to check on

20 **indefinitely** endlessly – 26 **futile** pointless, in vain – 31 **to convict at trial** to be found guilty in court *(bei einem Prozess überführen)*

conditions. He had not been let out of the cellblock once, and had been let out of the cell only to shower; the shower itself had bars. If they had refused him a phone call for seven days now, why would they change their policy in the future?

He had one hope, which was to impart his name and innocence to every prisoner he might meet, so that in the event that one of them was someday released they might not only remember his name, but also bother to call Kathy or tell someone where he was. But again, who among them would believe he was one of the true innocents in the prison? How many other names and promises had they known and made?

When he was originally arrested, Zeitoun had not been sure his country of origin had anything to do with his capture. After all, two of the four men in their group were white Americans born in New Orleans. But the arrest had taken on an entirely different cast by the time they were brought to Camp Greyhound. And though he was loath to make this leap, was it so improbable that he, like so many others, might be taken to an undisclosed location — to one of the secret prisons abroad? To Guantanamo Bay?

He was not the sort to fear such things. He was not given to conspiracy theories or believing that the U.S. government willfully committed human rights violations. But it seemed every month another story appeared about a native of Iran, Saudi Arabia, Libya, Syria, or any one of a number of other Muslim countries who was released after months or years from one of these detention centers. Usually the story was similar: a Muslim man came to be suspected by the U.S. government, and, under the president's current powers, U.S. agents were allowed to seize the man from anywhere in the

5 **to impart** to make known – 16 **entirely** totally – 16 **cast** *here:* feeling, image (his arrest felt completely different now: much more serious) – 17 **to be loath to do sth** to not want to do sth because it is too terrible – 17 **to make a leap** *here:* to draw a conclusion – 19 **undisclosed** secret

world and bring him anywhere in the world, without ever having to charge him with a crime.

How different was Zeitoun's current situation? He was being held without contact, charges, bail, or trial. Would it not behoove the Department of Homeland Security to add a name to their roster of dangerous individuals? In the minds of some Americans, the very thought of two Syrians paddling through New Orleans together after a hurricane would seem suspicious enough. Even the most amateur propagandist could conjure sinister implications.

Zeitoun did not entertain such thoughts lightly. They went against everything he knew and believed about his adopted country. But then again, he knew the stories. Professors, doctors, and engineers had all been seized and disappeared for months and years in the interest of national security.

Why not a house painter?

WEDNESDAY SEPTEMBER 14

The pain in Zeitoun's side was overtaking him. While standing or sitting in certain positions, he could barely breathe. He had to get help.

When he heard the nurse's cart making its way down the cellblock, he jumped up to meet her at the bars.

"Did you give the doctor my form?" he asked her.

She said she did, and that she would hear back soon.

"You look sick," Nasser said.

"I know," Zeitoun said.

"You've lost too much weight."

"The pain. It's so bad now."

Zeitoun had a sudden and strange thought, that the pain in his side could be caused not by infection or injury, but by sorrow. Maybe there wasn't a medical reason for it. Maybe it

5 **to behoove** *(AE)* to suit, be good for – 6 **roster** list – 9 **to conjure sinister implications** to invent evil stories – 31 **sorrow** suffering, despair

was just the manifestation of his anger and sadness and helplessness. He did not want any of this to be true. He did not want it to be true that his home and his city were underwater. He did not want it to be true that his wife and children were fifteen hundred miles away and might by now presume him to be dead. He did not want it to be true that he was now and might always be a man in a cage, hidden away, no longer part of the world.

<u>THURSDAY SEPTEMBER 15</u>

Now Zeitoun knew the rhythmic ticking of the nurse's cart like his own heartbeat. He leapt to the bars again to meet her.

"What did the doctor say?" he asked.

"About what?" she said.

"About my condition," he said. "You gave him the form."

"Oh, you know, I don't think he got it. You better fill it out again," she said, and handed him another form.

He did not see her again that day or the next.

Zeitoun began to feel faint when he rose to his feet. He was not eating enough. It seemed that every meal had pork at its center. And even when he could eat what was offered, he was often too agitated or despondent to do so.

After lunch three guards arrived. The gate to the cell opened, and they entered. Zeitoun was handcuffed and his legs were shackled, and he was led out from the cell. He was walked to another building, and was put into another, empty cell. Now he was alone.

He and Nasser had not spoken much, but the contrast in being alone was stark.

Zeitoun tried to remember how much his life insurance policy was worth. He should have bought a larger one. He had

22 **agitated** upset – 22 **despondent** sad, depressed – 25 **to shackle** to put in chains

not thought hard enough about it. The woman at Allstate had tried to convince him to insure his life for more than a million dollars, given that he had four children, and how much the business relied on him. But he could not envision his death. He was only forty-seven. Too early to contemplate life insurance. But he knew that by now Kathy would have checked the value of the policy. She would have begun to imagine a life without him.

When he pictured his wife having to make such plans, presuming him to be dead, his heart raged. He had wrathful thoughts about the police who had arrested him, the jailors who kept him here, the system that allowed this. He blamed Ronnie, the stranger who had come to the house on Claiborne, whom he didn't know and couldn't account for — whose presence might very well have brought suspicion upon all of them. Maybe Ronnie *was* guilty, maybe he *had* done something wrong. He cursed Nasser's bag of cash. What a fool! He should never have been carrying around money like that.

Kathy. Zachary. The girls. The girls might grow up without a father. If Zeitoun was transferred to a secret prison, their lives would be reversed completely: they would go from the well-off children of a successful man to the disgraced children of a presumptive sleeper-cell mastermind.

And even if he got out tomorrow or next week, their father had now been in prison. The scarring was inevitable — to live in fear of their father's death, and then to find out he had been taken to prison at gunpoint, made a prisoner, made to live like a rat?

He clutched his side, pushing back at the pain, trying to contain it.

1 **Allstate** large insurance company – 22 **to reverse** to turn around – 30 **to clutch** to hold tightly – 31 **to contain** to keep within limits

FRIDAY SEPTEMBER 16

The news came down to the prisoners that after lunch they would be allowed to go outside. It had been a week since Zeitoun had seen the sun.

During the hour they were allowed in the yard, Zeitoun tried to jog, but felt light-headed. He walked around the yard, overhearing one bewildered story after another.

He met a man who said he had been moving furniture in his house just after the storm hit. The police spotted him and broke in. When he protested his innocence, they beat him up and left. A few days later, he came to the Greyhound station to complain. They arrested him and sent him to Hunt.

No story was more absurd than the tale of Merlene Maten. One of the prisoners had just seen her story on TV. She had been held next door, at Hunt's sister prison for women.

Maten was seventy-three years old, a diabetic, and a deaconess at the Resurrection Mission Baptist Church. Before the storm, she and her husband, who was eighty, had checked into a hotel downtown, knowing that there they would be among other residents and guests. They would have access to help if they needed it, and would be safer, given that the hotel was on high ground. They drove to the hotel in their car and paid for the room with their credit card.

They had been at the hotel for three days when Maten went downstairs to get some food from their car. Mayor Nagin had told everyone in the city to have three days' food on hand, and she had duly packed enough into the car to last. The car was parked in the lot next to the hotel, and Maten had left a cooler inside, full of the foods her husband liked. She retrieved a package of sausages and was walking back to the hotel when she heard yelling and footsteps. It was the police, and they accused her of looting a nearby store.

17 **deaconess** Protestant woman who assists the minister of a church – 27 **duly** properly, obediently

The nearby Check In Check Out deli had just been looted, and the police were looking for anyone who might have benefited. They found Maten. She was handcuffed and charged with stealing $63.50 worth of groceries. Her bail was set, by a judge calling by phone, at $50,000. The usual bail for such a misdemeanor would be $500.

She was brought to Camp Greyhound, where she slept on the concrete. Then she was brought to the Louisiana Correctional Institute for Women, Hunt's sister prison, for more than two weeks. She was finally freed with the help of the AARP, volunteer lawyers, a private attorney, and an article about her plight published by the Associated Press.

The lawyers finally convinced a judge that a septuagenarian staying at a hotel would not need to loot a store for sausages. They proved that the store did not even sell the sausages she was carrying. Maten had never been in the store. Furthermore, to even enter the damaged store, strewn everywhere with debris and broken glass, would have required an agility that she did not possess.

In the late afternoon Zeitoun heard a group of guards enter the cellblock. He couldn't see them, but it sounded like at least four or five men. A cell down the hall rattled open. The guards yelled and cursed, and there was some kind of scuffle. Then quiet for a few minutes, and then the cell closed shut again. The process repeated itself half a dozen times.

Then it was his turn. First he saw their faces, five men on the other side of the blue bars. He had seen one of the guards before, but the other four were strangers. They were all wearing black riot gear, dressed like a SWAT team. They had shields, padding, batons, helmets. They waited at the ready for the door to open.

4 **bail** sum of money one pays for sb's release from prison *(Lösegeld)* – 11 **attorney** [əˈtɜːrni] lawyer – 13 **septuagenarian** [ˌseptuədʒəˈneriən] person who is over 70 years old but not yet 80 – 23 **scuffle** fight – 29 **riot gear** uniforms and equipment for use in a riot *(Ausschreitungen)* – 30 **padding** body protection – 30 **at the ready** prepared for anything

Zeitoun was determined not to struggle. He would not present any appearance of opposition. When the cell door slid open, he stood in the center of the floor, his hands in the air, his eyes level.

But still the men burst in as if he were in the process of committing a murder. Cursing at him, three men used their shields to push him to the wall. As they pressed his face against the cinderblock, they handcuffed his arms and shackled his legs.

They brought him into the hallway. Three guards held him while the other two ransacked the cell. They threw open the bedding, overturned the mattress, scoured the tiny room.

Two of the guards unlocked Zeitoun's handcuffs and shackles.

"Take off your clothes," one said.

He hesitated. He had not been given underwear when he arrived at Hunt, so if he took off his jumpsuit he would be naked.

"Now," the guard said.

Zeitoun unzipped the jumpsuit and pulled it off his shoulders. It dropped to his waist, and he pushed it to the floor. He was surrounded by three men fully dressed in black riot gear. He tried to cover himself. "Bend over," the guard said. Again he hesitated. "Do it."

Zeitoun complied.

"Farther," the guard said. "Grab ankles."

Zeitoun could not tell who was inspecting him or how. He expected something to enter his rectum at any moment. "Okay, get up," the guard said. They had spared him this one indignity.

Zeitoun stood. The guard used his foot to slide Zeitoun's jumpsuit back into the cell, and then pushed Zeitoun in, too. While Zeitoun was putting on his clothes, they backed away from him, shields up, and out of the cell.

11 **to ransack** to search in a violent way – 12 **to scour** [skaʊə˞] to search every last piece of sth

Zeitoun's door closed, and the guards assembled themselves at the next cell, ready for the next prisoner.

From the other prisoners Zeitoun learned that these searches were common. The guards were looking for drugs, weapons, any contraband. He should expect such a procedure every week.

SATURDAY SEPTEMBER 17

Zeitoun lay in bed much of the day, wrecked by fatigue. He had not slept. He had run the strip-search through his mind most of the night, trying to erase all memory of it, but every time he closed his eyes he saw the men in their riot gear, at the other side of the cell door, waiting to flood in and take him.

For weeks, it seemed, he had been stealing hours of sleep during the day, a few at night. He could not remember the last time he had strung more than three hours of rest together.

Why had he done this to his family? There was something broken in the country, this was certain, but he had begun all this. He had refused to leave the city. He had stayed to guard his property, to watch over his business. But then something else had overtaken him, some sense of destiny. Some sense that God had put him there to do His work, to glorify Him with good deeds.

It seemed ridiculous now. How could he have been guilty of such hubris? He had put himself in harm's way, and by doing so had put his family in danger. How could he not have known that staying in New Orleans, a city under something like martial law, would endanger him? He knew better. He had been careful for so many years. He had kept his head low. He had been a model citizen. But in the wake of the storm, he'd

10 **to erase** to get rid of – 24 **hubris** ['hju:brɪs] (too much) pride – 27 **martial law** temporary rule by military authorities in times of war

come to believe he was meant to help the stranded. He believed that that damned canoe had given him the right to serve as shepherd and savior. He had lost perspective.

He had expected too much. He had hoped too much.

The country he had left thirty years ago had been a realistic place. There were political realities there, then and now, that precluded blind faith, that discouraged one from thinking that everything, always, would work out fairly and equitably. But he had come to believe such things in the United States. Things had worked out. Difficulties had been overcome. He had worked hard and achieved success. The machinery of government functioned. Even if in New Orleans this machinery was sometimes slow, or poorly engineered, generally it functioned.

But now nothing worked. Or rather, every piece of machinery — the police, the military, the prisons — that was meant to protect people like him was devouring anyone who got close. He had long believed that the police acted in the best interests of the citizens they served. That the military was accountable, reasonable, and was kept in check by concentric circles of regulations, laws, common sense, common decency.

But now those hopes could be put to rest.

This country was not unique. This country was fallible. Mistakes were being made. He was a mistake. In the grand scheme of the country's blind, grasping fight against threats seen and unseen, there would be mistakes made. Innocents would be suspected. Innocents would be imprisoned.

He thought of bycatch. It was a fishing term. They'd used it when he was a boy, fishing for sardines by the light of the moon they'd made. When they pulled in the net, there were thousands of sardines, of course, but there were other

7 **to preclude** to exclude *(ausschließen)* – 8 **equitable** just – 19 **accountable** having to justify its actions to a higher authority – 21 **decency** good behavior *(Anstand)*

creatures too, life they had not intended to catch and for which they had no use.

Often they would not know until too late. They would bring their catch back to shore, a mound of silver, the sardines dying slowly. Zeitoun, exhausted, would rest against the bow, watching the fish slowly cease their struggles. And once on shore, when the crew unloaded the nets, they would sometimes find something else. One time there was a dolphin. He always remembered this dolphin, a magnificent ivory-white animal shining on the dock like porcelain. The fishermen nudged it with their feet, but it was dead. It had gotten caught in the net and, unable to reach the surface to breathe, it had died underwater. If they had noticed it in time, they could have freed it, but now all they could do was throw it back into the Mediterranean. It would be a meal for the bottom-feeders.

The pain in Zeitoun's side was growing, rippling outward. He could not stay here another week. He would not survive the heartbreak, the wrongness of it.

There was no way to come out of this prison improved. Not the way he was being treated. He had seen parts of Hunt that seemed well-run, clean, efficient. When he first arrived and was being processed, he saw prisoners milling about freely in a grassy courtyard. But he had been confined twenty-three hours a day to his cell, with no distractions, no companionship or beauty. The environment would drive any sane man mad. The grey walls, the blue bars, the strip searches, the showers behind bars watched by guards and cameras. The lack of any mental stimuli. Unable to work, to read or build or improve himself, he would waste away here.

He had risked too much in the hopes that he might do something to match the deeds of his brother Mohammed. No, it had never been a conscious part of his motivation — he had

9 **ivory** *Elfenbein* – 10 **to nudge** to touch

done what he could in the drowned city because he was there, it needed to be done, and he could do it. But somewhere in his gut, was there not some hope that he, too, could bring pride to the family, as Mohammed had so many years ago? Was there not some wish that he might honor his brother, his family, his God, by doing all he could, by circling the city looking for opportunities to do good? And was this imprisonment God's way of curbing his pride, tempering his vainglorious dreams?

As the prisoners awoke, with their rantings and threats, Zeitoun prayed. He prayed for the health of his family. He prayed that they felt at peace. And he prayed for a messenger. All he needed was a messenger, someone to tell his wife that he was alive. Someone to connect him with the part of the world that still worked.

SUNDAY SEPTEMBER 18

Zeitoun had been napping through the morning, dazed and sluggish from the heat. His sweat had soaked through his orange jumpsuit. He heard notice that they would be allowed to walk outside again after lunch, and he wasn't sure he could stand to make it.

He was disappointed in himself. Part of him had given up, and the part that still believed stood apart from the broken half of his soul, incredulous.

The wheels of the nurse's cart echoed down the hallway. He had no reason to think she would help him, but he stood up and made ready to plead with her again. But when he looked down the hall, it was not the nurse, but a man he had never seen before.

He was pushing a cart of black books, and had stopped a few cells away from Zeitoun's. He was talking to whichever prisoners were there, and Zeitoun watched him, unable to

8 **to curb** to limit, keep down – 8 **to temper** to modify – 8 **vainglorious** vain, proud – 18 **sluggish** lazy

hear the conversation. The man was black, in his sixties, and watching him interact with the prisoners down the row, it was clear he was a man of God. The books in his cart were Bibles.

When he finished and passed by Zeitoun's cell, Zeitoun stopped him. "Please, hello," he said.

"Hello," the missionary said. He had almond-shaped eyes, a wide smile. "Would you like to hear about Jesus Christ?"

Zeitoun declined. "Please sir," he said. "Please, I shouldn't be here. I committed no crime. But no one knows I'm here. I haven't gotten a phone call. My wife thinks I'm dead. Can you call her?"

The missionary closed his eyes. It was obvious he often heard things like this.

"Please," Zeitoun said. "I know it's hard to believe a man in a cage, but please. Can I just give you her number?"

Zeitoun could only remember Kathy's cell phone number, and hoped it would work. The missionary looked up and down the cellblock and gave a nod. "Be quick."

"Thank you," Zeitoun said. "Her name is Kathy. My wife. We have four children."

Zeitoun had no pen or paper.

"This is against the rules," the missionary said, finding a pen in his cart. He had no paper. Now they were both nervous. The missionary had been too long at his cell. He opened a Bible and tore a page from the back. Zeitoun gave him the number. The missionary stuffed the page into his pocket and moved his cart quickly down the block.

Hope rose in Zeitoun's heart. He couldn't sit down for hours. He paced, hopped in place, elated. He pictured the missionary leaving the prison, getting to his car, retrieving the number, calling Kathy from the road. Or maybe he would wait till he got home. How long could it take? He counted the minutes until Kathy would know. She would know! He

29 **elated** happy

estimated the hours until Kathy would arrive here to free him. If she knew he was alive, he could wait. The process might take days, he knew. But he could wait if it meant seeing her. It would be no problem. He pictured it all. He would be free in a day.

Zeitoun struggled to sleep that night. There was a man in the world who knew he was alive. He had found his messenger.

MONDAY SEPTEMBER 19

After breakfast two guards came to Zeitoun's cell. They told Zeitoun that his presence was requested.

"Where? With who?" Zeitoun asked. *Already it's begun,* he thought.

The guards told him nothing. They opened his cell, handcuffed him, and shackled his legs together. He was led out of the cell and down the hall. A few minutes later they arrived at another cell, where Zeitoun was deposited. He waited there for five minutes until the door opened again.

"Van's here," the guard said. The guard handed him to another guard, who walked him down another hallway and to a final gate. The gate opened, and Zeitoun was led to a white van waiting outside. He squinted in the full light of day. He was inserted into the van, the guard riding with him. They drove through the complex until they arrived at the main offices at the front of the prison.

Zeitoun was led out of the van and handed over to another guard, who led him into the building. Inside, they walked through an immaculate hallway until they arrived at a spare cinderblock office.

17 **to deposit** to put down (*here:* make him wait) – 28 **immaculate** [ɪˈmækjələt] very clean – 29 **cinderblock office** office built with hollow building blocks

Outside the office were Nasser, Todd, and Ronnie, sitting on folding chairs in the hallway. Zeitoun was surprised to see them all assembled, and they gave each other looks of mutual bewilderment. Zeitoun was led past them and into a small room.

In the room there were two men wearing suits. They sat down and gestured to Zeitoun that he could take a seat. They were from the Department of Homeland Security, they said. They smiled warmly at Zeitoun and told him that they needed to ask him some simple questions. They asked him what he did for a living. He told them that he was a painter and contractor. They asked him why he hadn't left the city when everyone had evacuated. He told them that he never left New Orleans during storms, and that he had a number of properties he wanted to watch over. They asked about Todd, Nasser, and Ronnie — how he knew them. He explained his relationship to each. They asked him why he didn't have any money on him.

"What am I going to do with money in a canoe during a flood?" Zeitoun said.

"But Nasser had money," one of the men said.

Zeitoun shrugged. He could not account for why Nasser had money with him.

The interview lasted less than thirty minutes. Zeitoun was struck by how friendly the men were, how easy the questions were. They did not ask about terrorism. They did not accuse him of plotting against the United States. At the end, they apologized for what Zeitoun had been through, and asked if there was anything they could do for him.

"Please call Kathy," he said.

They said they would.

3 **mutual** common *(gegenseitig)* – 4 **bewilderment** perplexity, confusion

MONDAY SEPTEMBER 19

Kathy was in a state. She'd just gotten the call from the missionary a few hours before. And now the phone was ringing again. Yuko, who had been fielding calls for days, no longer knew what to do. Kathy picked it up.

A man introduced himself as belonging to the Department of Homeland Security. He confirmed that Zeitoun was at the Elayn Hunt Correctional Center.

"He's fine, ma'am. We have no more interest in him."

"You have no more interest in him? Is that good or bad?"

"That's good."

"Well, what was he in there for?"

"Well, they have 'looting' on his arrest sheet. But those charges will be dropped."

The call was brief and businesslike. When she hung up, Kathy praised and thanked God for his mercy. She shrieked and jumped around the house with Yuko.

"I knew he was alive," Yuko said. "I knew it."

"God is good," they said. "God is good."

They called Yuko's husband and made plans to get the kids out of school early. They had to celebrate. And plan. There were so many things to do.

First of all, Kathy had to go. She knew she had to go. She had to leave that day for the prison. She didn't know where it was yet, but she had to go. Where was it? She looked it up online. St. Gabriel, less than an hour from Baton Rouge.

She called Hunt and was bounced around the various automated extensions until she reached a person. She could barely speak. She wanted to fly through the phone and be there with him.

"I'm trying to reach my husband. He's in there."

"The prisoner's name?" the woman asked.

2 **to be in a state** to be very nervous – 27 **to be bounced around various automatic extensions** to have to stay on the line while automatic voices are heard

Kathy had to take a breath. She could not stomach the idea of her husband being called a prisoner. By naming him she was expanding this lie, the one being told by everyone involved in his incarceration thus far.

"Abdulrahman Zeitoun," she said, and spelled it.

Kathy heard the typing of computer keys.

"He's not here," the woman said.

Kathy spelled the name again.

Again the sound of typing.

"We have no one by that name," the woman reiterated.

Kathy tried to remain calm. She told the woman that she had just received a call from someone from Homeland Security, and that that man had told her that Abdulrahman Zeitoun was at that very prison.

"We have no record of him," the woman said. She went on to say that Hunt had no records for anyone who came via the hurricane. None of the prisoners from New Orleans were in their computer system. "All of those records are on paper, and we don't have that paper. We have no actual records of any of those people. They're FEMA's."

Kathy almost collapsed. She was spinning, helpless. She didn't have a number for the Homeland Security man who had called; she cursed herself for not asking for a way to contact him. And now she was being told that her husband was not in the institution where the Homeland Security people and the missionary had seen him. Was this some kind of game? Had he been there at all? He might have been moved already. He had been a prisoner at Hunt but then some other agency wanted him. He had been spirited away to a secret prison somewhere—

She had to go. She would go to Hunt Correctional Center and insist she see him. She had a right to see him. If he wasn't there she would demand they tell her where he'd been taken. It was the only way.

She told Yuko and Ahmaad she was going.

"Where?" they asked.

"Hunt. The prison," she said.

They asked her if she was sure he was there. She was not. They asked if she was sure she would be allowed to visit. She was not. They asked where she would stay. Kathy didn't know. Already she was crying again. She didn't know what to do next.

They convinced her to stay in Phoenix for the time being, until she could be sure of Zeitoun's whereabouts and how she could actually help him. She needed to be smart, they said. They didn't want to worry about her, too.

Kathy called Raleigh Ohlmeyer, an attorney they had worked with before. Raleigh had helped a few of the Zeitouns' workers who had legal issues to straighten out. Raleigh's father was a well-known and powerful lawyer in New Orleans, and Raleigh, though in the family business, had chosen to break away, at least in his appearance. He wore his brown hair long, usually pulled back in a ponytail. He worked downtown and took on a wide variety of cases, from traffic tickets to criminal defense. Kathy was sure he would know how to straighten out this Hunt business.

There was no answer. She left a message.

Kathy called Ahmad in Spain and woke him up. She didn't care.

"He's alive!" she said.

He yelled a string of Thank Gods and Praise Gods.

"Where is he?" he asked. "With you?"

"No, he's in prison," Kathy said. "But it's okay. I know where he is. We'll get him out."

Ahmad was silent. Kathy could hear him breathing.

"How? How will you get him out?" he asked.

14 **to straighten out** to work on, put straight

Kathy did not have a plan just yet, but she had a lawyer, had put in a call to him, and—

"You need to go there," Ahmad said. "You have to see him and get him out. You must."

Kathy was unsettled by Ahmad's tone. He seemed almost as worried by Zeitoun's incarceration as he had been by his disappearance.

Fahzia, Zeitoun's sister in Jableh, called soon after.

Kathy told her the good news. "We know where he is. He's in prison. He's okay."

Another long silence.

"Have you seen him?" she asked.

Kathy said she had not, but that she was sure she would soon.

"You need to see him," Fahzia said. "You need to find him."

In the afternoon, Raleigh Ohlmeyer called Kathy back. He had fled the city just before the storm and had been staying in Baton Rouge. His house in New Orleans was under six feet of water.

Kathy told him what had happened to Zeitoun.

"What?" Raleigh said. "I just saw him on TV." He had seen the local news broadcast of Zeitoun in his canoe.

Kathy told him about the calls from the missionary and the Homeland Security officials, how they had seen him at Hunt.

Raleigh was reassuring. He already knew all about Hunt. After the storm he had set up a makeshift office in Baton Rouge and was already working with prisoners brought to the prison.

The system's broken, he said. There was no means to post bail. It would take some time before it could be rectified. Raleigh promised that he would get Zeitoun released, but

31 **to rectify** to correct

given the state of the courts — there were none to speak of — he could not predict or guarantee a timeline.

TUESDAY SEPTEMBER 20

In the morning Ahmad called Kathy, tense.

"Did you tell Fahzia that Abdulrahman was in prison?"

His tone was severe.

"Yes, she asked and—"

"No, no," he said, and then softened. "Let's not do that. Don't worry them. We cannot tell them he's in prison. We cannot do that."

"Okay, but I just thought—"

"We'll call them and tell them he's fine, he's home, it was a mistake. Okay? We need to tell them this. You don't understand the worry they'll have if they think he's in jail."

"Okay. Should I—"

"I'll call them and tell them he's fine. If they call you, tell them the same. He's at home, he's safe, all is fine. You made a mistake. Okay? This is what we tell them. Okay?"

"Okay," she said.

Ahmad wanted to know which prison he was in. Kathy told him it was in St. Gabriel, and that because the legal system was in limbo, it would be some time before they could even hope to get Abdulrahman out. But she had spoken to a lawyer, and he was on the case. It was only a matter of time.

But Ahmad was thinking beyond simple cases of attorneys and bail. He did not want his brother in prison at all. A Syrian in an American prison in 2005 — this was not to be trifled with. Abdulrahman had to be seen. He had to be freed immediately.

The next time Kathy checked her email she saw a message from Ahmad; she had been cc'ed. He was trying to find

22 **in limbo** at an unfinished, uncertain stage

Zeitoun, but he had gotten the city wrong. He had done an internet search for San Gabriel in the United States, had found a match, and had written this:

From:	CapZeton
To:	ACOSTA, ALEX
Subject:	Urgent from Spain
	The San Gabriel Police Department
	San Gabriel, CA

Dear Sires,

My name is: Ahmad Zeton, from Spain

Reason: I'm looking for my brother (New Orleans Katrina evacuated). On Sept. 7th I missed the contact with my brother which we talked daily by phone after the Hurricane Katrina batch, I asked every place in order to have any news about him, lastly I learned that the Police Force him on Sept. 6th to evacuated his house in New Orleans and tacked him for San Gabriel, and he is actually still arrested at San Gabriel.

Kindly would you please if there is a possibility to learn if he is all right, and if it's possible to talk to him, or to call me by a collected call to my phone [number omitted].

The detail of my brother is:

Name: Abdulrahman Zeitoun.

Date of berth: 24/10/1957

Address: 4649 Dart St., New Orleans, LA

Well be very kind from you just to let me know if he's all right,

Thanking you indeed,

Ahmad Zeton

Malaga-Spain

Kathy began to see the situation through Ahmad's eyes. What if the prosecutors, hoping to justify Zeitoun's

30 **prosecutor** lawyer that represents the state (against an accused person) *(Staatsanwalt)*

incarceration, tried to make a case against him—a connection, any distant connection, to some terrorist activity? Any connection, no matter how specious, might be used to justify his incarceration and extend it.

Kathy did not want to think this way.

THURSDAY SEPTEMBER 22

She called Raleigh Ohlmeyer again. He had just called Hunt, and they had confirmed that Zeitoun was there.

Kathy called Ahmad and told him the news.

"Yes, but has anyone seen him?" he asked.

"No," she said.

"Then we can't be sure," he said.

"Ahmad, I'm sure that—"

"You have to go," he said. "Kathy, please."

He apologized; he knew that he was pushing too hard, that he was calling Kathy too often, but his mind was filled with images of his brother on his knees, in an orange jumpsuit, in an outdoor cage. Every additional hour Zeitoun was in custody increased the chances of something taking a turn for the worse.

"I'll fly to New Orleans," he said.

"And do what?" Kathy asked.

"I'll find him," he said.

"Don't. Don't," she said. "They'll put you in jail, too."

FRIDAY SEPTEMBER 23

By now Raleigh was familiar with some of the judges and administrators working to process the post-storm prisoners being kept at Hunt. Hoping to get Zeitoun's case dismissed, Raleigh told Kathy it was time to come to Baton Rouge. She should fly out and be ready to come to the prison at a moment's

1 **to make a case against** to argue against (*usu* in a court) – 19 **custody** prison *(Gewahrsam)*

notice; there was a chance she could visit him on Monday. Kathy booked a flight and called Adnan, Zeitoun's cousin.

"Abdulrahman?" he asked, hesitant.

"He's okay," she said.

He exhaled. She told him the story of her husband's incarceration, and that she was coming to get him.

"You'll stay with us," Adnan said. After sleeping on the floor of a Baton Rouge mosque for that first week, he and his wife had rented an apartment for the month, and were living there.

Adnan would pick her up and drive her to the prison.

SUNDAY SEPTEMBER 25

There was something wrong with the airplane. They were flying so low, descending too quickly. Kathy was certain the plane would crash. She no longer trusted anything about New Orleans, even the sky above the city. She gripped the armrest. She looked around to see if anyone else was alarmed. The pilot's voice came on the intercom. He announced that they were flying low over the city so the passengers could survey the damage. Kathy couldn't look.

When they landed, the airport was desolate. There were airport security officers, New Orleans police, National Guardsmen, but few civilians. The passengers of Kathy's plane seemed to be the only people in the building. All the stores were closed. The lights were dim. There was detritus all over the floors — garbage, papers, bandages and other medical supplies.

Adnan picked her up and they drove to the apartment he and Abeer had rented in Baton Rouge. Kathy, exhausted and overwhelmed, fell asleep with her shoes on.

1 **at a moment's notice** immediately

MONDAY SEPTEMBER 26

Zeitoun knew nothing about the work Kathy and Raleigh were doing. He still had not been allowed a phone call. All he knew was that he had been assured by both the missionary and the Homeland Security men that they would call his wife. But since then, he had no assurance that contact had been made.

After lunch, Zeitoun was taken from his cell and again handcuffed and brought to the same building near the front gate of the prison. Inside he was brought to a small cinderblock room, where a table and a handful of chairs had been arranged. Sitting on one side of the table was a man in his late fifties, wearing a suit. On the other side were two men in coats and ties. Three other prisoners were seated in chairs at the back of the room. It was some kind of courtroom.

A young man introduced himself to Zeitoun as the public defender. He would be representing Zeitoun that day. Zeitoun began to explain his case, the mistakes that had brought him to prison, and asked for an immediate phone call to his wife. The public defender closed his eyes to indicate that Zeitoun should stop talking.

"You're not here to be judged," he said. "This is just a hearing to set bail."

"But don't you want—"

"Please," the young man said, "just don't say anything. Let me speak for you. Just sit and be quiet if you can. Don't say a word."

The charges against Zeitoun were read: possession of stolen property valued at $500. The prosecutor suggested setting bail at $150,000.

The defender countered that Zeitoun had no prior record, and that the bail should be far lower. He suggested $35,000.

31 **prior record** i.e. criminal record *(Vorstrafe)*

The judge set the bail at $75,000. That was the end of Zeitoun's hearing. The defender extended his hand to Zeitoun, and Zeitoun shook it. He was led out of the room as the defender opened the file for the next prisoner. On his way out, Zeitoun again asked for a phone call. The defender shrugged.

"But why set bail when I can't tell anyone I'm in prison?" Zeitoun asked.

From the judge, the prosecutor, and the defender, there was no answer. Zeitoun was brought back to his cell.

TUESDAY SEPTEMBER 27

Raleigh called Kathy.

"Okay," he said, "they finally have a system arranged, and we've got a court date. They want to clear the docket as much as we want him out of there. So gather as many people as you can to come to court and testify on his behalf. Character witnesses."

This seemed sensible enough to Kathy. It was a clear-cut task, and she dug in. But while making a list of friends to call, she realized she had forgotten to ask Raleigh where the courthouse was. She called him back and got his voicemail.

She called the New Orleans District Attorney's office. A recording gave her a number in Baton Rouge. She called it, expecting to get a recording, but to her surprise a woman answered the phone on the second ring. Kathy asked for the address of the courthouse.

"We don't have one right now," the woman said.

"What?" Kathy said. "I just need the address of the courthouse where the hearings are, the hearings for prisoners at Hunt? I just need the court address."

"We don't have one of those," the woman said.

"A court?" "Right."

"Where are people going to pay tickets?"

"No one's paying tickets right now," the woman said.

13 **docket** *(AE)* list of cases in a court – 15 **to testify** to be a witness *(bezeugen)*

Kathy asked to speak to a supervisor.

She was transferred, and this time a man picked up the phone. Kathy explained that she had just gotten word that her husband had been arrested, and now there was a court date. She only wanted to know where court hearings were being held.

"Oh, we can't tell you that," the man said.

"What? You can't tell me?"

"No, that's privileged information," he said.

"Privileged for who? I'm his wife!"

"I'm sorry, that's private information."

"It's not private! It's public!" Kathy screamed. "That's the point! It's a public court!" She asked to speak to another, more knowledgeable person. The man sighed and put her on hold.

Finally a third person, a woman, picked up the phone.

"What is it you want?" she asked.

Kathy composed herself, hoping that perhaps the other two officials hadn't heard her clearly. She said, "I want to know the location of the court. The court where sentencing and bail hearings are being held."

The woman's voice was even and firm: "That is private information."

Kathy fell apart. She wailed and screamed. Somehow this, knowing that her husband was so close but that these layers of bureaucracy and incompetence were keeping her from him — it was too much. She cried out of frustration and rage. She felt like she was watching a baby drown, unable to do anything to save it.

When she'd gathered herself, she called CNN.

She reached a producer and told her the story: her husband's incarceration, the call from Homeland Security, the stonewalling, the courts that didn't even exist. The producer said she would investigate, and took Kathy's number.

14 **knowledgeable** informed – 17 **to compose oneself** to calm down – 32 **stonewalling** refusing to cooperate, blocking

Raleigh called back. He apologized. Now he knew where the hearing would be held — at Hunt itself. He told Kathy to call anyone she could and tell them to be at Hunt the next day, at nine a.m.

"I'm going to try to see Zeitoun today," he said.

Kathy prayed that he would.

Kathy began calling friends, neighbors, and clients. In two hours she managed to secure at least seven people who said they would come, including the principal of her daughters' school.

Zeitoun was again called out of his cell for a meeting. He was handcuffed, his legs were chained, and again he was led to the white van. He was driven to the front of the prison complex and was brought to another small cinderblock room, where he saw Raleigh, the first representative of the outside world he'd seen since his arrest.

He smiled, and they shook hands warmly.

"I want to get out," Zeitoun said.

"You have to pay to get out," Raleigh said. He sighed deeply. "We've got a situation with this bail."

Zeitoun could either find and pay $75,000, and if he eventually won his case he would be refunded the full amount. Or he could pay thirteen percent of the bail to the courts and three percent to the bondsman — about $10,000 total. And regardless of the outcome of his case, he would lose that amount.

"Isn't $75,000 a lot for petty theft?" Zeitoun asked.

Raleigh agreed it was. It was about a hundred times what it should be. Zeitoun could find the $10,000, but it seemed silly to him to throw away that much money. It would be, in effect, paying the government for incarcerating him for a month.

24 **bondsman** man who sells bonds *(Schuldscheine)* so that prisoners get out of prison on bail

"Can't you reduce it?" Zeitoun asked.

"I'll have to fight for it," Raleigh said.

"Well, then fight for it," Zeitoun said.

"What if it doesn't work?" Raleigh asked.

"Then check if we can use my property as bail," Zeitoun said.

"You don't want to pay the bond?"

"No," Zeitoun said.

If he paid for his release, what would he do, after all? He couldn't work. There was nothing to do in New Orleans, not yet. And by now he knew that Kathy and his kids knew he was alive. He trusted that he would be released. So he would be paying $10,000 to be free for a few extra days — and he would spend that time pacing around Yuko and Ahmaad's living room. He would see his daughters, yes, but they knew he was safe now, and that money would be better spent elsewhere — in their college trusts, for example. He had already been kept two and a half weeks; he could wait a few more days.

"I'll check about using your property as collateral," Raleigh said.

"Call Kathy," Zeitoun said.

WEDNESDAY SEPTEMBER 28

Kathy drove into Hunt, holding her breath. It was a surreal sight — the tidy white fencing, the bright green lawn. It looked like a golf course. White birds scattered as she made her way down the long driveway and up to the gate.

In the parking lot, she stood outside and waited. It was eight-thirty in the morning, and she needed all the friends they had. They began to arrive a few minutes later. Rob and Walt had driven from Lafayette. Jennifer Callender, who worked with Walt and whose house Zeitoun had renovated, arrived with her husband and father. Tom and Celeste Bitchatch, neighbors on Claiborne, had driven from Houston.

17 **trust** legal firm that keeps and invests money for others – 19 **collateral** security

Nabil Abukhader, the principal at the girls' school, had driven from the French Quarter.

They all embraced. No one had been sleeping. They all looked terrible, and were shocked that such a thing had brought them together. But they were heartened, somewhat, to know that they would be able to speak about the character of Abdulrahman Zeitoun. They were confident that when the judge heard from them all and realized that the police had imprisoned a well-known businessman, the judge might very well release him that day. Perhaps they could all celebrate together.

Kathy couldn't stop thanking them. She was a wreck of tears and gratitude and anticipation.

When Raleigh arrived, he was impressed. He gathered everyone together and gave them a brief rundown of how the proceedings would go. He wasn't sure exactly where the hearing would take place, or even what time. But he was confident that between Zeitoun's reputation, lack of any prior infractions, and this showing of character witnesses — a wide swath of upstanding New Orleanians — the judge would release Abdulrahman Zeitoun with profuse apologies.

They waited through the morning. No word. Finally Raleigh went to see what was happening. He came back out, his face a cloud.

"They won't see any of you," he said.

The hearing had been canceled. There was no explanation why.

Now the only chance was to post bail. Kathy would have to go back into the city and find papers proving ownership of their office building. They would use the building as collateral against the bond.

5 **to hearten** to encourage - 19 **infraction** breaking the law - 21 **profuse** many

Adnan insisted he drive Kathy into the city.

They took I-10 and exited at Carrollton. Immediately they were struck by the smell. It was so many things —acrid, rotten, and even, from the branches and trees lying in the sun, sweet. But most of all the smell was overpowering. It was loud. Kathy wrapped her scarf around her face to blunt its power.

The city looked like it had been abandoned for decades. The cars, their colors washed grey from the toxic water, were strewn about like playthings. They took Carrollton to Earhart, and at one point had to cross over to the opposite lane to avoid downed trees. The debris was everywhere and bizarre — tires, refrigerators, tricycles, couches, a straw hat.

The streets were deserted. They saw no one — no human or vehicle — until a police cruiser pulled up behind them a few blocks from the office. Kathy told Adnan to let her do the talking. It was a long-held strategy she developed with Zeitoun. It was always easier and quicker when she did the talking; a Middle Eastern accent would only provoke more questions.

Two officers approached their car, both with their hands on their sidearms. The officer at the driver's side window asked Adnan what he was doing in the city. Kathy leaned over to explain and extended her driver's license through the window.

"I live in the house down the street," she said. "Just coming back to assess the damage, pick up anything that survived."

He listened to Kathy but turned back to Adnan. "What are you doing here?"

Kathy preempted him. "We're contractors," she said. She gave the officer her business card.

The officer took it back to the squad car. He and his partner spent ten minutes there before returning to Adnan's window.

"Okay," the officer said, and let them go.

They decided to drive straight to the office, for fear that the next time they were stopped they would not be so fortunate.

When they reached the building on Dublin, Kathy could see the remains of the homes that had burned to the ground. It seemed miraculous that the fire had stopped only a few yards away. The office appeared damaged from the outside, but not in a way that would hint at what they would find within. Kathy went to the door. Her key didn't work. The lock was rusted inside and out.

Across the street, Adnan spotted something. He jogged over to a neighbor's house and came back carrying an ancient, ruined ladder.

"I'm going up," he said. "You stay here."

He set the ladder against the building and began to climb. The steps were crooked and some of them broken, but he went up carefully, and when he arrived at the second-floor window, he climbed through and quickly disappeared inside.

Kathy heard some thumps and scraping, and then it was quiet. Soon there was a voice from the other side of the door.

"Move away," he said. "I'm kicking the door down."

He kicked it four times and the door gave way, falling flat.

"Be careful when you're going up the stairs," he said.

Inside, the building was ruined. It looked like it hadn't been inhabited in decades. The ceiling was half-destroyed, dotted with jagged holes. Exposed wiring and papers everywhere. A grey sludge covered the floor. The smell was strong. Mildew and rain and sewage.

Kathy and Adnan carefully climbed the stairs to the office. It was unrecognizable. The carpet squished with every step. She could smell the presence of animals, and there were scurrying sounds as they walked through the office. She opened a closet door and a dozen roaches fell onto her hands. She screamed. Adnan calmed her.

"Let's just get the papers and go," he said.

But nothing was where she remembered it. The file cabinets had shifted. The desk organizers were all over the floor. She

23 **jagged** uneven *(ausgefranst)* – 30 **roach** cockroach *(Kakerlake)*

searched through the cabinets and desk drawers, sweeping bugs off the few files left undamaged. Some of the files were so wet and soaked in mud that they were useless. She made a pile of the files that were unreadable, hoping that among the few that she could recognize was proof that they owned this building. It seemed so absurd, that she was searching through her own building, widely known as the headquarters of their well-known business, for a simple, filthy piece of paper that a makeshift court would accept in exchange for her husband. And what if she didn't find it? Her husband might fall deeper into the abyss of this broken judicial system for lack of this piece of paper?

"Please help," she asked Adnan, choking on the words.

They searched for an hour. They opened every drawer and every file, until she thought they were simply examining the same, few, undamaged files they'd already read repeatedly. But finally, in a drawer she was sure contained nothing of value, she found it, the act of sale for 3015 Dublin. She was on her knees, her abaya filthy, and she held it in her hands, and cried. She sat back and shook.

"This better work," she said.

With the papers in hand, they returned to Raleigh's office in Baton Rouge. Raleigh prepared the paperwork and faxed it over to the bondsman. The bondsman confirmed that he had received it and that the bond had been paid. Raleigh called Hunt to confirm that all the paperwork had gone through for the surety bond. He was told that they had the paperwork, but that the office had closed early. It was three p.m.

Zeitoun would have to spend another night at Hunt.

THURSDAY SEPTEMBER 29

In the morning, Kathy and Adnan drove to the prison, arriving before eight. They went into the office and were told Zeitoun

11 **abyss** black hole, chaos – 27 **surety bond** *Sicherheitsschuldschein*

would be released that day. They waited in the same room where Zeitoun's friends had gathered two days earlier.

They waited until eleven. No word. Twelve. Nothing. It wasn't until one o'clock that they were given notice that he would be released any moment. Kathy was told to wait for him outside. A bus would be dropping him off at the gate.

Zeitoun was in his cell praying.

In the name of God, the Most Beneficent, the Most Merciful:
Praise be to God, the Lord of the Heavens and the Earth.
The Most Beneficent, the Most Merciful.
Master of the Day of Judgment.

"Zeitoun!"

A guard was calling to him.

The guard can wait, Zeitoun thought. He had no idea that Kathy was at the prison and his release was imminent.

He continued his prayers.

You alone we worship, and You alone we ask for help.
Guide us to the straight way;
The way of those whom you have blessed,
not of those who have deserved anger,
nor of those who are astray.

"Zeitoun!" Now the guard was at his cell, yelling through the bars. "Get ready!"

Zeitoun continued his prayers until he was finished. The guard waited silently. When Zeitoun stood, the guard nodded to him.

"Get your stuff. You're getting out today."

"What?" Zeitoun said.

15 **imminent** about to happen at any moment

"Hurry up."

Zeitoun fell against the wall. His legs had given way.

Kathy waited outside the prison with Adnan.

A white bus arrived at the gate. A figure moved from within, from left to right, and then stepped down onto the pavement. It was Abdulrahman, her husband. He had lost twenty pounds. He looked like a different man, a smaller man, with longer hair, almost all of it white. Tears soaked her face. *He's so small,* she thought. A flash of anger overtook her. *Goddamn those people. All of you people, everyone responsible for this.*

Zeitoun saw her. He smiled and she went to him. Tears all over her face, she could barely see. She ran to him. She wanted to protect him. She wanted to take him in the crescent of her arms and heal him.

"Get back!"

A heavy hand was on her shoulder. A guard had stopped her.

"Stay here!" he yelled.

Kathy had crossed a barrier. It wasn't visible to her, but the guards had delineated an area within which the prisoners' relatives were not allowed.

She waited, standing a few yards away from her husband. They stared at each other, smiling grimly. He looked like a sad old man. He was wearing denim pants, a denim shirt, orange flip-flops. Prison clothes. They hung off him, two sizes too big.

A few minutes later he was free. He walked to her and she ran to him. They held each other for a long moment. She could feel his shoulder blades, his ribs. His neck seemed so thin and fragile, his arms skeletal. She pulled back, and his eyes were the same — green, long-lashed, touched with honey — but

20 **to delineate** [dɪ'lɪnieɪt] to fix an area, draw a line

they were tired, defeated. She had never seen this in him. He had been broken.

Zeitoun hugged Adnan, and then quickly pulled away.

"We should go," Zeitoun said.

The three of them quickly got in the car. They didn't want whoever was responsible for this to change their minds. It wouldn't have surprised them. Nothing at all would have surprised them.

They left the prison as fast as they could. They felt better after they passed through the main gate, and felt better still as they drove down the long white-fenced driveway and reached the road. Zeitoun turned around periodically, to be sure no one was following them. Adnan checked his rearview mirror as they sped down the rural route, trying to put as much distance as possible between themselves and the prison. They passed through a long corridor of tall trees, and with each mile they felt more sure that Zeitoun was absolutely free.

Kathy sat in the back seat, reaching forward, stroking her husband's head. But she wanted to be closer. She wanted him in her arms, she wanted to hold him and restore him.

They were only ten minutes away from the prison when Ahmad called Kathy's cell phone.

"We've got him!" she said.

"What? You do?"

She handed the phone to Zeitoun.

"Hello brother!" he said.

"Is it you?" Ahmad asked.

"It's me," Zeitoun said.

"Praise God. Praise God. How are you?"

Ahmad's voice was trembling.

"Okay," Zeitoun said, "I'm okay. Were you worried?" He tried to laugh.

Now Ahmad was crying. "Oh praise God. Praise God."

PART V

FALL 2008

Kathy has lost her memory. It's shredded, unreliable. The wiring in her mind has been snapped in vital places, she fears, and now the strangest things have been happening.

She was at the bank in November, just to deposit checks from clients and withdraw cash for the week. She comes to this bank, Capital One, so often that everyone there knows her. This morning, like any other, the employees greeted her when she entered.

"Hi, Mrs. Zeitoun!" they sang, and she waved and smiled.

She walked to one of the tellers and removed her checkbook and picked up a pen. She needed to write two checks, one for cash and the other to move money into the company's payroll account.

She wrote the first check and gave it to the teller, and when she returned her attention to her checkbook, she paused. She didn't know what to do next. She couldn't remember what her hand was supposed to be doing. She didn't know how to write, or what to write, or where. She stared and stared at the checkbook; it became more foreign by the moment. She couldn't identify the purpose of the checkbook on the counter or of the pen in her hand.

She looked around, hoping to see someone with these tools in their hands, to see how they were using them. She saw people, but they provided no clues. She was lost.

The teller said something but Kathy couldn't understand the words. She looked at the young woman, but the sounds coming from her mouth were garbled, backward.

Kathy couldn't speak. She knew, inwardly, that she was beginning to worry the teller. *Focus,* she told herself. *Focus, focus, focus, Kathy!*

The teller spoke again, but the sounds were more distant now, coming, it seemed, from underwater, or far away.

2 **shredded** torn to pieces – 28 **garbled** mixed up

Kathy's eyes locked on to the sliding wooden partition that separated this teller from the others. She lost herself in the blond wood grain, slipping into the elliptical lines of age on the wood's surface. Then she realized what she was doing, staring at the grain on the wood, and urged herself to snap out of it.

Focus! she thought. *C'mon.*

Her hands felt numb. Her vision was blurry.

Come back! Come back!

And slowly she returned. The teller was talking. Kathy made out a few words. Kathy felt herself re-enter her body, and suddenly everything clicked into place again.

"Are you okay, Mrs. Zeitoun?" the teller asked again.

Kathy smiled and waved her hand dismissively.

"Just spacing out for a second," she said. "Busy day."

The teller smiled, relieved.

"I'm fine," Kathy said, and wrote the second check.

She's been forgetting numbers, names, dates. She has trouble concentrating. She tells friends that she's going crazy, and laughs it off. She's not going crazy, she is sure and they are sure — she's still the same Kathy almost all the time and certainly to most of the people she knows — but episodes like the one at the bank are accumulating. She's not as sharp as she once was, and there are things she can't count on doing as she did before. One day she'll be unable to place the name of one of the workers she's known for ten years. Another day she'll find herself with the phone in her hand, the other end of the line ringing, and will have no idea who she is calling or why.

It is the fall of 2008 and the Zeitouns are in the process of moving into a new house. It's the same house, really — the one

15 **to space out** *(inf)* to be disoriented – 23 **to accumulate** to add up, become more, increase – 23 **sharp** clever

on Dart — but it's been gutted, expanded, tripled. Zeitoun designed an addition that will give all the children their own rooms, and will allow Kathy to work at home. There are balconies, gabled roofs, a large kitchen, four bathrooms, two sitting rooms. It is the closest thing to a dream house they will ever have.

The office on Dublin was a total loss. They went there a few days after Zeitoun's release from prison and found only mud and insects. The roof had given way, and everything inside was covered in the same grey mud. Kathy and Zeitoun took the few things they could salvage and eventually sold the building. They planned to move their office to their home. Now their house has an entrance on Dart, the residential address, and another one on Earhart Boulevard.

The Zeitouns have lived in seven apartments and houses since the storm. Their Dublin Street office was leveled and is now a parking lot. The house on Dart is still unfinished.

They are tired.

When they returned from Hunt, they stayed for two days on Adnan's floor in Baton Rouge, then moved into the studio apartment of their rental unit on Tita Street, on New Orleans' West Bank. There was no furniture, but it had been undamaged in the storm. Those first few nights, Kathy and Zeitoun lay on the floor, with borrowed blankets, talking very little. He did not want to talk about prison. He did not want to talk about Camp Greyhound. He was ashamed. Ashamed that his hubris, if that was what it was, had caused all this. Ashamed that he had been handcuffed, stripped, caged, treated like an animal. He wanted it all erased from their lives.

On that night and for many nights after, they lay on the floor and held each other, bitter and thankful and frustrated, and they said nothing.

1 **to gut** to take out the inner parts

Kathy fed him as much as she could each day. The day after his release, Kathy and Adnan took Zeitoun to Our Lady of the Lake Regional Medical Center, where the doctors found no major injuries. They could find no reason for the stabbing pain in his side. But he had lost twenty-two pounds. It would be a year before he was back to his previous weight. He'd lost hair, and what was left had gone grey. His cheeks were hollow, his eyes had lost their spark. Slowly, he regained himself. He grew stronger. The pain in his side dissipated, and this convinced Zeitoun it had been caused not by anything visible on an X-ray, but by heartbreak, by sorrow.

After Zeitoun's release, their friend Walt loaned them a car from his Lexus dealership, and Kathy and Zeitoun drove it back into the city and to the house on Dart.

The smell was overpowering, a mixture of mold, sewage, and dead animals. Kathy pulled part of her hijab to her mouth to mute the stench. Zeitoun tried to flush one of the toilets and sewage poured out. More water had made its way into the rooms on the second floor. A shelf of books was ruined, as well as most of the electronics.

Without Zeitoun there to plug holes as they arose, the house had been devastated. He looked at the gaps in the roof and sighed.

Kathy leaned against the wall in the hallway. She was overwhelmed. Everything they owned was filthy. To think she had cleaned this house a thousand times!

"You okay?" he asked her.

She nodded. "I want to leave. I've seen enough."

They took the computer and some of the kids' clothes and put them in the car. Zeitoun started the engine but then ran back inside, retrieved the box of photos, brought it down, and

8 **spark** brightness *(Funken)* – 8 **to regain oneself** to get back to normal – 9 **to dissipate** to dissolve, to disappear – 17 **to mute the stench** to make the smell less bad

put it in the trunk. He backed out of the driveway, turned down Dart, and remembered something else.

"Wait!" he said. "Oh no..." He jumped out of the car, leaving the door open. *The dogs.* How long had it been? He ran across the street and down the block, his stomach spinning. *The dogs, the dogs.*

He knocked on the front doors of the two houses where he had fed them. No answer. He looked in the first-floor windows. No one. The owners had not come back.

Zeitoun went back to the tree. His plank was still there, and he leaned it against the trunk. He climbed up to his usual perch and then pulled the plank up. He stretched the plank across to the house on the right and walked to the roof. Usually the dogs were barking for him by now, but today he heard nothing.

Please, he thought. *Please God.*

He lifted the window and slipped inside. The stench hit him immediately. He knew the dogs were dead before he saw them. He found them together in one of the bedrooms.

He left the roof, stepped back to the tree, and arranged the plank to reach the second house. The dogs were just under the windowsill, a tangle of limbs, heads to the heavens, as if they had been waiting, for weeks, for him.

After two weeks, Kathy and Zeitoun were still in the studio apartment, and the kids were ready to return to New Orleans. Zeitoun was nervous. "Do I look like me?" he asked Kathy. He was afraid he would scare them, having lost so much weight and hair. Kathy didn't know what to say. He did not look like him, not yet, but the kids needed to see their father. So Kathy and Zeitoun flew to Phoenix, and amid much crying and hugging, the Zeitouns were reunited. They drove back to New Orleans and returned to the apartment on Tita. For a month they slept together on the floor.

12 **perch** place (*usu* high up somewhere) – 22 **tangle of limbs** body parts mixed together

One day Kathy opened a letter from the Federal Emergency Management Agency. They were offering the Zeitouns a free trailer, a two-bedroom portable unit that would be delivered to them at their request.

Kathy filled out the appropriate forms and sent them back. She didn't expect much from the process, so she was startled when, in December 2005, an eighteen-wheeler pulled up in front of their apartment with a gleaming white trailer in tow.

Zeitoun was on his rounds, so he didn't see them install it. When he returned, he was puzzled. They hadn't connected the trailer to water or electricity. And it had been installed on a rickety tower of cement blocks, easily four feet off the ground. There were no steps to reach the door. It was so high that there was no way to get inside without a stepladder.

And even if one reached the door, you couldn't enter the trailer, because the delivery team had failed to leave a set of keys.

Kathy called FEMA and let them know about these issues. They said they were doing the best they could, and would get to it as soon as possible. Weeks passed. No key was delivered. The Zeitouns watched every day for signs of any FEMA personnel. The trailer stayed where it was, unused, unconnected, and locked.

After a month, a FEMA pickup truck arrived and dropped off a set of steps, about four feet high. They left no equipment that might attach the steps to the trailer. There was a foot-wide gap between the steps and the door. To get inside, one would have to jump. But the door still couldn't be opened. They had yet to provide the key.

After another six weeks or so, a FEMA inspector appeared and gave Kathy the key to the trailer. But when he saw the trailer, he noted that because it was leaning, it was unsafe to use. He left, telling Kathy that someone would come to fix it.

Zeitoun and Kathy began to buy houses in their neighborhood. Their next-door neighbor had fled the storm and hadn't returned. She put the house on the market and the Zeitouns made an offer. It was half the value of the house before the hurricane, but she accepted. This was the most satisfying of all the transactions they made. Before the storm, they'd also bought the house on the other side of their own. Soon they were living in this house, while renovating their original house on Dart, and renting out the other house next door.

Meanwhile, the FEMA trailer was still parked in front of the house on Tita. It had been there eight months, and had never been connected to water or electricity. A practical way to enter the trailer had never been devised, and now the Zeitouns didn't need it. It was an eyesore. Zeitoun had repaired all the damage to the Tita house, and they were trying to sell it. But the trailer was blocking the view of the house, and no one would buy a house where an immovable leaning trailer was parked out front.

But FEMA wouldn't pick it up. Kathy called every week, telling FEMA officials that the trailer had never been used and now was decreasing the value of their property. She was told each time that it would be removed soon enough, and that, besides, thousands of people would love to have such a trailer; why was she trying to get rid of it?

In June 2006, a FEMA representative came to collect the keys. He said they would return to take away the trailer. Months went by. There was no sign of anyone from FEMA. Kathy called again, and FEMA had no record of anyone picking up the keys.

Finally, in April of 2007, Kathy wrote a letter to the *Times-Picayune* detailing the saga of the trailer. At that point, the trailer had sat, unused and unusable, for over fourteen months. On the morning the letter ran, a FEMA official called Kathy.

12 **to devise** to form, to plan – 13 **eyesore** sth that is unpleasant to the eye

"What's your address?" he asked.

They took it away that day.

Kathy's problems with memory gave way to other difficulties, equally difficult to explain. She began to have stomach problems. She would eat any small thing, a piece of pasta, and her stomach would swell to double its original size. Soon she was choking on anything she tried to eat. Food would not go down some days, and when it did, she would have to gag and fight it down.

She grew clumsier. She knocked over glasses and plates. She broke a lamp. She dropped her phone constantly. Some days, when she walked, she would feel tipsy, swaying side to side, needing to rest against walls as if struck by vertigo. Some days her hands or feet would grow numb while she was doing normal everyday things like driving or working with the kids on their homework.

"Honey, what's happening to me?" she asked her husband.

She went in for tests. One doctor suggested she might have multiple sclerosis; so many of her symptoms seemed to indicate some kind of degenerative illness. She was given an endoscopy, an MRI, and a barium swallow to test her gastrointestinal tract. Doctors administered tests of her cognitive skills, and she did poorly on those that measure memory and recognition. Overall the tests pointed to post-traumatic stress syndrome, though she has yet to decide on the strategy to manage it.

Kathy and Zeitoun had no intention of suing anyone over his arrest. They wanted it in the past. But friends and relatives

10 **clumsy** awkward *(ungeschickt)* – 14 **numb** [nʌm] unfeeling – 19 **multiple sclerosis** disease of the central nervous system – 21 **endoscopy** examination of inner parts of the body – 21 **MRI** use of a nuclear magnetic resonance spectrometer to produce electronic images of the body – 22 **gastrointestinal tract** [ˌgæstroʊ.ɪnˈtestənəl] stomach and intestines *(Darm)* – 27 **to sue** to try to get compensation (money) from sb because you believe they did you wrong (by going to court)

fanned their outrage, and convinced them that those responsible needed to be held accountable. So they hired a lawyer, Louis Koerner, to pursue a civil suit against the city, the state, the prisons, the police department, and a half-dozen other agencies and individuals. They named everyone they could think of — the mayor, Eddie Jordan, and everyone in between. They were told by everyone who knew anything about the New Orleans courts to get in line. There were hundreds, perhaps thousands, of cases against the city, the federal government, FEMA, police officers, the Army Corps of Engineers. Three years after the storm, few of the lawsuits had gone anywhere.

A few months after Zeitoun's release, Louis Koerner found his arrest report. Kathy was shocked that it even existed, that any records had been made or kept. Finding the names of those who arrested her husband was satisfying at first, but then it only fueled her rage. She wanted justice. She wanted to see these men, confront them, punish them. The arresting officer was named Donald Lima, and this name, Donald Lima, seared itself into her mind. The other officer named on the report was Ralph Gonzales. Lima was identified as a police officer from New Orleans. Gonzales was a cop from Albuquerque, New Mexico.

Out-of-state police could not make arrests, Kathy discovered, so on any arrest, a local officer had to be present along with any Guardsmen or contractors. Kathy and Zeitoun decided to name Donald Lima, the officer on the arrest report, in the lawsuit. The Zeitouns' lawyer contacted the New Orleans Police Department and found that Lima was no longer employed there. He had resigned in 2005, a few months after the storm. The department had no forwarding address.

1 **to fan an outrage** to support and stir up anger – 2 **to hold accountable** to make sb take responsibility for sth

Gonzales was easy to find. On the arrest report, he was identified as being an officer from Albuquerque, and he was still with that department in the fall of 2008. When he was reached by phone, he told his side of the story.

Gonzales had been a police officer for twenty-one years when, in August of 2005, his captain suggested that they send a team to New Orleans. The New Orleans Police Department had put out a nationwide request for law enforcement help, so Gonzales agreed to go, along with about thirty other officers from Albuquerque.

The New Mexico team arrived a few days after the storm, were sworn in as deputies, and began to assist with search and rescue operations. Before arriving in New Orleans, Gonzales and his fellow officers had heard a lot about the conditions in the city, and they were tense. They had heard about shootings, rapes, gangs of heavily armed and fearless men. They saw no such crime, but they saw plenty of death. They were one of the first units to investigate one of the hospitals. Gonzales didn't remember which one, but they found dozens of bodies. The smell was indescribable.

Conditions worsened every day. He and his fellow cops wouldn't go out at night. They could hear windows breaking and shots fired after dark. The entire city smelled of death and decay. "Everyone was on guard," he said of his fellow cops. "We thought we were in a third-world country."

On September 6, Gonzales was at the Napoleon—St. Charles staging ground. Cops and soldiers and medical personnel gathered there every day to share information and receive assignments. Gonzales got word that there would be a search of a house down the road, occupied by at least four suspects presumed to have been looting and dealing drugs. It could be very dangerous, he was told, and they needed as many cops and soldiers as possible. It was the first law-and-order assignment he'd been part of since he had arrived.

He jumped on the boat wearing a bulletproof vest and carrying a pistol and an M-16. He was one of six cops, National Guard soldiers, and soldiers-for-hire on the boat. When they arrived, Gonzales was one of the first to enter. He saw a pile of computer components and stereo equipment on the dining room table, and he saw the four men. There was something in their attitude, he thought, which signaled that "they were up to no good."

They arrested the four men, brought them to the staging ground, handed them to the authorities there. They were finished with the assignment in fifteen minutes. That was the extent, Gonzales asserted, of their duties. He never went to Camp Greyhound and was only vaguely aware that a jail had been installed there. Neither he nor any part of the arresting party secured the house or collected any evidence. In fact, none of them returned even once to the house on Claiborne.

The arrest of Zeitoun and the other three men on Claiborne Avenue was one of two arrests Gonzales made while he was in New Orleans. Every other task he performed was related to search and rescue. Ten minutes after bringing the four men to the staging ground, he was on another boat, looking for people in need.

Gonzales was asked how he felt about the fact that Abdulrahman Zeitoun, a middle-aged businessman and father of four, had done a month in maximum-security prison.

Gonzales seemed regretful. "If he was innocent, then I feel very bad," he said. "Here's the bottom line: I wouldn't want something like that to happen to me personally."

Gonzales talked about how the system is supposed to work: police officers investigate, make arrests, and then hand the process over to the judicial system. Under normal circumstances, if the men were innocent, he maintained, they would have been given a phone call and the opportunity to post bail.

"They should have gotten a phone call," he said.

Lima was more difficult to track down, but he had not gone far. He had left the New Orleans Police Department in 2005 and was living in Shreveport, Louisiana.

He knew that Zeitoun and the others had spent time in jail. He knew about Zeitoun's case because he'd been served papers when the lawsuit was undertaken. He didn't know how long the other men had spent in prison. He was quick to note that their imprisonment wasn't his doing. He only made the arrest.

At the time of Katrina, he was living in a five-thousand-square-foot house on Napoleon. During and after the storm, he stayed in the city with members of his family, guarding his house. He had two generators and enough food and water for three weeks. He also had over forty pistols and automatic rifles. During the day he traveled the city with other police officers and National Guard troops, making rescues. Each day he met with other law-enforcement personnel, and they would map out a plan of action. They divided up tasks and territory.

The National Guardsmen in the city had plenty of gasoline but were low on other supplies. In exchange for gasoline, Lima and other New Orleans police officers broke into convenience stores and took cigarettes and chewing tobacco. A majority of the National Guardsmen, Lima said, chewed tobacco and smoked Marlboros, so this arrangement kept both sides well supplied. Lima considered the looting a necessary part of the mission. The gasoline, he said, helped them make the rescues they did. He also needed it to power his home generators. When he couldn't find Guardsmen who had gas, Lima siphoned fuel from cars and trucks. His throat was sore from all the gas-siphoning he did after the storm, he said.

"The whole place was anarchy," he said.

While making his rounds on a motorboat one day, Lima observed four men leaving a Walgreens carrying stolen goods. They left the Walgreens and put the goods into a blue-and-white motorboat. Lima had two rescues with him, so he couldn't pursue the thieves at the time, but he made a mental note. He continued to make rounds, seeing dead bodies and being confronted by angry residents, many of them armed.

"My state of mind was rattled," he said.

Two days later he passed a house on Claiborne and saw the same blue-and-white boat tethered to the porch. He raced to the Napoleon—St. Charles staging ground and gathered a crew of police and military personnel. They were "heavily armed" with sidearms and M-16s. He didn't know the other four men or the one woman who joined in the mission. Together they took a flatboat to the house. Lima was the lead cop on the arrest.

When they entered, they saw what they thought were stolen goods on the dining room table. They found four men inside, and something about them and the scene seemed amiss. Lima was sure that these were the same four men he had seen leaving the Walgreens, so they arrested them and brought them to the staging ground.

"It was a fairly routine arrest," he said. "All four of the guys were very quiet."

They handed the men over to National Guardsmen, and the Guardsmen put them in the white van. Lima filled out paperwork about the arrest and gave it to the Guardsmen, and they drove the arrestees to Camp Greyhound. Later, Lima went to Greyhound, where he saw the men's property laid out on a table. He saw Todd's maps, Nasser's cash, and the memory chips. "They'd been up to something," he said.

Lima was not sure what goods he had seen the four men stealing. And he did not see any goods customarily sold by Walgreens in the house on Claiborne. He did not secure the house on Claiborne as a crime scene. No stolen goods were recovered. But he was certain the men in the house were guilty of something, though the extraordinary circumstances of post-storm New Orleans did not allow for the same degree of thoroughness as he would have liked.

15 **amiss** wrong

Nor was the post-arrest procedure standard or fair, he said. In a normal situation, Lima said, they would have been arraigned properly, given a phone call and an attorney, and would have been out on bail within days. When he was a cop, he was frustrated by the revolving-door nature of the justice system. He would arrest someone in the morning and they would be out on the street in the afternoon. It was maddening for a police officer, but he admitted that this element of checks and balances would have been useful in this case.

"They should have gotten a phone call," he said.

Lima quit the NOPD in November 2005, and moved with his wife and daughter to Shreveport. He was a police officer in Shreveport for a time, but was treated, he said, "like a second-class citizen." The officers there assume that all cops from New Orleans are corrupt, he said. So he quit, and now he's looking for a new career. Before joining the force, he was a stockbroker, and he was considering going back to that.

The Zeitouns were conflicted about what they heard about Lima and Gonzales. On the one hand, knowing that these two police officers had not purposely hunted and arrested a man because he was Middle Eastern gave them some comfort. But knowing that Zeitoun's ordeal was caused instead by systemic ignorance and malfunction — and perhaps long-festering paranoia on the part of the National Guard and whatever other agencies were involved — was unsettling. It said, quite clearly, that this wasn't a case of a bad apple or two in the barrel. The barrel itself was rotten.

Soon after, a friend emailed Kathy a document that seemed to shed light on the state of mind of the soldiers and law-enforcement agencies working in New Orleans at the time.

5 **revolving door** *Drehtür* – 8 **checks and balances** procedures that stop things from going wrong – 17 **stockbroker** sb who buys and sells company shares *(Börsenmakler)* – 23 **malfunction** failure to function – 24 **to fester** to become rotten and sick *(eitern)*

The Federal Emergency Management Agency had been its own freestanding agency for decades, but after 9/11 had been folded into the Department of Homeland Security. FEMA had historically been granted broad powers in the wake of a federal emergency; they could take command of all police, fire, and rescue operations. This was the case after Katrina, where it was necessary for FEMA to assume the responsibility for all prisoners being evacuated from New Orleans. And thus the prisoners, including Zeitoun, were overseen by the Department of Homeland Security.

While Katrina bore down on the Gulf Coast, a four-page document was apparently faxed and emailed to law-enforcement agencies in the region, and to National Guard units headed to the Gulf area. The document, issued in 2003 by the Department of Homeland Security, was written by a "red cell" group encompassing representatives of the Department of Homeland Security, the CIA, the Marines, corporate security firms, and Sandia National Laboratories.

The authoring committee had been asked to "speculate on possible terrorist exploitation of a high category hurricane." And though the authors admitted that it was unlikely that terrorists would act during or after a hurricane, they nevertheless enumerated the many ways they might do so. "Several types of exploitation or attacks may potentially be conducted throughout the hurricane cycle — hostage situations or attacks on shelters, cyber attacks, or impersonation of emergency response officials and equipment to gain access." These terrorists "might even hope that National Guard and other units are less able and well-equipped to respond... because of deployments overseas."

Then they broke their findings into three categories: Pre-Event, During Event, and Post-Event. Before the storm, the committee wrote, the terrorists would be most likely to use the occasion "to observe precautionary measures to gauge

34 **precautionary measures** things you do to stop sth bad happening *(Vorsichtsmaßnahmen)* – 34 **to gauge** [geɪdʒ] to measure precisely

emergency response resources and continuity of operation plans at critical infrastructures." They also warned that terrorists might target evacuation routes, creating "mass panic" and "loss of public confidence in the government." Terrorist activity during the storm, the committee felt, was "less likely due to the severe weather, unpredictability of the storm path and the difficulty of mobilizing resources." After the storm, the options for terrorists were few but potent. They might "build on public panic to further destabilize the system by disseminating rumors" and therefore "increase media coverage" and "stress the public health system."

The committee had several recommendations to reduce the threat posed by such terrorists. They included: "Institute increased security procedures (e.g. identification checks) at evacuation centers and shelters"; "Advise the first responder community, telecommunications personnel, and power restoration personnel to increase identification procedures to prevent imposters from gaining unauthorized access to targets"; and "Increase patrols and vigilance of staff at key transportation and evacuation points (for instance, bridges and tunnels), including watching for unattended vehicles at these locations."

The "red cell" committee thought it unlikely that an established terrorist group would work in the United States during a hurricane. Instead, they felt that "a splinter terrorist cell, or a lone actor... would be more likely to exploit a hurricane on site. This includes persons pursuing a political agenda, religious extremists, or other disgruntled individuals."

Kathy isn't sure whether hearing things like this is helpful or not. She has moved on from Katrina in many ways, and yet the residual effects arrive at unexpected times. There are

10 **to disseminate** to spread – 18 **imposter** sb who gets into a situation by deceit – 19 **vigilance** watchfulness – 21 **unattended** empty (*here:* without a driver) – 28 **disgruntled** discontent – 32 **residual** remaining *(übrig bleibend)*

plenty of normal days. She drives the kids to school and picks them up, and in between she manages the affairs of the painting and contracting company. When the kids get home she makes them a snack and they watch TV and do their homework.

But the other day Kathy had to ask for Nademah's help. She was trying to get onto the Internet but couldn't make it work. She looked behind the computer and the wires were a chaos she couldn't decipher. "D, can you help me get connected?"

Nademah came to help. It was Kathy who had set up all the computers in the house, Nademah reminded her, and Kathy who had taught Nademah how to use them. Kathy knew this, but at that moment she couldn't remember which wires went where, which buttons did what, how everything was connected.

Camp Greyhound has been the subject of investigative reports and a source of fascination for the city at large. Even employees of Greyhound and Amtrak are amazed at what became of the station after the storm. Clerks at the Amtrak desk will happily show visitors the place where prisoners were fingerprinted, where their heights were determined. The height chart is still there. Under a poster next to the counter, the handwritten marks are still there. You just have to move the poster to see them, just as they were in the days of Camp Greyhound.

As Zeitoun had suspected, the jail was built largely by hand. When he was incarcerated there, he couldn't imagine what workers were available and ready to work long hours a day after the hurricane, but the answer makes a certain amount of sense. The work was completed by prisoners from Dixon Correctional Institute in Jackson, Louisiana, and from the Louisiana State Penitentiary in Angola.

Angola, the country's largest prison, was built on an eighteen-thousand-acre former plantation once used for the breeding of slaves. Meant to hold those convicted of the most serious crimes, it has long been considered the most dangerous, most hopeless prison in the United States. Among the five thousand men held there, the average sentence is 89.9 years. Historically the inmates were required to do backbreaking labor, including picking cotton, for about four cents an hour. In a mass protest decades ago, thirty-one prisoners cut their Achilles tendons, lest they be sent again to work.

At the time of the hurricane, Marlin Gusman, sheriff of Orleans parish, knew that there was a chance that the Orleans Parish Prison, where most offenders were kept while awaiting trial, would flood. So he called Burl Cain, warden of Angola. An arrangement was made to build an impromptu prison on high ground in New Orleans. Warden Cain rounded up fences and portable toilets, all of which he had available at the Angola campus, and sent the materials on trucks to New Orleans. They arrived two days after the hurricane struck the city.

Cain also sent dozens of prisoners, many of them convicted of murder and rape, and tasked them with building cages for new prisoners and those forced out of Orleans Parish Prison. The Angola prisoners completed the network of outdoor jails in two days, sleeping at night next door to the Greyhound station. Cain also sent guards. When the cages were finished, the Angola prisoners were sent back north, and the guards remained. These were the men who guarded Zeitoun's cage.

When the prison was completed, Cain said it was "a real start to rebuilding" New Orleans. In the weeks that followed, more than 1,200 men and women were incarcerated at Camp Greyhound.

This complex and exceedingly efficient government operation was completed while residents of New Orleans were trapped in attics and begging for rescue from rooftops and highway overpasses. The portable toilets were available and working at Camp Greyhound while there were no working bathrooms at the Convention Center and Superdome a few blocks away. Hundreds of cases of water and MREs were readily available for the guards and prisoners, while those stranded nearby were fighting for food and water.

There have been times when someone speaks to Kathy in English and she can't understand what the person is saying. It happened the other day with Ambata, a woman the Zeitouns recently hired to help with office work. The kids had just come home from school, the TV was on, a stereo was playing — there was noise throughout the house. Kathy and Ambata were sending out invoices when Ambata said something Kathy couldn't understand. She saw Ambata's mouth moving, but the words conveyed no meaning.

"Can you repeat that?" she asked.

Ambata repeated herself.

The words made no sense.

"I'm sorry," Kathy said. "I have no idea what you're saying." She grew scared. She jumped up and, frantic, she turned off the TV, the stereo, and the computer. She wanted to eliminate any variables. She sat down again with Ambata and asked her to repeat what she said.

Ambata did, but Kathy still could not parse the words.

One day, in 2006, Zeitoun was visiting his cousin Adnan at his Subway franchise downtown. Zeitoun occasionally stopped there for lunch, and was eating there that day when he saw an exceptionally tall African American woman enter. She was in tan-and-green fatigues, evidently a National Guard soldier. She looked very familiar.

Zeitoun realized why he recognized her. She was, he was almost certain, one of the people who had arrested him. She had the same eyes, the same short hair. He stared for a few long moments and tried to muster the nerve to say something. He couldn't devise the right thing to say, and soon she was gone.

Afterward he asked Adnan about her.

"Have you seen her before?"

"I'm not sure. I don't think so."

"If she comes in again, you have to ask her questions. Ask her if she was in New Orleans after the storm."

Zeitoun spent the day reliving his arrest and the weeks afterward. It wasn't every day that the arrest came to him, but late at night it was sometimes difficult to send away his anger.

He knew he couldn't live in the city if he felt he would continue to encounter people like this soldier. It was painful enough to pass by the Greyhound station. It was almost unavoidable, though, given how central it was — within sight of the Home Depot. He had adjusted his habits in a dozen small ways. He was exceedingly careful not to commit any minor traffic infraction. He feared that because of the lawsuit he would be a target of local police, that they would manufacture charges against him, try to justify his arrest. But these were fleeting thoughts. He fought them off every day.

One confrontation was unavoidable.

Four days after his release, Zeitoun had had time to sleep, and to eat a bit. He felt stronger. He didn't want to return to Camp Greyhound. But Kathy had insisted, and he knew she was right. They had to get his wallet back. It held his driver's license, and without it the only identification he had was the prison ID he had been given at Hunt. He and Kathy needed to fly to Phoenix to gather their children and drive home, and the only way he could do so was with his driver's license. They thought about it a dozen ways but couldn't find a better way. They had to return to the Greyhound station and retrieve the wallet.

They pulled into the crescent-shaped drive. All around were police cars, military Humvees, jeeps, and other military vehicles.

"How do you feel?" Kathy asked.

17 **fleeting** impermanent, moving quickly

"Not good," Zeitoun said.

They parked and stayed in the car for a minute.

"Ready?" Kathy asked. She was primed for a fight.

Zeitoun opened his door. They walked toward the station. Outside the entrance, there were two soldiers.

"Please don't say anything," Zeitoun said to Kathy.

"I won't," she said, though she could barely contain her rage.

"Please don't," he repeated. He had warned her repeatedly that they could both be put in jail, or he could be returned to prison. Anything could happen. Anything *had* happened.

As they approached the bus station, Zeitoun was trembling.

"Please be calm," he said. "Don't make it worse."

"Okay, okay," Kathy said.

They walked past a dozen military personnel and into the building. It looked much like Zeitoun remembered. For the first time in his life, he tried to shrink. Trying to hide his face — the very people who caged him might still be there — he followed Kathy through the doors.

They were stopped by a pair of soldiers. They patted Zeitoun down and searched Kathy's purse. They directed them both through a metal detector. Zeitoun's eyes darted around the building, looking for anyone he recognized.

They were directed to a set of chairs, the same chairs Zeitoun had been questioned in, and were told to wait for a chance to meet with the assistant district attorney. Zeitoun wanted badly to get out as soon as possible. The situation was far too familiar. He had no faith that he would leave again.

As they waited, a man holding a tape recorder approached them. He told them that he was a reporter from the Netherlands, and that his friend had been held overnight at the station in one of the cages, and had just been released.

3 **primed** prepared

He began asking Zeitoun and Kathy why they were there. Kathy didn't hesitate, and began to tell him that her husband had been wrongfully arrested, sent to a maximum-security prison, held there for twenty-three days, and that now they were trying to retrieve his possessions.

"Get away from them!"

Kathy looked up. A female officer in her fifties, wearing full camouflage, was glaring at them, and barking at the Dutch reporter. "Get out of here," she said to him. "Interview's over." Then she turned to a pair of National Guardsmen. "If that man is seen in here again, arrest him and put him in a cage." The soldiers approached the reporter.

Kathy stood up and strode toward the woman.

"Now you take away my freedom of speech? Really? You took away my husband, you wouldn't let me speak to or see my husband, and now you take away my ability to speak freely? I don't think so! You know anything about freedom of speech?"

The officer turned away from Kathy and ordered that the reporter be removed. Two soldiers guided him to the front door and led him outside.

The assistant district attorney, a heavyset white man, approached them and asked how he could help. Kathy reiterated that she needed her husband's wallet. The man led them to the gift shop, which had been converted into an office. It was a glass box in the middle of the station, full of Mardi Gras T-shirts and paperweights. Kathy and Zeitoun explained their situation.

The assistant DA said he was sorry, but the wallet was still being used as evidence. Kathy blew up. "Evidence? How could his ID be used as evidence? You know his name. Why would you need his ID? He didn't commit a crime with his wallet."

The man sighed. "I'm sympathetic, but you can't have it without permission of the district attorney," he said.

24 **to reiterate** [ri'ɪt̬əreɪt] to repeat

"You mean Eddie Jordan?" Kathy asked. "Where is he?"

"He's not here," he said.

"When will he be here?" Kathy asked.

The assistant DA didn't know.

Kathy and Zeitoun walked into the station lobby, not knowing what their next step was. But then, through the station's front window, she saw Eddie Jordan. He was standing out front, surrounded by a phalanx of reporters.

Kathy marched out the door to confront Jordan. He was dressed in a three-piece suit.

"Why can't we have his wallet?" she asked.

"Excuse me?" Jordan said.

Kathy told him a brief version of Zeitoun's situation, and reiterated her demand that the wallet be returned.

Jordan said that there was nothing he could do about it, and turned around, resuming his conversation.

Now Kathy saw that the Dutch reporter was nearby. She wanted him and the other reporters to hear what was happening. She spoke as loudly as she could.

"You arrested my husband in his own house, and now you won't give him his wallet back? What's going on here? What is wrong with this city?"

Jordan shrugged and turned away.

"We're going back inside," Kathy said to Zeitoun.

Zeitoun didn't see the point, but the fire in her eyes did not encourage debate. They went back in and walked directly up to the assistant DA. Kathy wouldn't allow that damned prison ID to define her husband, to be the only government-issued identification he owned.

"You have to do something," she said. She was near tears now, a mess of frustration and rage.

The assistant DA closed his eyes. "Let me see what I can find," he said. He left the office. In ten minutes, he came back with the wallet and handed it to Zeitoun.

Zeitoun's driver's license and permanent-resident card were there, but all his cash, business cards, and credit cards were gone.

"Where are the other things?" Zeitoun asked.

The man didn't know. "That's all there was."

Kathy didn't care. All she wanted, for now, was proof that her country recognized her husband as a citizen.

"Thank you, sir," she said. "Thank you." She wanted to hug him. He was the first person representing any part of the city or state government who had shown any humanity at all. Even this one easily executed task, retrieving the wallet of a man they'd held in a cage a few yards away, seemed, in the context, an act of great courage and empathy.

They left, satisfied that they had gotten the most crucial thing, the driver's license. Given the nature of the city's judicial system, it was miraculous that the wallet had been kept at all. Kathy had already canceled the credit cards. The rest they could replace.

That was the last time Kathy felt that focused, that angry. Now she is more diffuse. She gets angry, but not as often, and she can't focus her rage as she once could. Where she was once ready and willing to fight any battle, she prefers now to retreat, reinforce her defenses, double the locks on the doors. She finds herself fearful, always, that something will happen to her family. She doesn't like her kids playing in the neighborhood. She wants them where she can see them, even Nademah, who is thirteen now, and almost as tall as Kathy herself. She watches them sleep. She never did that before. She checks on them frequently during the night. She wakes up and has trouble getting back to sleep.

Nademah, always responsible, always whip-smart, is now sharing in the care of her sisters. Zachary is eighteen, lives with friends in New Orleans, and works at one of Adnan's Subway restaurants. Safiya and Aisha are the same as always: blithe, full of joy, given to bursts of song. All of the kids make life very easy for little Ahmad, born on November 10, 2006 at East Jefferson Hospital.

Ahmad is, by all accounts, a preternaturally content baby. He never wants for attention, with his sisters taking turns holding him, taking dangerous things out of his mouth, reading to him, dressing him in their old clothes.

Zeitoun was so thankful for a boy. And the name was never an issue. Ahmad was the first and only name.

Zeitoun's brother Ahmad, still living in Spain, now works as a ship inspector. He's waiting for his brother to bring the new baby to Malaga. It's time he saw his nephew, his namesake.

Kathy is working less these days. There's the baby to care for, and her mind is not sharp enough, not lately, to handle all the paperwork on her own. They have some help now, from Ambata and others, which gives Kathy some room to breathe, to be a mother, to try to make sense of the last three years.

There are appointments with doctors. Doctors to try to figure out why her hands go numb without warning. Doctors to investigate her digestive problems, memory problems.

Doctors have asked Kathy what she thinks the most traumatic part of the Katrina experience was. She surprised herself and the doctors when she realized that it was after she knew Zeitoun was alive, and had been told he was at Hunt Correctional Center, but wasn't allowed to see him or even know where a court hearing might be held. It was that moment, being told by the woman on the phone that the hearing's location was "private information," that did the most damage.

"I felt cracked open," she says.

That this woman, a stranger, could know her despair and desperation, and simply deny her. That there could be trials

3 **preternatural** extraordinary

without witnesses, that her government could make people disappear.

"It broke me."

She finds herself wondering, early in the morning and late at night and sometimes just while sitting with little Ahmad sleeping on her lap: *Did all that really happen? Did it happen in the United States? To us?* It could have been avoided, she thinks. So many little things could have been done. So many people let it happen. So many looked away. And it only takes one person, one small act of stepping from the dark to the light.

She wants to find out who that missionary was, the man who met her husband in prison and took her phone number — the messenger. The man who risked something in the name of mercy.

But did he risk so much? Not really. Usually you needn't risk so much to right a wrong. It's not so complicated. It's the opposite of complicated. To dial a number given to you by a man in a cage, to tell the voice on the other end, "I saw him." Is that complicated? Is that an act of great heroism in the United States of America?

It should not be so.

Kathy worries that her husband is working too hard now. He works every day, even Sundays. He's home for meals, and bedtimes, but he works whenever he can. And how he does it while fasting on Mondays and Fridays — he's become more religious — is beyond her. He seems to eat even less than before, and works harder than ever.

Friends who know what happened to Zeitoun after the storm ask why he hasn't left, why he hasn't gone to another city, another country — even back to Syria — anyplace removed from the memories embedded into New Orleans. He does have dark feelings when he passes by the Greyhound station, when he drives past the house on Claiborne where he and two friends and a stranger were carried off. When he drives by the home of Alvin and Beulah Williams, the pastor and his wife, he says a quick prayer for them. Beulah Williams died in 2007. Reverend Alvin Williams died in 2008.

When he passes by the home of Charlie Ray, his neighbor on Claiborne, he waves if Charlie is on his porch, which he often is. One day after the storm, Charlie was visited by the National Guard. They told him that he should leave the city, and that they would help him. They waited for him to pack, and then carried his bags to their boat. They ferried him to an evacuation point, whereupon a helicopter flew him to the airport and he was given a free plane ticket to New York.

His rescue took place the same day Zeitoun was arrested. A few months after the storm, Charlie returned to New Orleans and still lives on Claiborne.

Todd Gambino now lives in Mississippi. He spent over five months at Hunt Correctional Center. He was released on February 14, 2006. All charges against him were dropped. More than $2,400 had been confiscated from him when he was processed at Camp Greyhound, and when he was released, he attempted repeatedly to recover it. He was unsuccessful. He was not compensated in any way for the five months he spent at the maximum-security prison.

After his release, he went to work on an oil rig in the Gulf of Mexico but was laid off in the fall of 2008.

Nasser Dayoob spent six months at Hunt. All charges against him were eventually dropped; when he was released, he tried to recover the $10,000 he'd had with him when he was arrested. No authorities had any record of it, and he never recovered the money, his life savings. In 2008 he moved back to Syria.

Ronnie spent eight months at Hunt. Since his release in the spring of 2006, the Zeitouns have not heard from him.

Frank Noland and his wife have moved. Just about everyone in the Zeitouns' neighborhood has moved. Gone, too, is the woman Zeitoun found in her foyer — the woman whose cries he heard because he paddled quietly. The new occupant of her house doesn't know where she went, but he has heard the story of Zeitoun's rescue.

Zeitoun thinks of the simple greatness of the canoe, of the advantages of moving quietly, of listening carefully. When he was released from prison, he and Kathy looked for the canoe where he'd last seen it, at the Claiborne house, but it was gone. The house had been robbed, too. Everything was stolen, because the soldiers and police who arrested Zeitoun had left the house unlocked and unguarded. Thieves walked in unimpeded and made off with all the tenants' belongings, everything

Todd had gathered there in the front rooms to keep dry.

All those things were replaced, but he misses the canoe. He keeps his eye out for it, hoping he'll see it at a yard sale or in someone's sideyard. He'd pay for it again. Maybe he should get a new one, he thinks. Maybe his girls will like it more now. Maybe little Ahmad, like his uncle and father and grandfather and countless Zeitouns before them, will feel the lure of the sea.

Some nights Zeitoun struggles to sleep. Some nights he thinks of the faces, the people who arrested him, who jailed him, who shuttled him between cages like an animal, who transported him like luggage. He thinks of the people who could not see him as a neighbor, as a countryman, as a human.

Eventually he finds his way to sleep, and in the morning he awakens to the sounds of his children — four young ones in the house now, so many voices in this now-bigger house, the smell of fresh paint filling the home with possibility. The kids fear water, yes, and when a pipe burst last year there were screams and nightmares, but slowly they're growing stronger. For them he has to be strong, and he needs to look forward. He needs to feed them, to hold them close, and he needs to show them that God had a reason for their trials. He tells them that perhaps God, by allowing him to be jailed, saved him from something worse.

"Everything happens for a reason," he tells them. "You do your duty, you do what's right, and the rest is in God's hands."

He has watched the progress of the rebuilding of the city. The first few years were frustrating, as legislators and planners bickered over money and protocols. New Orleans, his home, needs no speeches, no squabbling, and no politics. It needs new flooring, and new roofing, new windows and doors and stairs.

For many of his clients, it took time for the insurance money to come through, for the FEMA money to appear, for any number of complications to work themselves out. But now things are moving. The city is rising again. Since Hurricane Katrina, Zeitoun A. Painting Contractor LLC has restored 114 houses to their former states, or improved versions thereof.

Zeitoun bought a new van and drives through the city, through Uptown, the Garden District, the French Quarter, Lakeview, the West Bank, Broadmoor, Metairie, Gentilly, the Lower Ninth, Mirabeau Gardens — and every time he sees a home under construction, no matter who's doing it, he smiles. *Build,* he thinks. *Build, build, build.*

And so he makes his rounds, checking in on his crews. They're working on some very good and important projects. Even with a slowing economy, there is much to do.

There's McDonough #28, a three-story junior high school on Esplanade. It's been closed since the storm, but it can come back. Zeitoun is fixing the woodwork with caulk and putty,

11 **to bicker** to fight – 12 **to squabble** to argue – 32 **caulk** *(AE)* material used to fill spaces *(Dichtungsmaterial)* – 32 **putty** soft material used as caulk

repainting the interiors with medium grey and sage-green and bone-white. That shouldn't take too long. It'll be good to see that school open again.

It would be easy, he knows, with that building and so many others, to simply tear them down and begin again. As a builder, it certainly is easier starting with a piece of flat, cleared land. But so much is lost that way, far too much is lost. And so for three years of rebuilding he has always asked, first, "What can be saved?"

There's the Leidenheimer Bakery on Simon Bolivar Avenue. The building is a wonderful brick structure, over a hundred years old, and the bakery is still run by the descendants of George Leidenheimer, an immigrant from Germany. Zeitoun was proud to get the job, as he always is with buildings of significance; he hates to see them torn down. The masonry weathered the storm just fine, but the windows and wood need refinishing or replacing. So he and his crew are doing that, and remodeling the inner office, installing some cabinets, painting the vents.

And there's the St. Clement of Rome Parish Church on West Esplanade and Richland. The interior woodwork needs priming and re-finishing. The exterior sustained some damage, so they'll pressure-wash it, sand and caulk it, and repaint every wall and window. He intends to oversee that project very carefully. He always does when hired to restore any house of worship. He is sure that God is watching the work he and Kathy and his men are doing, so it must be done with great care and even, he tells his crews, with soul.

More than anything else, Zeitoun is simply happy to be free and in his city. It's the place of his dreams, the place where he was married, where his children were born, where he was given the trust of his neighbors. So every day he gets in his white van, still with its rainbow logo, and makes his way through the city, watching it rise again.

It was a test, Zeitoun thinks. Who among us could deny that we were tested? But now look at us, he says. Every person is stronger now. Every person who was forgotten by God or country is now louder, more defiant, and more determined. They existed before, and they exist again, in the city of New Orleans and the United States of America. And Abdulrahman Zeitoun existed before, and exists again, in the city of New Orleans and the United States of America. He can only have faith that will never again be forgotten, denied, called by a name other than his own. He must trust, and he must have faith. And so he builds, because what is building, and rebuilding and rebuilding again, but an act of faith? There is no faith like the faith of a builder of homes in coastal Louisiana. And there is no better way to prove to God and neighbor that you were there, that you are there, that you are human, than to build. Who could ever again deny he belonged here? If he needs to restore every home in this city, he will, to prove he is part of this place.

As he drives through the city during the day and dreams of it at night, his mind vaults into glorious reveries — he envisions this city and this country not just as it was, but better, far better. It can be. Yes, a dark time passed over this land, but now there is something like light. Progress is being made. It's so slow sometimes, so terribly so sometimes, but progress is being made. We have removed the rot, we are strengthening the foundations. There is much work to do, and we all know what needs to be done. We can only do the work, he tells Kathy, and his children, and his crew, his friends, anyone he sees. So let us get up early and stay late, and, brick by brick and block by block, let us get that work done. If he can picture it, it can be. This has been the pattern of his life: ludicrous dreams followed by hours and days and years of work and then a reality surpassing his wildest hopes and expectations.

And so why should this be any different?

20 **to vault into** to rise (*here:* create a vision of) – 20 **revery** dream

THE ZEITOUN FOUNDATION

All author proceeds from this book go to the Zeitoun Foundation, founded in 2009 by the Zeitoun family, the author, and McSweeney's. Its purpose is to aid in the rebuilding of New Orleans and to promote respect for human rights in the United States and around the world. The Zeitoun Foundation will serve as a grantor of funds generated from this book; the first group of recipients include the following nonprofit organizations.

REBUILDING TOGETHER

Rebuilding Together's Gulf Coast operations have focused on preserving and rehabilitating one thousand houses of low-income homeowners, which were damaged in the wake of Hurricane Katrina and Rita.

www.rebuildingtogether.org

THE GREEN PROJECT

The Green Project obtains and resells building materials salvaged in the New Orleans area. The purpose is to encourage recycling, thereby reducing waste; to enable residents of New Orleans to purchase low-cost materials; and to preserve the architectural history of the area.

www.thegreenproject.org

THE LOUISIANA CAPITAL ASSISTANCE CENTER

After Hurricane Katrina, the LCAC was a leading force in locating the thousands of inmates who had been displaced, highlighting the plight of the prisoners who had been evacuated into terrible conditions, and securing the release of hundreds of inmates who were wrongfully imprisoned. The LCAC now aims to provide legal representation for defendants in Louisiana who are facing capital punishment, and seeks to address racism in the criminal justice system.

www.thejusticecenter.org/lcac

INNOCENCE PROJECT OF NEW ORLEANS

This New Orleans—based organization provides legal aid for people who have been wrongfully convicted, and helps them in their transition from incarceration to liberty. They focus on the states where incarceration rates (and rates of wrongful conviction) are highest — Louisiana and Mississippi.

www.ip-no.org

MEENA MAGAZINE

Meena ("port" in Arabic) is a bilingual literary journal based in the port cities of New Orleans and Alexandria, Egypt. The journal publishes poetry, fiction, essays, travel writing, mixed-genre media, and art. *Meena* hopes to exist as a port between the Western and Arab worlds by exchanging ideas about culture, language, conflict, and peace through writing and dialogue.

www.meenamag.com

THE PORCH SEVENTH WARD CULTURAL ORGANIZATION

An organization committed to the Seventh Ward in New Orleans, The Porch is a place to come together and share culture and community. The Porch seeks to promote and sustain the cultures of the neighborhood, the city, and the region, and to foster exchange between cultural groups.

www.ny2no.net/theporch

CATHOLIC CHARITIES, ARCHDIOCESE NEW ORLEANS

Catholic Charities works with the entire community of New Orleans to respect the dignity of every human person. They are currently operating eleven community centers in the Greater New Orleans area to help with hurricane recovery. These centers provide case-management services, direct assistance, and other services as needed.

www.ccano.org

ISLAMIC RELIEF USA

Islamic Relief strives to alleviate suffering, hunger, illiteracy, and diseases worldwide, without regard to color, race, or creed. In the event of man-made or natural disasters, it aims to provide rapid relief. Working with the United Nations World Food Program (UNWFP) and the Department for International Development, Islamic Relief establishes development projects in needy areas to help tackle poverty at a local level.

www.irw.org

THE MUSLIM AMERICAN SOCIETY

The Muslim American Society (MAS) is a charitable, religious, social, cultural, and educational not-for-profit organization. Its mission is to build an integrated empowerment process for the American Muslim community through civic education, local leadership training, community outreach, and coalition building. MAS also strives to forge positive relationships with other institutions outside of its community, in order to facilitate the protection of civil rights and liberties for American Muslims and all Americans.

www.masnet.org

THE NEW ORLEANS INSTITUTE

The New Orleans Institute is dedicated to engaged citizenry and is determined to cultivate local solutions. This is a networking alliance with a shared interest and commitment to fostering the resilience of New Orleans through innovation.

www.theneworleansinstitute.org

THE NEIGHBORHOOD STORY PROJECT

In 2004, the Neighborhood Story Project was founded by Rachel Breunlin and Abram Himelstein as a book-making project based in New Orleans, for New Orleanians. The NSP conducts workshops and facilitates the publishing of books by first-time authors in New Orleans, in an effort to tell the story of the city and its citizens.

www.neighborhoodstoryproject.org

MUSLIM STUDENT ASSOCIATION

The MSA is dedicated to developing an understanding of Islam and the Islamic culture among the Tulane University community. They seek to create a sense of awareness of Islam among the Tulane community by increasing their basic knowledge of Islam. The MSA aims to give the Tulane community a first-hand experience with Islam and the Islamic culture.

www.tulane.edu/~msa/

THE NEW ORLEANS LENS

The New Orleans Lens is a nonprofit news-reporting site, dedicated to journalism in New Orleans. The Lens's strength lies in a highly qualified editorial and research staff, as well as a collaborative network of affiliated organizations including the Center for Public Integrity, Project on Government Oversight, and the national Investigative News Network.

thelensnola.org

NEW ORLEANS CENTER FOR CREATIVE ARTS

The New Orleans Center for Creative Arts is a regional, pre-professional arts training center that offers secondary school—age children intensive instruction in dance, media arts, music (classical, jazz, vocal), theatre arts (drama, musical theatre, theatre design), visual arts, and creative writing, while demanding simultaneous excellence.

www.nocca.com

VOICE OF WITNESS

Voice of Witness is a nonprofit book series that empowers those most closely affected by contemporary social injustice. Using oral history as a foundation, the series depicts human rights crises around the world through the stories of the men and women who experience them.

http://www.voiceofwitness.com/index.php

RESTORE WESLEY UNITED

Restore Wesley United is rehabilitating the building that was home to New Orleans' second-oldest African-American church, the Wesley United Methodist Church, and transforming that building into a Digital Arts and Training Center for the 21st Century. It will train and employ members of its surrounding community to increase Louisiana's homegrown capabilities in the creation and business of entertainment.

http://www.savewesleyunited.org/

THE JEREMIAH GROUP

The Jeremiah Group is comprised of religious congregations and other institutions in the metropolitan New Orleans area, with the mission to transform the practice of politics in this City, from the neighborhood to the metro-level.

http://www.jeremiahgroup.org/

ACKNOWLEDGMENTS

THE ZEITOUN FAMILY WOULD LIKE TO ACKNOWLEDGE:

Ahmad Zeton; Mrs. Trufant; Yuko and Ahmaad Alakoum for putting up with us in our darkest hours; Mary Amarouni; Crystal and Keene Kelly; Celeste and Tom Bitchatch; the Callender family; Tom and Luke; Nabil Abukhader; Mohammed Salaam; Rob Florence; and all of those who helped us.

THE AUTHOR WOULD LIKE TO ACKNOWLEDGE THE WORK OF THE FOLLOWING JOURNALISTS AND RESEARCHERS:

Gwen Filosa, Rob Nelson, Bruce Nolan, Emmet Mayer III, Mark Schleifstein, John McCusker, *New Orleans Times-Picayune;* Dr. Daniel L. Haulman, the Air Force Historical Research Agency; Tech. Sgt. Mark Diamond, the Air Force Medical Services Monthly Newswire; Jenny Carchman, Michelle Ferrari, Stephen Ives, Lindsey Megrue, Amanda Pollak, Mark Samels, *The American Experience;* Donna Miles, Rudi Williams, the American Forces Press Service; Marina Sideris, Amnesty Working Group; Betty Reid, *Arizona Republic;* Joseph R. Chenelly, *Army Times;* Craig Alia, *Army Magazine;* Lolita C. Baldor, Wendy Benjaminson, Rick Bowmer, Allen G. Breed, Melinda Deslatte, Linda Klein-dienst, Marilynn Marchione, Brett Martel, Janet McConnaughey, Kevin McGill, Adam Nossiter, John Solomon, the Associated Press; Kelly Bradley, Lt. Col. Tim Donovan, Larry Sommers, *At Ease Magazine;* Mickey Noah, *Baptist Press;* Olenka Frenkiel, BBC; Amy Goodman, *Democracy Now!;* Brandon L. Garrett, Tania Tetlow, *Duke Law Journal*; Charlie Savage, *Boston Globe;* Patrik Jonsson, the *Christian Science Monitor,* Jamie Wilson, the *Guardian*; Jason Carroll, Anderson Cooper, Jacqui Jeras, Chris Lawrence, Ed Lavandera, Rob Mar-ciano, Ed Zarrella, Jeanne Meserve, Betty Nguyen, CNN; Tamara Audi, *Detroit Free Press;* Neil deMause, Steve Rendall, *Extra!;* Todd Stubing,

Fort Myers News-Press; Dave Reynolds, *Inclusion Daily Express;* Adnan Bounni, Iran Chamber Society; Guy Siebold, *Journal of Political and Military Sociology;* Stacy Parker Aab, The Katrina Experience Oral History Project; Alan Zarembo, *Los Angeles Times;* Capt. David Nevers, *Marines Magazine;* Jeremy Scahill, the *Nation;* Staff Sgt. Jon Soucy, National Guard Bureau; Daniel P. Brown, Richard D. Knabb, Jamie R. Rhome, National Hurricane Center; John Burnett, Jeff Brady, National Public Radio; Ken Munson, *Nautical Notes;* Diane E. Dees, *Mother Jones;* Curtis A. Utz, Naval Historical Center; Ruth Berggren, *New England Journal of Medicine;* Lou Dolinar, *New York Post;* David Carr, Melissa Clark, N.R. Kleinfield, Merrill Perlman, Shadi Rahimi, Joseph B. Treaster, Richard W. Stevenson, Alex Berenson, Sewell Chan, Paul von Zielbauer, *New York Times;* Sarita Sarvate, Pacific News Service; Kevin Callan, paddling.net; Yvonne Haddad, Fariborz Haghshenass, *PolicyWatch;* Peter Henderson, Michael Christie, Jane Sutton, Reuters; Richard Burgess, *Sea Power Magazine;* Jordan Flaherty, *Southern Studies: An Interdisciplinary Journal of the South;* Morris Merrill, *Southern Quarterly;* Fred Kaplan, *Slate;* Angie Welling, *Salt Lake City De-seret News;* Ken Kaye, Robert Nolin, *South Florida Sun-Sentinel;* Jeff Schogol, *Stars and Stripes;* Harry Mount, the *Telegraph;* Amber McIlwain, *Times of London;* Matthew Van Dusen, *Times of Northwest Indiana;* Joel Stein, *Time Magazine;* Anna Mulrine, Dan Gilgoff, *US News and World Report;* Douglas Brinkley, *Vanity Fair;* Renae Merle, Guy Gugliotta, Peter Whoriskey, Eugene Robinson, the *Washington Post;* Michael Pope, Christiana Halsey, *Customs and Border Protection Today;* the Center for Human Rights and Global Justice; Charles Janda, Chucksphotospot.com; Jordan Flaherty, *ColorLines;* Eugen Tarnow, PhD, Cogprints.org; Amy Belasco, Steve Bowman, Lawrence Kapp, Department of Defense; Maj. Mark Brady, Capt. Lisa Kopczynski, Sgt. Les Newport, First U.S. Army in the News; Gary Mason, the *Globe and Mail;* Hugh Hewitt, *The Hugh Hewitt Show;* The Indy Channel; Indiana University, Bloomington; The Innocence

Project; staff, *Killeen Daily Herald;* Jason Brown, *Lafayette Daily Advertiser;* Jamie Doward, *London Observer;* Rosa Brooks, *Los Angeles Times;* Chris Kelly, *MichelleMalkin.com;* Michael Robbins, *Military History;* staff, *Naples Daily News;* staff, *NGAUS Notes;* Lt. Col. Deedra Thombleson, National Guard; Erick Studenicka, National Guard Bureau; Navy Office of Information; Carl Quintanilla, Tony Zumbado, NBC News; New Orleans Copwatch; Jayne Huckerby, New York University Center for Human Rights and Global Justice; Gregory Smith MD, Woodhall Stopford MD, *North Carolina Medical Journal;peopleshurricane.org;* Keith Woods, Poynter Institute; Eric Barr, Taylor Rankin, John Baird, *ThinkQuest;* David Crossland, *Times of London;* United States Coast Guard; Marina Sideris, University of California Berkeley Law School; Jerry Seper, the *Washington Times;* Wrongful-Convictions.blogspot.com; Kelly Leosis, Katherine Yurica, *yuricareport.com; Neworleans.indymedia.org.*

THE FOLLOWING BOOKS AND REPORTS WERE CRUCIAL TO THE WRITING OF *ZEITOUN*:

The Great Deluge: Hurricane Katrina, New Orleans, and the Mississippi Gulf Coast by Douglas Brinkley (William Morrow, 2006); *Severe and Hazardous Weather* by Bob Rauber, John Walsh, Donna Charlevoix (Kendall Hunt Publishing, 2005); *On Risk and Disaster: Lessons from Hurricane Katrina,* edited by Ronald J. Daniels, Donald F. Kettl and Howard Kunreuther (University of Pennsylvania Press, 2006); *Hurricane Katrina: America's Unnatural Disaster,* by Jeremy I. Levitt and Matthew C. Whitaker (University of Nebraska Press, 2009); *Come Hell or High Water* by Michael Eric Dyson (Basic Civitas, 2006); *Disaster: Hurricane Katrina and the Failure of Homeland Security* by Robert Block and Christopher Cooper (Henry Holt Books, 2006); *Down in New Orleans: Reflections from a Drowned City* by Billy Sothern and Nikki Page (University of California Press, 2007); *The Essential Koran,* translated and presented by Thomas Cleary (HarperCollins, 1993); *A Modern*

History of Syria by A.L. Tibawi (St. Martin's Press, 1969); *Fifty Years of Modern Syria and Lebanon,* by George Had-dad (Dar-al-Hayat, 1950); *Modern Syria, from Ottoman Rule to Pivotal Role in the Middle East,* edited by Moshe Ma'oz, Joseph Ginat, and Onn Winckler, (Sussex Academic Press, 1999); *Supporting the Future Total Force,* by John G. Drew, Kristin F. Lynch, James Masters, Sally Sleeper, and William Williams (RAND, 2007); *By the Numbers: Findings of the Detainee Abuse and Accountability Project* by Human Rights Watch (Human Rights Watch, 2006); *Irreversible Consequences: Racial Profiling and Lethal Force in the War on Terror,* by the Center for Human Rights and Global Justice (NYU School of Law, 2006); *Public Safety, Public Spending: Forecasting America's Prison Population 2007—2011,* by the JFA Institute, the Public Safety Performance Project, and the Pew Charitable Trusts (Pew Charitable Trusts, 2007); *Abandoned and Abused: Orleans Parish Prisoners in the Wake of Hurricane Katrina,* by the National Prison Project of the American Civil Liberties Union, the American Civil Liberties Union of Louisiana, the American Civil Liberties Union Racial Justice Program, Human Rights Watch, the Juvenile Justice Project of Louisiana, the NAACP Legal Defense and Educational Fund, Inc., and Safe Street/ Strong Communities (American Civil Liberties Union and the National Prison Project, 2006); *Enabling Torture: International Law Applicable to State Participation in the Unlawful Activities of Other States,* by the Center for Human Rights and Global Justice (NYU School of Law, 2006); *BeyondGuantanamo: Transfers to Torture One Year After Rasul v. Bush,* by the Center for Human Rights and Global Justice (NYU School of Law, 2005); *Louisiana National Guard Timeline of Significant Events, HurricaneKatrina,* by the Louisiana National Guard (Louisiana National Guard, 2005); *Torture by Proxy: International Law applicable to "Extraordinary Renditions"* by the Association of the Bar of the City of New York and the Center for Human Rights and Global Justice (ABCNY and the NYU School of Law, 2004); *Use of Force: ATF Policy, Training and Review Process Are*

Comparable to DEA's and FBI's, by USGAO (United States General Accounting Office, 1996).

THE FOLLOWING AGENCIES AND ORGANIZATIONS PROVIDED ESSENTIAL INFORMATION:

44th Medical Brigade Public Affairs; Air National Guard 920 Rescue Wing; American Civil Liberties Union; Blackwater USA; Bureau of Alcohol Tobacco and Firearms; Camp Pendleton Public Affairs; Center for Disease Control; DynCorp International; Defense Logistics Agency Defense Supply Center; Federal Emergency Management Agency; First Army Public Affairs; Fort Hood Public Affairs; Fort Hood Media Relations; Fort Carson Public Affairs; Fourth Infantry Division Public Affairs; Immigration and Customs Enforcement Public Affairs; Louisiana National Guard Public Affairs; Louisiana State Police; NASA; National Guard Association of the United States; National Oceanic and Atmospheric Administration; National Weather Service; National Hurricane Center; Office of the Attorney General; SOPAKCO; State of Michigan Department of Military and Veterans Affairs; State of Wisconsin Department of Military Affairs; Texas National Guard Community Relations; U.S. Army Public Affairs; U.S. Capitol Police; U.S. Department of Homeland Security, Department of Public Affairs; U.S. Marine Corps Public Affairs; U.S. Marshals.

NOTES ABOUT THE QUR'AN QUOTED HEREIN

Many translations of the Qur'an into English exist and many were consulted. The translation quoted in this book is by Laleh Bakhtiar, published in 2007 by Kazi Publications under the title *The Sublime Quran.* As is evidenced in the quotations included in this book, the Qur'an contains very powerful and surpassingly beautiful language, and this English edition reflects that beauty exceedingly well.

AUTHOR NOTES ON PROCESS AND METHODOLOGY

The process behind this book started in 2005, when, shortly after Hurricane Katrina struck New Orleans, a team of volunteers from Voice of Witness, our series of books that use oral history to illuminate human rights crises, fanned out all over the Southeast to collect testimonies. From Houston to Florida, they interviewed residents and former residents of New Orleans about their lives before, during, and after the storm. The result was *Voices from the Storm*, edited by Chris Ying and Lola Vollen and published by McSweeney's/Voice of Witness in 2005. The book featured vivid narratives from dozens of New Orleanians, including Abdulrahman and Kathy Zeitoun. His story stuck with me, and the next time I was in New Orleans, to speak to students at the New Orleans Center for the Creative Arts (a great high school arts program), I visited the Zeitouns. From our first talk, it was clear that there was more to their story than we were able to include in *Voices from the Storm*. And so began an almost-three-year process of interviews and research that went into *Zeitoun*. During that time, I was able to get to know Abdulrahman and Kathy, as well as their beautiful family here and in Syria. Additional notes:

All events are seen through the eyes of either Abdulrahman or Kathy Zeitoun, so the view of events reflects their recollections. Todd Gambino was also a participant in the writing and fact-checking of this book. All conversations are reconstructed from the memories of the participants. Interviews with Officers Donald Lima and Ralph Gonzales were conducted by the author in 2008.

I visited the Elayn Hunt Correctional Center in 2008. It seemed to be a very well-run prison, a progressive and rational place with a keen eye toward rehabilitation and reentry, and toward giving prisoners the opportunity to advance their educations, whether academic or vocational. And yet Adbulrahman's experience there was not acceptable. I don't intend to denounce the operation of that prison; perhaps the institution was simply overwhelmed after Katrina and fell short of its higher standards.

AUTHOR THANKS

Chris Ying and Lola Vollen laid the groundwork for this book and deserve vast thanks for encouraging me to pursue this story further. Billy Sothern, the New Orleans lawyer and author who conducted the initial interviews with Abdulrahman and Kathy Zeitoun for *Voices from the Storm,* deserves profound thanks. He was a constant guide and mentor during the writing of *Zeitoun,* and his own book, *Down in New Orleans,* was both inspiration and roadmap. As deputy director of the Capital Appeals Project, he continues to fight every day in the defense of those left vulnerable to the judicial system's frailties and oversights. Annie Preziosi of the Louisiana Capital Assistance Center provided expert research at crucial junctures. Her colleague at LCAC, Julie Kilborn, was very helpful in providing context for the arrests and processing of prisoners after Katrina. Thanks also go to Pam Metzger at the Tulane University Law School and to Nikki Page, whose hospitality and warmth was appreciated always. Anne Gisleson, extraordinary New Orleans writer and teacher and activist, provided invaluable guidance and encouragement and was an expert reader of the manuscript. The courageous Todd Gambino provided fact-checking and context and important details. Elissa Bassist provided key and voluminous research early on. Yousef Mu-nayyer and Mohammed Khalil provided gentle guidance in Arabic and Islamic matters. Naor Ben-Yehoyada provided expert counsel on the history and practice of *lampara* fishing. Farah Aldabbagh translated a rare book about Mohammed Zeitoun from Arabic to English in a timely and expert manner. Peter Orner and Stephen Elliott provided surgical notes and deeply appreciated encouragement. Proofing and copyediting was provided by Lindsay Quella, Juliet Litman, Tess Thackara, Emily Stackhouse, and Henry Jones. Thanks to all at McSweeney's

— Jordan Bass, Heidi Meredith, Angela Petrella, Eli Horowitz, Mimi Lok, and especially to Andrew Leland, whose early read of the manuscript was crucial. Extraordinary and tenacious fact-checking was also performed by the indefatigable Chris Benz. Michelle Quint, associate editor at McSweeney's, was the day-to-day research director for this book. Her dedication, reliability, intelligence, and efficiency will never be forgotten, as this book would have been impossible without her. And of course life generally would not be possible without my wife Vendela, our children, and my brothers Bill and Toph.

Finally, profound thanks go to the Zeitouns of America, Spain, and Syria. Captain Ahmad Zeton — there are many ways to spell the name — and his family in Malaga, Spain (Laila, Lutfi, and Antonia) were generous hosts and brought forth crucial memories. Ahmad was not only a champion of this project from the beginning, but also a meticulous record-keeper, and his photos, emails, and calls from before and after the storm were invaluable. Warm thanks and greetings go to the Zeitoun family in Syria, and to Qusay and young Mahmoud in Jableh in particular. The hospitality of all the Zeitouns knew no limits, and the beauty and laughter and warmth permeating every part of their extraordinary clan was inspiring and enriched this book and this author beyond measure. Most of all, thanks go to Abdulrahman and Kathy, and to their remarkable children, for their stunning personal generosity and for their unwavering commitment to the writing of this book. The process of bringing their story to print required a great deal of them, but they fought through unpleasant memories in the hopes that something constructive might come from their days of personal struggle. Their courage knows no bounds, and their faith in family and in this country renews the faith of us all.

Additional material

Map 1: New Orleans

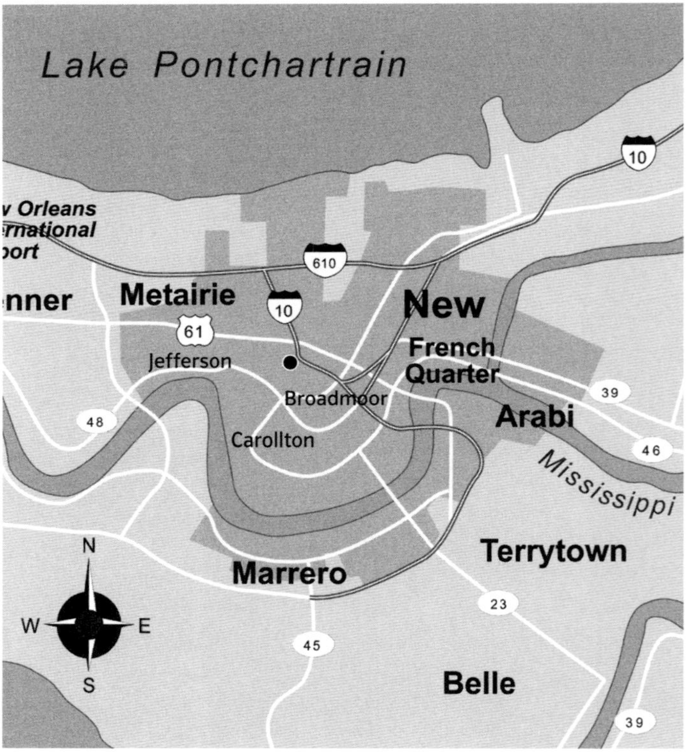

● Dart Street (Zeitoun's home)

Map 2: The U.S. and the Gulf of Mexico

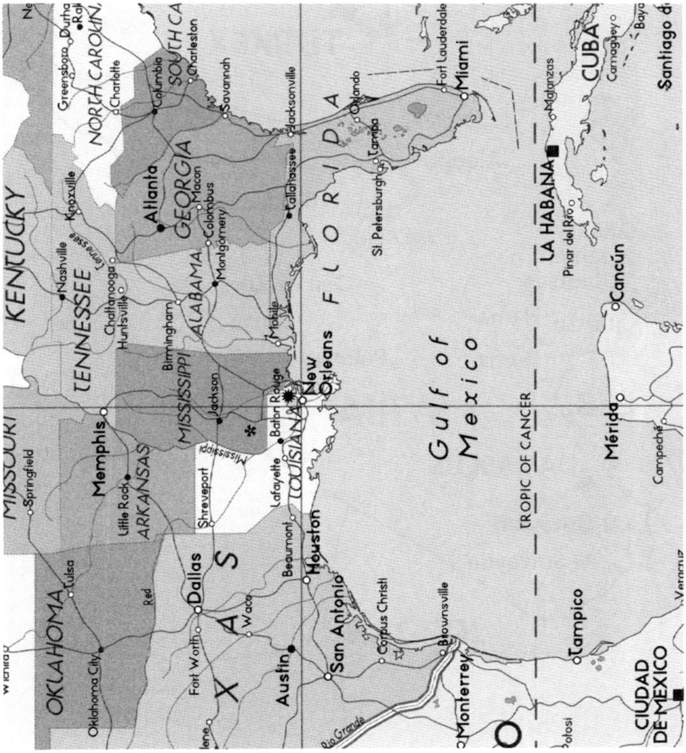

* Angola Prison

✹ Covington

Map 3: Syria

Tigris
TURKEY
Aleppo
Al-Hasakah
Raqqa
Latakia
Lake Assad
Jableh
Med.
Sea
Baniyas
Euphrates
Deir ez-Zor
Tartus
Hama
Homs
Palmyra
LEB.
SYRIA
DAMASCUS
IRAQ
Al-Qutayfah
As Suwayda
JORDAN

1. Hurricane Katrina: The Essential Time Line

by Willie Drye in *National Geographic News,* September 14, 2005

TUESDAY, AUGUST 23, 2005

5 p.m.: The National Hurricane Center in Miami, Florida, issues its first advisory about the tropical system that will become Hurricane Katrina. The advisory notes that the season's 12th tropical depression has formed over the Bahamas. The weather system is about 350 miles (560 kilometers) east of Miami.

WEDNESDAY, AUGUST 24

11 a.m.: The storm has strengthened, become more organized, and been given a name. It is now tropical storm Katrina, the 11th named storm of 2005, about 230 miles (370 kilometers) east of Miami. Its strongest winds are blowing at about 40 miles an hour (65 kilometers an hour).

THURSDAY, AUGUST 25

5 p.m.: Katrina has continued to strengthen and is now a hurricane. Its strongest winds are about 75 miles an hour (120 kilometers an hour), making it a Category One hurricane. The storm is about 15 miles (25 kilometers) east of Fort Lauderdale, Florida, and about to make landfall.

7 p.m.: The eye of Hurricane Katrina comes ashore between North Miami Beach and Hallandale Beach on Florida's southeastern coast. The storm's top winds are 80 miles an hour (130 kilometers an hour). Falling trees kill two people.

FRIDAY, AUGUST 26

1 a.m.: Katrina weakens and is reclassified as a tropical storm. Its center is about 45 miles (70 kilometers) northwest of Key

6 **advisory** piece of advice, warning – 22 **to make landfall** to reach (hit) land

Largo, Florida. Its strongest winds are about 70 miles an hour (115 kilometers an hour).

3 a.m.: The storm's center has emerged from the Florida peninsula and starts strengthening almost immediately as it touches the warm waters of the Gulf of Mexico

5 a.m.: Katrina reintensifies into a hurricane. Its strongest winds are about 75 miles an hour (120 kilometers an hour), and its eye is about 70 miles (115 kilometers) northwest of Key Largo. Keys residents are surprised by Katrina's strength as it passes offshore. "We went to bed last night expecting some possible rain and woke up this morning to learn that Katrina was 75 miles (120 kilometers) north of Marathon [Florida]," says Dan Gallagher, resident of Grassy Key. "A lot of the live-aboards [people living on houseboats] in Boot Key Harbor were surprised to find their boats in new spots."

11:30 a.m.: The National Hurricane Center reports that the hurricane is "rapidly strengthening" as it crosses the Gulf of Mexico's very warm waters. In only a few hours, the storm's strongest winds have increased to about a hundred miles an hour (160 kilometers an hour).

During the day: Governors Kathleen Blanco of Louisiana and Haley Barbour of Mississippi declare states of emergency in their respective states.

11 p.m.: The National Hurricane Center predicts that Katrina will become a major hurricane by the time it reaches the central Gulf of Mexico. The eye of the storm is now about 460 miles (740 kilometers) southeast of the mouth of the Mississippi River in Louisiana.

SATURDAY, AUGUST 27

5 a.m.: Katrina's strongest winds have reached 115 miles an hour (185 kilometers an hour), making it a Category Three hurricane.

4 **peninsula** *Halbinsel* – 15 **spot** place, position

During the day: Hurricane-hunter aircraft fly into Hurricane Katrina to measure wind speed, barometric pressure, ocean surface temperature, and other data.

"It was certainly very strong and also was very large," Chris Landsea said later. Landsea, a meteorologist with the National Oceanic and Atmospheric Administration, was aboard a flight into Hurricane Katrina. "When we were flying into it Saturday, its circulation covered the entire Gulf of Mexico."

SUNDAY, AUGUST 28

2 a.m.: Hurricane Katrina's winds have increased to 145 miles an hour (235 kilometers an hour), making it a Category Four storm. The eye of the storm is about 310 miles (500 kilometers) south of the mouth of the Mississippi River.

9:30 a.m.: New Orleans Mayor Ray Nagin issues a mandatory evacuation order. Tens of thousands of New Orleans residents begin streaming out of the city. "We're facing the storm most of us have feared," Nagin said. "This is going to be an unprecedented event."

11 a.m.: Hurricane Katrina has mushroomed into one of the most powerful hurricanes ever to form in the Atlantic. The storm's strongest winds are blowing at about 175 miles an hour (280 kilometers an hour), making it a Category Five storm. The center of the storm is about 225 miles (360 kilometers) from the mouth of the Mississippi River.

5 p.m.: The National Hurricane Center describes Katrina as a "potentially catastrophic" hurricane. "Some levees in the greater New Orleans area could be overtopped," the center warns. "Significant storm surge flooding will occur elsewhere along the central and northeastern Gulf of Mexico coast."

9:15 p.m.: A. J. Holloway, mayor of Biloxi, Mississippi, says his city is "getting some rain, a little wind, and some lightning

8 **circulation** *here:* active area – 14 **mandatory evacuation order** legalised command for everybody to leave – 18 **unprecedented** *(adj)* unique, never experienced before – 19 **to mushroom** to increase dramatically in size

and thunder" from Hurricane Katrina. Holloway survived Hurricane Camille in August 1969, and he's worried that this hurricane will be as bad or worse than that catastrophic storm. He's also worried that many new residents of Biloxi have no idea what they may soon be facing. "There's a lot of new people who moved into Biloxi with the advent of casino gambling who have never experienced a real hurricane, and they may be taking it lightly," Holloway tells National Geographic News. "And even some of the people who were here during Camille are not worried. But just because your house stood up during Camille don't mean it'll stand up to this hurricane."

Late Sunday night: Thousands of New Orleans residents who are unable to leave town or have chosen not to leave seek shelter in the Louisiana Superdome.

MONDAY, AUGUST 29

2 a.m.: Hurricane Katrina turns north toward the Louisiana coast, but the storm's strongest winds have diminished slightly to about 155 miles an hour (250 kilometers an hour). The center of the storm is about 130 miles (210 kilometers) from New Orleans. A weather buoy about 50 miles (80 kilometers) east of the river's mouth reports waves at least 40 feet (12 meters) high.

5 a.m.: The hurricane's strongest winds are now about 150 miles an hour (240 kilometers an hour), and its eye is about 90 miles (145 kilometers) from New Orleans and about 120 miles (195 kilometers) from Biloxi.

7 a.m.: Hurricane Katrina's eye is about to come ashore in Plaquemines Parish, Louisiana. The hurricane's strongest winds are about 145 miles an hour (235 kilometers an hour). The eye is about 70 miles (115 kilometers) from New Orleans.

8 a.m.: Mayor Ray Nagin reports that water is flowing over one of New Orleans's levees.

18 **to diminish** to reduce, become smaller

9 a.m.: The eye is about 40 miles (65 kilometers) from New Orleans and is expected to pass just to the east of the city. The storm's strongest winds are about 135 miles an hour (215 kilometers an hour).

11 a.m.: The hurricane's eye comes ashore again near the Louisiana-Mississippi border. The storm's strongest winds are about 125 miles an hour (200 kilometers an hour). Katrina's front-right quadrant—which contains its strongest winds and peak storm surge—slams into Biloxi and Gulfport, Mississippi, with devastating force, destroying much of both cities. Meanwhile, a major levee in New Orleans has failed. Water is pouring through the 17th Street Canal, and the city is beginning to flood.

1 p.m.: Hurricane Katrina continues to weaken as it moves farther inland. Its strongest winds are about 105 miles an hour (170 kilometers an hour).

3 p.m.: The center of the hurricane is about 20 miles (30 kilometers) west of Hattiesburg, Mississippi. Its winds are down to about 95 miles an hour (155 kilometers an hour).

TUESDAY, AUGUST 30

11 a.m.: The National Hurricane Center issues its last advisory on the storm that once was Hurricane Katrina. The storm has maximum winds of about 35 miles an hour (55 kilometers an hour), and its center is dumping heavy rainfall on Tennessee.

During the day: Floodwaters continue to pour into New Orleans from breaks in the city's levees.

WEDNESDAY, AUGUST 31

During the day: Health and Human Services Secretary Michael O. Leavitt declares a public health emergency in Louisiana, Mississippi, Alabama, and Florida. Meanwhile, Louisiana Governor Kathleen Blanco orders that all remaining residents leave New Orleans. But buses and trucks aren't available to carry out the order.

THURSDAY, SEPTEMBER 1

2 p.m.: On national television New Orleans Mayor Ray Nagin issues a "desperate SOS" for help from the federal government. Nagin says there's no food for those who took shelter at the Louisiana Superdome and New Orleans convention center.

FRIDAY, SEPTEMBER 2

During the day: A convoy of U.S. National Guard troops and supply trucks arrives in New Orleans and distributes food and water to residents stranded at the Superdome and convention center. Congress approves 10.5 billion dollars (U.S.) in aid for Hurricane Katrina rescue and relief, and President George W. Bush signs the bill. The work of repairing the city's levees, pumping out the floodwaters, and finding homes for tens of thousands of displaced residents is underway.

reproduced by permission of the National Geographic Society

9 **to be stranded** to be stuck somewhere, unable to get away – 14 **displaced** homeless, stranded

2. Excerpt from John Swenson's *New Atlantis: Musicians Battle for the Survival of New Orleans*, Chapter 3: "The Constantinople of the New World" (pages 16 – 20)

New Atlantis, *which was published in 2011, is a non-fiction book written by music journalist John Swenson. It is about the efforts of New Orleans musicians to help rebuild and restore their city after Hurricane Katrina, and it shows their courage and positive attitude to life, which is also typical of the city. After an opening chapter dealing with the* Voice of the Wetlands *project that had been initiated before Katrina, and a chapter on the Mardi Gras Indians, Swenson describes the atmosphere amongst members of the New Orleans music scene on their return to the city.*

When I [the author] returned to New Orleans after the federal flood the waters had finally receded after sitting for the better part of a month. The city was still under curfew and was essentially occupied by National Guard units from other states since the Louisiana Guard had been sent to Iraq.

[…]

Our neighborhood, a stretch of ground along the Mississippi River called Bywater, is part of the Ninth Ward. We're in what's known as the upper Ninth, separated from the lower Ninth by the Industrial Canal, which connects the Mississippi with the lake [Lake Pontchartrain]. During Katrina, a barge crashed through the levee on the downriver side of the Industrial Canal, causing the entire lower Ninth to flood to rooftops.

Those of us down in Bywater were the lucky ones, along with the rest of the city on the high ground close to the

16 **to recede** to go back or down, retreat – 17 **curfew** ['kɚfju:] law that states that nobody is allowed to leave their houses (Ausgangssperre) – 25 **barge** heavy cargo ship

Mississippi. Our houses were torn by wind and rain, but we were able to move back, to congregate at Markey's Bar down on Royal Street, and to tell our stories over and over. Our neighborhood was surrounded by devastation that stretched for miles towards the lake in one direction and downriver in the other. Much of the New Orleans we knew was dead and gone. The city had lost an essential part of its identity. The social clubs and neighborhood joints of African American enclaves like Treme, Mid-City, Gentilly, and the lower Ninth Ward, which nurtured the culture of street parades, brass bands, and the magnificence of the Mardi Gras Indians were gone, along with the departed residents of those ghost-town neighborhoods. Few believed that the intricate family-based institutions that had been built over the span of numerous generations would reassemble in force.

New Orleans has always attracted itinerant adventurers, runaways, bohemians, outcasts from conservative southern communities, and those who just didn't fit in with their local culture. Street musicians and self-described anarchist clowns had established a presence in our neighborhood before the flood, but they returned in greater number afterward, arriving by the busload and squatting in abandoned houses. [...] They were street corner clowns – mimes, actors, artists, jugglers, amateur musicians, and sideshow performers more than comedians dressed in colorful, disheveled thrift-store outfits, and they fit the dysfunctional mood of the city perfectly. The capacity of New Orleanians to be whimsical in the face of disaster was never more needed than it was then.

2 **to congregate** to get together (*usu* sitting and talking) – 3 **over and over** again and again – 8 **joint** *(inf)* bar, pub, meeting place – 9 **enclave** here: area of town – 10 **to nurture** to encourage, to feed – 15 **to reassemble** to grow back together, to be repaired – 16 **itinerant** wandering around, with no fixed home – 22 **to squat** [skwɑːt] to live in a house that you do not own or rent officially (i.e. for free) – 25 **disheveled** old, untidy, full of holes – 25 **thrift-store outfit** clothes bought at a cheap shop – 27 **whimsical** treating things with humour, taking things lightly

It was early November, and my brother and a group of friends from the Blue Nile nightclub were sitting outside after a day's work on our house, cooking chicken legs on a propane stove, and listening on a battery-powered CD player to Davis Rogan singing "Hurricane", a song about staying in New Orleans during a hurricane. The song is steeped in the carefree, whistle-past-the-graveyard spirit that New Orleaneans have long exhibited in the face of imminent disaster, a kind of defiant innocence that makes the ultimate irony of "Hurricane" not the fact that it was written before Katrina but that it would be that much harder to write in the face of all that had happened since.

[...]

All across New Orleans, musicians were returning and looking to play anyplace that would let them. All kinds of venues opened up to accommodate them despite problems with intermittent electricity service and the curfew. Mayor Ray Nagin had issued an evacuation order for the city, and a dusk-to-dawn curfew enforced by National Guard units made New Orleans even more of a city of isolated neighborhoods than it had been before the flood. Residents were forced to stay close to home, and neighborhood bars became key places to trade information, unwind with a few beers, and hear reassuring music of New Orleans played by returning musicians. Even in some of the blighted areas the music was back in action almost immediately.

[...]

[In an interview of the author with singer/songwriter Shannon McNally she said:]

"The energy that's trapped here [in New Orleans], that lives here, is very unique, and it's very powerful, and I think that's what we all feel. It's transmitted in a million ways. That's why

6 **to be steeped in** to be full of – 9 **defiant** refusing to conform or obey – 17 **intermittent** here: unreliable – 23 **to unwind** [ʌnˈwaɪnd] to relax, recover from stress – 25 **blighted** [ˈblaɪt̬ɪd] very badly damaged

the music is like it is. I believe music comes out of the ground. I don't think it comes out of the sky or your head. It ... has something to do with the vibrations of the earth wherever you are.

The earth here ... it's a combination of elements – the fact that [much of it is] below sea level; the heat; its history as a port town and a portal into the whole western hemisphere for Europeans and Africans; and then the millions and millions of people who lived here already. It's like the Constantinople of the New World. Everything is exaggerated here: The beauty is exaggerated, the poverty is exaggerated, the brutality, the music, the food. If you're a person whose senses are acute, there's no way of getting around it. You just feel it."